RESIDENTIAL KITCHEN AND BATH DESIGN

FAIRCHILD
BOOKS

RESIDENTIAL KITCHEN AND BATH DESIGN

Anastasia Wilkening

NCIDQ certified, CKD, CBD, ASID

FAIRCHILD BOOKS
New York

Fairchild Books
An imprint of Bloomsbury Publishing Inc

175 Fifth Avenue
New York
NY 10010
USA

50 Bedford Square
London
WC1B 3DP
UK

www.fairchildbooks.com

First published 2013

Library of Congress Cataloging-in-Publication Data
A catalog record for this book is available from the Library of Congress.
2012936303

ISBN: PB: 978-1-60901-125-3

Typeset by Alicia Freile, Tango Media
Cover Design by Sarah Silberg
Cover Art: Thomas Loof/trunkarchive.com; Courtesy of Pamela Polvere Designs and Dennis Jourdan Photography Inc.
Printed and bound in China

CONTENTS

EXTENDED CONTENTS

CHAPTER 7: KITCHEN AND BATH DESIGN: PLUMBING 163

CHAPTER 8: KITCHEN AND BATHROOM WORKING DOCUMENTS 197

CHAPTER 9:
KITCHEN AND BATH DESIGN:
LIGHTING AND ELECTRICAL PLANS 213

CHAPTER 10:
PROJECT MANAGEMENT FOR
KITCHEN AND BATH 233

PREFACE

*R*esidential Kitchen and Bath Design takes a real-world approach to teaching the student the skills needed to be a kitchen and bath designer. This book navigates through the complete kitchen and bath design process, from the first meeting with a client, to measuring and interviewing, and through the project management phase. Students will learn how to space plan, about the various products involved in the kitchen and bath, how to draft the necessary documents, and current information about sustainability and universal design concerns for these specific rooms.

Residential Kitchen and Bath Design is intended for the upper-level student who has learned the basics about construction, codes, drafting, and material selection. Although this book would be best used for a specific kitchen and bath class, it is also useful as a resource for students taking residential design classes.

The text is organized with the comprehensive project process in mind. **Chapter 1** (Overview of Kitchen and Bath Design) discusses and explains the initial steps when working with a client, including preliminary con-

sultation, interviewing, estimating, and measuring. **Chapter 2** focuses on the next step, space planning. Students will gain knowledge of how to create a functional kitchen or bath. **Chapter 3** concentrates on universal design and sustainable design, with numerous detailed suggestions on how to accomplish these strategies. Materials, cabinetry, appliances, and plumbing are covered in separate chapters **(Chapters 4–7)**, providing thorough information so that the student understands the specifications of these items. Working documents are explained in **Chapter 8** because kitchen and bath drafting style varies slightly from the general interior designer's drafting style. Once the plan is drafted, lighting and electrical plans are decided on and are explained in **Chapter 9**. The various options for lighting are discussed as well as how to illustrate these selections on the lighting and electrical plan. Appropriately, the book ends with **Chapter 10** on project management. This topic is often covered in a separate class of its own; Chapter 10 highlights suggestions relevant for kitchen or bath project installation.

TEXT FEATURES

Residential Kitchen and Bath Design provides many exciting features that help bring to life the kitchen and bath industry for the student. Each chapter contains numerous color illustrations, photographs, drawings, floor plans, tables, charts, and boxes demonstrating examples of each design element for the kitchen and bath. We believe these features will make learning about this topic engrossing. Features include design scenarios, key terms, designer's dialogue, and trade talk boxes found throughout each chapter; end-of-chapter exercises, including discussion questions and design checklists; and additional print and online resources.

DESIGN SCENARIOS

Each chapter opens with a case study pertaining to the specific content of each chapter. The case study is followed by discussion questions, which allow students to pursue the techniques, principles, and practices found throughout the chapter.

OBJECTIVES

Each chapter contains a bulleted list of learning objectives provided for the student to comprehend by the time he or she is finishing reading and learning the chapter's content.

KEY TERMS

Key terms are found in boldface at first mention in each chapter. The definitions, found in the margins of each chapter, provide the student with the vocabulary needed to speak in an educated manner.

DESIGNER'S DIALOGUE

In "Designer's Dialogue," real-world kitchen and bath designers from around the country share their project experiences with the beginning designer. This feature is found in every chapter and makes the chapter information more real for the student.

TRADE TALK

Similar to Designer's Dialogue, "Trade Talk" is essential advice from tradespeople within the kitchen and bath industry. This information also helps bring the chapter information to life for the student.

SUMMARY AND REVIEW

The chapters conclude with student-oriented activities designed to reinforce the material. A summary provides a brief recollection of key concepts, techniques, and practices found in each chapter.

CHAPTER EXERCISES

This section also facilitates discussion among students in the classroom. It includes questions about the major concepts presented in each chapter while revisiting the projects from the Design Scenarios to afford students a chance to work on real-life kitchen and bath projects.

DESIGN CHECKLISTS

Checklists are found at the end of each chapter and remind the student of the many considerations required throughout a kitchen or bath project. These checklists will be practical references for a student and for working kitchen and bath designers.

ACKNOWLEDGMENTS

This book could not have been written without the help of many people. I am grateful for the hard work and thoughtful insight of Development Editor Julie Vitale. Your suggestions, guidance, and impeccable editing are greatly appreciated. My thanks to Fairchild Books, particularly Executive Editor Olga Kontzias, for your patience and to Senior Development Editor Joseph Miranda for helping guide the process.

My heartfelt gratitude goes to Pamela Polvere, my mentor and friend. I cannot sufficiently express my appreciation for your unwavering encouragement and support; thank you. Thank you to Lisa Godsey for your unceasing aid, advice, and confidence in my abilities. I'm fortunate to continue being your student long after I've passed your classes. Thank you to Dana Mowat for the extra push I needed to begin the process of writing this book.

I am indebted to the many designers and tradespeople who were generous with their time, allowing this book to share their industry experience and insights. Thank you for taking the time to speak with me so that students can learn from what you've learned. A special thank you to Aga Tersh for your expertise and suggestions regarding information on tile covered in this book. Sincere thanks to all the individuals, photographers, design firms, and companies that allowed us to reprint photos or graphics.

I want to thank the following interior design educators, selected by the publisher, for their reviews and recommendations: Donna Weaverling Daley, The Art Institute of Philadelphia; Nancy Wolford, Canada College; Cheryl A. Glazier, University of Nebraska Kearney; Catherine Azcarate, Art Institute of Colorado; Amy Bodell-Hersch, Western Kentucky University.

Thank you to my family and friends for your encouragement. An ardent thank you to my remarkable husband, Brad Wilkening; thank you for all of your love and support, and the photography you generously provided for this book. This book is dedicated to my parents Sylvia and Stanley Sowinski and my daughter, Sylvia Wilkening, three people who have inspired me to work at being the best I can be.

OVERVIEW OF KITCHEN AND BATH DESIGN

OBJECTIVES

After reading this chapter, you will:

- Grasp the essentials of kitchen and bath design.

- Understand the history and significance of the kitchen and bath.

- Distinguish how various design companies work with payment and showroom use, so you can decide how you would prefer to work.

- Know how to hold an effective initial consultation with the potential client.

- Recognize the tasks required to carry out a successful client meeting after being retained, including the following: measuring for different situations, taking photographs, and efficiently interviewing the client for his or her design wants and needs (Figure 1.1).

- Learn how to be successful in the kitchen and bath design industry.

DESIGN SCENARIO

You are working at a kitchen and bath design firm, when Mr. and Mrs. Sowinski walk in the door. This couple has recently hired an architect to design an addition to their home. Part of the new addition is an expanded kitchen and they are very excited about the design options available. The Sowinskis want to discuss your experience, the costs associated with the project, and what the next steps will involve.

1. How will you accurately estimate this kitchen project?

2. What should you do when you have to work with other hired professionals on a project?

3. What steps do you need to take if the clients decide to hire you?

The purpose of this chapter is to provide guidance in deciding how you would like to work as a kitchen and bath designer and the various steps in the beginning of the design process. The first section describes different types of design firms, from individual designers to multiple-person studios, and how each works and the different ways designers are paid. This is important to help you decide what type of company you would like to work for, or if you prefer being your own boss. The next section of the chapter provides detail about the various initial tasks before and after the client is retained, if a retainer is used. The designer will provide information for the potential client to help him or her decide if he or she wishes to work with that designer. Once the designer is hired, the programming process begins with gathering information by taking measurements and photographs. Additional information is gathered by interviewing the client, which is made easier when using a standard survey. Once these first steps are handled, the designer can start to think about all the other aspects that will be discussed further in this book, such as how to lay out the space and what materials to use.

Kitchen and bath design is a popular specialization in the profession of Interior Design. These two rooms of a home are extremely significant to their residents. The kitchen often has been referred to as "the heart of the home" in current North American cultures. Beginning in the seventeenth century, the kitchen was the central component in a house because it was used as the pri-

Figure 1.1 The kitchen is a gathering place for families. © *Shutterstock.com.*

mary heat source and was a gathering spot for families. This has remained true to the present day, whether it is an ordinary weeknight or a large family party; people often end up in the kitchen.

Bathrooms are used every day throughout homes across the globe. Hygiene has become more important than ever before in daily life. Not only is the importance of good hygiene recognized, but the bath is often seen as a place to relax. Baths were used, starting around 3000 B.C., for purification. Bathhouses became a place to relax and socialize and remained that way for centuries. During the Renaissance, it was feared that water carried disease, which led to less personal hygiene. Today, a bathroom is frequently a highly sought-after retreat. Many people want their bathrooms to mimic a spa, where they can unwind from their busy days (Figure 1.2).

Remodeling a kitchen or bath is an investment in the home. When a home has an up-to-date kitchen or a bath its value increases. Many people are aware of this fact and therefore consider remodeling either of these rooms if they have the means. The average time between kitchen remodels has recently been approximately 14 years. That length of time has been decreasing as technology advances. In addition, more people are living comfortable lifestyles. The number of people who have the desire and means to hire a designer keeps growing (Figure 1.3).

Figure 1.2 The kitchen and bath are investments in a home. © *Shutterstock.com.*

Figure 1.3 Designers are being hired more frequently to assist with projects. © *Shutterstock.com.*

TYPICAL PAY STRUCTURE FOR THE DESIGNER

A career in the kitchen and bath industry can be rewarding and potentially very profitable. Frequently, designers working for a design firm in this industry earn a wage on a commission basis. Although a commission-based wage may be intimidating to some, it can be an opportunity for great financial success. The percentage of commission earned for a project depends on the company the designer works for. Salaried or hourly designers are less common in the kitchen and bath industry, but do exist. The commission style of pay makes the most sense given the nature of the job. Although many kitchen and bath designers may argue they are not salespeople, they really are. They design a kitchen or bath and typically sell the product to the client. The space is designed with the client's wants, needs, and budget in mind, but ultimately products still are being sold. Designers who do not sell products usually work on an hourly fee for the client, or possibly for a lump-sum fee. How much commission the designer makes is affected by a few factors, primarily whether the designer works for a firm or is independent.

WORKING FOR A FIRM VERSUS WORKING INDEPENDENTLY

There are two major types of kitchen and bath designers: those who work for a design firm and those who are independent designers. There are advantages and disadvantages to each of these options. Although some designers may decide to start out independently in hopes of making more money, there are advantages to starting out working for a firm.

WORKING FOR A FIRM

A designer who works for a firm has the advantage of support through resources and knowledge. The extent of the support is based on the size of the company. At the minimum, the designer probably has a colleague to double-check ideas and contracts. In general, the company owner is someone with years of experience and who has a great deal of knowledge to share. In larger design firms, designer assistance may be available for a wide range of tasks. Companies sometimes have support staff for tasks, such as drafting, gathering samples, assembling contracts, placing orders, or project management. Working for a firm is a great way for the new kitchen and bath designer to start out because it provides a structure for the designer to learn from. The designer

will likely be taught a certain method to organize and manage a project from start to finish. It is easier to learn this from a firm that has it figured out than to learn as you go, working in the field.

The potential disadvantage of working for a design firm is the salary paid. Larger companies, with more support staff, have more overhead; the more overhead a company has, the smaller the commission rate for the designer. The other disadvantage of a design firm is if the designer has a desire to be his or her own boss. Some designers have a great drive to own their own businesses and will not be happy working for someone else.

WORKING INDEPENDENTLY

A designer who wants to be his or her own boss has the desire to be an independent designer or business owner. Oftentimes an independent kitchen and bath designer will work out of his or her home. The advantage to this is that he or she will have little to no overhead. No overhead means larger profits. Independent designers also do not have to answer to anyone other than the client. They are given the freedom to make decisions on the client's behalf without someone else's opinion infringing on their ideas.

The disadvantage of a designer owning his or her own business is that he or she must carry the weight of the business. If a client is unhappy or if something goes wrong, the designer is the one who has to handle it. The designer ultimately takes on any risk of the business. Being a business owner in any profession is a big responsibility and the kitchen and bath field is not any different. Among the many things to consider as a business owner is whether it is wise to invest in a showroom for the company. See Table 1.1 for a comparison of different designer working styles.

TABLE 1.1 COMPARISON OF THE WORKING STYLES OF VARIOUS DESIGNERS		
Working Style	**Pros**	**Cons**
Independent: A designer who works for him- or herself	1. Only has to answer to the client 2. Typically less overhead, so more profit to the designer	1. All mistakes, problems, expenses, and risk fall on the designer
Small Firm: A designer who works for a smaller-sized firm	1. Generally there is some support 2. There may be a showroom, which can be helpful	1. Less profit for the designer 2. The designer will typically have to answer to the owner of the firm, in addition to the client, in the event of costly mistakes or problems
Large Firm: A designer who works for a larger-sized firm	1. There is typically a lot of support 2. The firm would likely have a showroom, which can be beneficial	1. More people involved in a project can lead to more errors 2. There are more people to answer to in the event of a mistake or problem 3. There is less profit for the designer because there is more overhead

SHOWROOMS

Most commonly a larger design firm will have a showroom. It is rare that an independent designer would have a showroom. The usefulness of a showroom for a kitchen and bath designer is debatable. Most designers would say it is very beneficial to have a showroom. A showroom is a place where the designer can feature the cabinet lines or other products that he or she represents or prefers to specify. It is an opportunity for the designer to display his or her creativity and the different products he or she can provide. It is especially helpful if the designer sells multiple cabinet lines, so as to be able to compare and present the different cabinets in one place to the client. Some showrooms even have a working kitchen, which can be useful. The disadvantage of having a showroom is the investment. For the showroom to be most effective it has to remain current. Manufacturers typically offer deeper discounts to display their products, but the business still pays for the displays. Another decision the firm owner has to

make is whether the showroom will be open to the public or will be open by appointment only.

OPEN SHOWROOMS

An open showroom needs to have someone available for people who walk into the showroom without an appointment, sometimes called **walk-ins.** This could simply be a receptionist who records contact information or a designer who walks the showroom floor. Sometimes firms will have both a receptionist and designer available for those who walk into the showroom. The benefit of having a designer available is that he or she can immediately answer any questions a potential client may have specifically about a project.

The disadvantages of an open showroom are the need to always have a person staffed to watch for people walking in, and the probability of people walking in who are not really potential clients. Some people will walk into a showroom simply to waste time or just to browse. People who are working on their kitchen or bath by themselves may enter a showroom to get ideas, and have no intention of hiring a designer.

BY APPOINTMENT ONLY

Another type of showroom is by appointment only. The benefit of this style of showroom is that there is no need for someone to be present at all times. Having a showroom by appointment only also tends to attract clients who have a serious interest in hiring a designer. Someone who just wants to browse to waste time will generally not call to make an appointment.

NO SHOWROOM

Independent designers rarely have a showroom. The cost to keep an up-to-date showroom may be something the designer does not want to deal with. However, kitchen and bath designers who do not have a showroom still have a way to show prospective clients their products and creativity: their previous clients. It is common for a designer to ask permission from past clients to allow new prospects to view their homes. This also is a great opportunity for the prospective client to ask a past client questions about how the designer works and the client's level of satisfaction.

The disadvantage of not having a showroom is the inconvenience of having to ask past clients to allow potential clients into their homes. Some past clients will not allow this. For the designer starting out, it can be difficult to show examples when he or she has not had many, or any, clients. Having a showroom also reassures the potential client that the business has a solid location and so is less likely to close and disappear with the client's deposit.

EMPLOYED VERSUS RECOMMENDED CONTRACTORS

Another difference among kitchen and bath designers concerns whether they have contractors that they employ or whether the client hires his or her own contractor directly. Again, there are advantages and disadvantages to each (Figure 1.4).

EMPLOYED CONTRACTORS

The advantage to the designer employing the contractor is that he or she will almost always be working with someone he or she is familiar with. The designer can work closely with the contractor and installers to ensure that the project is installed as it was intended. The designer also can give the client an overall project price, all at once. When the designer employs the contractor, the designer or contractor will estimate how much the labor and construction materials will cost.

RECOMMENDED CONTRACTORS

If the designer does not employ the contractor, the client must hire one on his or her own. Designers who do not employ their own contractors typically have a list of those with whom they like to work and can refer to the client. When the client hires the contractor directly, the contractor reports to the client. If the designer knows the client is hiring his or her own contractor, then the designer needs to make contact with the contractor. The designer should make sure the contractor has the most current drawings before starting the project. It also is best if the designer contacts the contractor to introduce him- or herself. In this introduction, the designer should share the best way to be reached if any questions arise. It is important that the designer do this, as often clients will not know answers to the contractor's questions. The advantage to the client hiring his or her own contractor is more flexibility in labor pricing, as the client can obtain several bids. The disadvantage is that the designer will not necessarily know the contractor the client selects, and will have to learn to work with whoever it is.

Now that we know who we work for, our showroom status, and how we will work with a contractor, let's discuss the first step with a new client: the retainer agreement.

RETAINER AGREEMENTS

Designers in the kitchen and bath industry often use retainer agreements. A **retainer** is money given up front by the client to officially hire, or **retain**, the designer. Once the client pays the retainer the designer can begin to work. Retainers differ in the amount paid and how the money is applied. For example, some retainers are arranged so that the designer keeps a portion as a

Figure 1.4 The contractor can be employed by the designer or directly by the client. © *Shutterstock.com.*

design fee while the remainder is applied to the contract. Other retainers are arranged so that the whole amount is applied to the contract. In either case, the client can apply the money to a contract only if he or she signs a contract. If the client decides not to continue with the design at any point in the process, the designer is entitled to keep the entire retainer.

Having a retainer is a wise decision for the designer. It protects the designer's time invested in a project. Without a retainer, a designer who does not charge an hourly fee could have hours of work wasted if the client ceases working with the designer.

INITIAL CONSULTATION

The initial consultation with the client is an important meeting. The client may still be deciding whether or not to hire a designer for the project. Often, clients will interview several different designers to make sure they are choosing the right person for them. It is a very personal thing to hire someone who will be in your home. The client must be comfortable with the designer. Depending on how the design firm works, this first meeting could be a free in-home consultation, or it could just be the first meeting in the showroom with the designer. In the next sections we review the typical steps of the initial consultation, before the client has paid a retainer (Figure 1.5).

An in-home estimate typically starts with the designer explaining the design process to the potential client. The designer will also ask the client questions, in order to fully understand the project. This meeting creates the client's first impression of the designer, so it is very important. One of the best things the designer can do is to really listen to the client. A successful designer listens closely, takes notes, and follows up with actions based on the client's thoughts.

Figure 1.5 The designer and client first meet during the initial consultation. At this point no work has been done to design the space, but the designer may review existing plans. © of Shutterstock.com.

ESTIMATING

One of the first questions that a potential client will ask concerns how much his or her project will cost. This is a question that can be difficult to answer. There are many factors to consider, such as the grade of materials that will be used and how much labor is needed. In addition, slightly different methods may be used to estimate the cost of a kitchen, versus a bath, remodel. The designer can give a rough estimate or a more realistic estimate based on the cabinets the designer sells. Let's take a closer look at these different methods of estimating.

ROUGH ESTIMATING THE COST OF A KITCHEN REMODEL

Often homeowners do not know typical prices for a remodel. They may know someone who has done a remodel, but no two homes are the same and material prices range widely. However, there is a general industry standard method to estimate kitchen remodel costs. Typically, a kitchen remodel will cost approximately 10 percent to 20 percent of the home's value. Of this total one third is the cost of appliances, fixtures, and finishes. Another third of the total is the cost of the cabinets. The remaining third is the fee for the labor. The percentage of the remodel total that will be gained in home value depends on several factors including the location of the home and the total cost of the project. It is safe to say that the closer the kitchen remodeling cost is to the 10-percent end, in terms of current home value, the more likely the money invested will be regained.

More often than not, kitchen and bath renovations are not done solely for investment purposes. If homeowners are taking on a kitchen or bath remodel and hiring a designer, they most likely want to create a space they can enjoy.

A remodel not only needs money, but time and space as well; these also factor into the cost, and can determine whether potential clients will have the patience or will to undertake the inconvenience of a renovation. The homeowners have to live with the remodel process and most likely will not have a functional kitchen or bath for a month or longer. Renovations are also very messy. Even the cleanest contractor cannot entirely prevent dust from getting throughout the house. In addition, not all kitchen and bath projects are renovations; some are new construction projects. In the case of new construction, the earlier the designer is involved, the better: The designer can have more contribution to the best wall and window placement for the layout of the space.

ROUGH ESTIMATING THE COST OF A BATH REMODEL

Estimating the cost of a bath remodel is a little more challenging than for a kitchen. There is no standard equation to determine a rough estimate. Because the work is usually more complicated in a bathroom, the cost of labor often is about the same as for all the materials combined. Of course, the cost of labor will be affected by the extent of changes intended for the bathroom remodel. Shifting a toilet waste stack or moving any plumbing will be more costly than leaving items in their existing locations. As for the kitchen, there are many products offered at various prices. For both kitchen and bath remodels, it is useful to look back at old projects done by the design firm to estimate the cost. If there are no old projects to review, a budget can be created simply by looking up prices for all the pieces that will be needed. If the designer is providing cabinets, he or she also can use the following estimating procedure to determine approximately what that part will cost.

MORE REALISTIC CABINET ESTIMATING

Another way to estimate the cost for a kitchen or bath is for the designer to give a more realistic estimate based on the particular project. Many design firms use this technique. This process is done by the designer adding up the number of cabinet boxes or linear feet of cabinets. If the project is a remodel the designer can get this number by looking at the existing kitchen or bath and determining whether additional cabinets are expected. If the project is new construction the designer can look at the architect's plans.

To estimate cabinet cost as accurately as possible for the client is to know standard average prices. Every design studio sells different lines of cabinetry and materials at different prices. The designer can determine the average individual cabinet price by looking at old project costs or by pricing a sample project. If the company carries several cabinet lines the designer may want to give the client a price range into which their project would most likely fall.

Let's look at an example. For this project, the average individual cabinet price is $500 on the lower end, and $2,000 on the higher end. Each individual base and wall cabinet will count as one cabinet each. Each tall cabinet will count as two cabinets. Refrigerator panels and the hood will be considered two cabinets while the dishwasher panel will count as one cabinet. Look at the floor plan example to see how the cabinets were added (Figure 1.6).

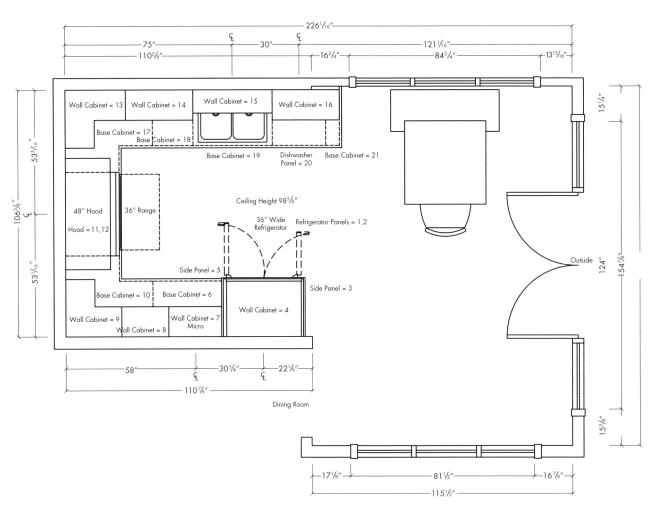

Figure 1.6 Here is a sample kitchen for estimating.

Based on this floor plan, there are 21 cabinets. If a lower-end cabinet line without much detail were used the cabinets could cost approximately $10,500. If the client prefers a higher-end cabinet line with many details, the cabinet cost would be closer to $42,000. This example shows the wide range in cabinet pricing that is available. The designer will have to determine, depending on the client's wants and budget, where he or she might end up in that price range. This technique is accurate only if it is based on the cabinet company or companies the designer's firm uses.

ESTIMATING LABOR COST AND THE COST OF OTHER MATERIALS

The designer can also estimate the price for other materials and for labor. Remember that the total cost of a kitchen is broken down as one third for cabinets, one third for labor, and one third for appliances and miscellaneous materials; the labor cost is usually about the same as for the cabinets. When cabinets are more expensive it is typically because the client selected a higher-end line with more detail. This requires more labor to install, therefore increasing the labor price. As stated earlier, labor for a bathroom project will typically be equivalent to or higher than the cost of all the materials for the bathroom project. Materials, such as countertops, tile, and appliances, also range as widely in price as cabinets. Again, it is best to look at previous, already priced projects and set standard price ranges on the basis of that information. Countertop and tile square footage can be estimated quickly by multiplying the estimated square footage by the average price per square foot. Appliance prices vary, depending on the manufacturer and specific series. A useful trick is to have several different manufacturers already priced. The designer can assemble a few different appliance package options as a starting point. After the space is designed the appliances can be switched to whatever is needed to fit the space. These package prices can at least be discussed and the designer will have a better understanding of where the client would like to be with pricing.

AFTER THE RETAINER, TIME TO MEASURE

If the client decides to hire the designer and pay the retainer, the design process can begin. The first step is for the designer to obtain measurements of the space. If the project is new construction, the designer can start planning the space, based on the architect's plans. If the project is a remodel, the designer will need to measure the space. Measuring a space is a very important task. Accurate measurements are crucial to a successful design (Figure 1.7).

In a remodel project, dimensions are typically taken once by the designer. New construction projects may need to be measured multiple times. The architect may supply plans for the designer to work from, but no building is ever built exactly as planned. The designer may have planned a kitchen based on it having a 115-inch-long wall, only to discover it was built at 101 inches long. This may seem insignificant, as it is only a 14-inch difference; but there is a problem if the designer ordered cabinets based on the original dimension. If the cabinets have already been ordered they will not fit on the wall as built. For this reason, cabinets should never be ordered based from an architect's plan. The

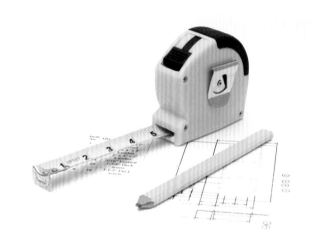

Figure 1.7 Measuring is an important initial step.
© *Shutterstock.com.*

designer may plan the space to have it ready, but orders should not be placed until physical measurements can be taken. There are instances when a designer may need to measure again; this happens occasionally when the designer measures the space when the studs are installed but the drywall has not been hung. The wall size could still change at this point. The designer should wait to measure until after the drywall has been installed. We talk about the process of measuring in the case of framing without drywall in the section Measuring before Drywall Installation (below).

DESIGNER'S DIALOGUE 1.2

"When you go out to measure the project, sketch it to scale. It has a dual purpose, you can transverse numbers, but drawing to scale is a double-check. You can then trace on top and instantly put your ideas on paper."
—*Joanne Giesel, Kitchen and Bath Designer*

MEASUREMENT ACCURACY IS CRUCIAL

Taking accurate measurements is so important because of the nature of kitchen and bath design. The exact space available is critical to determine what will fit in the space. Measurements being recorded should never be rounded. If a window was being measured and the tape measure reads 24⅜ inches it should never be rounded to 24½ inches. For those who are uncomfortable reading a tape measure, there are types available that have these fractions of an inch marked. However, an interior designer should be proficient in taking exact measurements, as he or she will have to do so often.

WHAT NEEDS TO BE MEASURED

Items that need to be measured in a space include the following: overall walls, windows, doorways, ceiling heights, soffits, existing vents, existing toilet and plumbing **centerlines**, and existing centerlines of outlets, doorways, and windows.

Figure 1.8 demonstrates how window width should be determined: from the outside of the trim on one side of the window to the outside of the trim on the other side of the window. If a window is even slightly irregular in shape, take this measurement at the widest point. This is important, as it is best to avoid cabinets intersecting with this area. The height of a window should be taken from the lowest part of the trim to the highest part (Figure 1.9). It is important to determine a window's height above the finished floor (Figure 1.10). This is a crucial dimension to get right if base cabinets are to fit under the window.

Measurements also should be taken for outlet and switch centerlines. It is important when space planning to know where these existing items are located. When the designer starts working on the electrical plan he or she can decide whether more outlets are required (Figure 1.11).

Doorways should be measured in the same manner as windows (Figures 1.12 and 1.13). The width and height dimensions are taken from the outside edge of the casing.

Figure 1.8 Window width should be measured at the widest point. *Courtesy of Brad Wilkening.*

Figure 1.10 A window's height above the finished floor is also important to determine. *Courtesy of Brad Wilkening.*

Figure 1.9 Window height should be measured from the lowest point to the tallest point. *Courtesy of Brad Wilkening.*

Figure 1.11 Outlet and switch centerline measurements should be taken. *Courtesy of Brad Wilkening.*

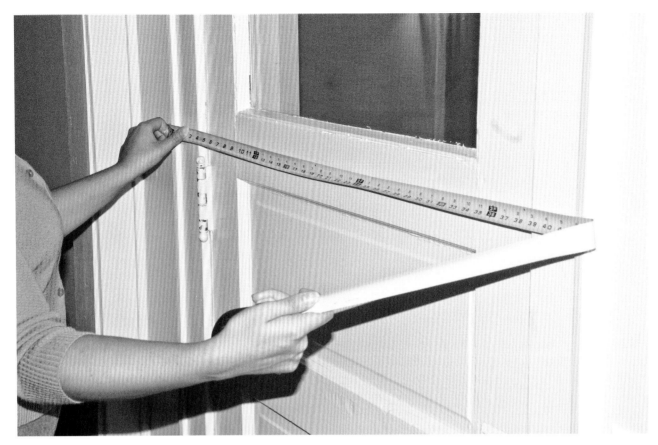

Figure 1.12 Doorway measurements are taken from the outside edges of the casing. *Courtesy of Brad Wilkening.*

It is crucial to measure existing plumbing accurately, as having to move plumbing can be a very expensive task. The best way to be accurate is to measure the total width of the area taken up by the pipes, and the center-lines of the pipes (Figure 1.14).

The ceiling height is another important dimension. This height will determine the options for how high the wall and tall cabinets can be (Figure 1.15).

MEASURING BEFORE DRYWALL INSTALLATION

Sometimes measurements are taken before the dry-wall has been hung. Occasionally, it happens that a client will hire a designer for new construction after the framing has been installed. At this point, it is better for the designer to plan the space based on the studs that have been installed, rather than the architect's plans, which may no longer be as accurate. If this is the case, the designer must be very careful in accounting for the drywall that will eventually be added. Drywall is available in thicknesses of 1/2 inch or 5/8 inch, so the designer should confirm which size will be used. In the example shown in Figure 1.16, 1/2-inch drywall and 3-inch casing are being used.

In Figure 1.16, start with wall A. Measure from the corner stud to the stud by the door opening. Subtract 1/2 inch from this number to account for the drywall that will be applied to the perpendicular wall. Then deduct 3 inches for the standard casing because this is where the door is located. Drywall is not added inside a door opening because that is where the door frame is

Figure 1.13 Doorway heights should be measured to the top of the casing. *Courtesy of Brad Wilkening.*

Figure 1.14 When measuring existing plumbing, determine the width of the area taken up by the pipes, and their centerline. *Courtesy of Brad Wilkening.*

Figure 1.15 Be sure to get the ceiling height. In older homes where the floor may be uneven, it is good to measure the ceiling in a few different locations. *Courtesy of Brad Wilkening.*

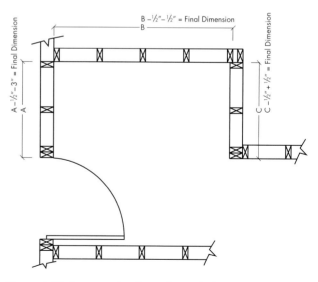

Figure 1.16 An example of a wall's stud placement.

attached. If wall A had been measured as having a 55-inch **rough dimension,** it would be a 51½-inch finished wall dimension.

The dimension for wall B is needed next. This wall is between two perpendicular walls, so once the drywall is attached it will become smaller from both sides. This final dimension would be B (rough dimension) minus 1/2 inch from one side and another 1/2 inch from the other side. From stud corner to the stud corner, wall B measured 70 inches in width. Your finished wall dimension would be 69 inches wide.

Finally, we have wall C. For this wall, measure from the corner to the exposed end. Again, 1/2 inch will be lost because the perpendicular wall will have drywall attached. In this case, we also will be gaining 1/2 inch on the other side because drywall will be attached. For wall C, the number measured from stud to stud, that is, the rough dimension, will also be the final dimension. If you measure the studs, and get 50 inches for the width, this will also be the finished dimension.

ADDITIONAL MEASURING ADVICE

There are a few other things to keep in mind to complete a successful measure. Be sure to arrive prepared. Bring all the supplies that might be needed. As mentioned earlier, there are tape measures marked to one-sixteenth of an inch, which makes measurement easier. A pen or pencil and paper obviously also will be needed. Some designers like to use graph paper to make sketching the space easier and neater. Some even use the graph paper as a tool to sketch the space to scale as they are measuring. For the tech savvy, there are now applications that can be used to store this information electronically. If measuring at a construction job site appropriate footwear should be considered; often construction sites are exposed to the elements and have makeshift temporary walkways and stairs, which can be dangerous to navigate. Other items that may come in handy include a calculator, string to help measure circular situations, and a straightedge to help align for hard-to-reach areas.

TAKING PHOTOGRAPHS

Another important aspect of the initial consultation is the taking of photographs. It is a sensible idea that the design firm have an office camera. It is useful to take photographs at the initial consultation for several reasons. Designers typically have multiple projects occurring simultaneously, and sometimes it may be difficult for the designer to remember details from every project. If the designer takes photographs he or she can review them when designing the space. There may be architectural details of the home that should be incorporated into the design. Perhaps the client has a stained glass window in the dining room that has colors he or she wants to incorporate into the kitchen. Photographs also are good to have when remembering any unique details about a space, such as different soffit or ceiling heights that may affect the design. "Before photographs" also are useful to have in case the designer decides to submit the project in a contest. Even if the contest is not specifically a before- and after-type contest, photographs help the judges see the difference the designer has made in the space. Magazines that scout for projects to publish also typically ask to see before photographs. In addition to being useful for the design or for potential contest entry, an office camera is also beneficial in the case of issues with products or installation. If a cabinet was delivered in a damaged state a photograph could be taken and e-mailed to the cabinet company. This would help expedite replacement of the cabinet, as oftentimes the cabinetmaker wants to see the problem first.

INTERVIEWING THE CLIENT FOR WANTS AND NEEDS

After the retainer agreement is signed, measurements have been recorded, and photographs taken, the designer can sit down with the client to get more details about his or her wants and needs. The most efficient way that designers may use to get this information is to go through a survey with the client. Many design firms use this technique to ensure they remember to ask all the important questions. An example of a basic survey is presented in Figure 1.17. Many design studios will have more detailed versions of this survey. The example shown here consists of three pages, but it would not be unusual to find a similar survey about 10 pages long.

As always, it is extremely important that the designer be a good listener. Bring a notepad and pen to all meetings to take notes on everything the client says pertaining to the project. Clients always appreciate a designer who listens and addresses their needs.

Clients describing what they are looking for often don't know the words to express what they want. Typically, a client is not involved in the design industry, other than possibly watching television shows, and so is unaware of the standard vocabulary used. It is very helpful to suggest that the client look through magazines or browse the Web and pull images of kitchens or baths they like. There are clients who will pull images and still cannot explain what it is they like. As the designer, discuss the photographs with them to break down what is being shown. The designer can ask the clients: what it is they like about the image? Do they like the layout, the finishes, or the style? Is there anything they do not like about the image? The designer also can observe any similarities between photos that have been pulled. There may be certain features that the designer will decide to incorporate into his or her design.

DESIGNER'S DIALOGUE 1.3

"It's the designer's job to guide the client through the process. Typically, clients want to pick materials right away, but the designer needs to first gather information."
—*Gail Drury, CMKBD, Kitchen and Bath Designer*

WORKING WITH OTHER PROFESSIONALS

Kitchen and bath designers often find themselves working with other design professionals on a project. Some clients may additionally hire an interior designer or architect. This is not always the case, but clients do exist who prefer a team to find the solution to their space. The kitchen and bath designer also works with the general contractor for the project.

The client may also hire an interior designer if the project entails more than the kitchen and bath. Even if the project includes only the kitchen or bath, the client may still hire an interior designer. The client may have worked with someone previously, or simply would like to get another opinion. It is important if this is the case that communication be clear. The kitchen and bath designer should communicate with the interior designer and client about who is responsible for what and include that in documented forms, such as the purchase agreement.

An architect is sometimes necessary for a project. Typically, the client will hire an architect if the project involves an addition or new construction, and involvement depends on the architect. After the architect's plans are drafted, the general contractor takes the lead on managing the project. If issues arise regarding updates needed or the plans not meeting code, the architect would need to become involved again.

Building codes were created to protect the public's safety and welfare and impose minimum standards. The majority of construction requires a building permit. Permits are needed so it can be verified that the proposed project will meet all necessary codes. The type of project, the size, and the location determine the number of codes that need to be met and the type of building permit required. Permits must be obtained for every project. Some designers or installers may try to avoid obtaining them, as they can be a hassle. Not obtaining necessary permits puts any project at risk. If a nonpermitted project is discovered after it has been installed, some municipalities will force the homeowner

Kitchen Survey

Date: _____ **Client Name:** _____

HOUSE INFORMATION

1. When was the house built? _____

2. What type of house is it architecturally? _____

3. What type of architectural details do you like about the house? _____
_____

PROJECT INFORMATION

4. When do you want to start the project and when would you like it completed? _____
_____

5. Do you plan on using an interior designer or architect on the project? _____
_____

6. Do you have a contractor, or do you need a recommendation? _____

7. What is your budget? _____

8. How many people are in your household? _____

9. What family members will share in the decision making process? _____
_____

KITCHEN INFORMATION

10. What do you like about your present kitchen? _____
_____

11. What do you dislike about your present kitchen? _____
_____

    Have you gathered any images of kitchens or features you like? _____

12. Who is the primary cook? How many household members cook? _____
_____

Figure 1.17 A sample kitchen survey.

13. Are you right or left handed?   Primary Cook_____ Secondary_____

14. How tall are you?   Primary Cook _____ Secondary_____

15. Do you frequently bake or specialty cook?   _____

16. Do you sit while preparing food?   _____

17. Would you like a desk or message center?   _____

18. Approximately how many cookbooks do you have? _____
Would you like them hidden or in view? _____

19. How many sets of dishes do you have in the kitchen? _____

20. How much glassware do you have? _____

21. How much silverware do you have in the kitchen? _____

22. Are meals served in the kitchen? _____

23. How frequently do you entertain and for how many? _____

24. Do you store liquor or wine in the kitchen? If yes, do you require a lock?
_____

25. Is there anything you want to display? (wine, pottery, china, etc.)
_____

26. Do you have pets? _____

27. Do you store any medications or vitamins in the kitchen?
_____

28. How often do you go grocery shopping? Do you buy any food in bulk?
_____

29. Do you need a cabinet for brooms, mops and cleaning supplies?
_____

30. Do you have a preference between cabinets with drawers or doors?
_____

31. Would you like any cabinets that are open or have glass doors?
_____

32. Would you like a TV in the kitchen? If yes, would you like the ability to hide it?
_____

ACCESSORIES (circle)

Spice rack	Roll out shelves
Spice drawer	Cutlery dividers
Appliance garage	Utensil dividers
Plate rack	Knife block
Swing-out pantry system	Plate storage in drawer
Pull-out pantry	Bread box
Tray dividers	Waste basket/Recycle bin
Door can racks	Tilt out sink front
Pull out can racks	Pull-out towel bar
Base lazy susan	Swing-up mixer

APPLIANCES (size, finish, gas, electric or dual fuel, wood panels and style).

Free Standing Range_____   Cooktop_____

Single/Double Ovens_____   Microwave_____

Warming Drawer_____   Ventilation_____

Refrigerator_____   Under counter Refrigerator_____

Ice Maker_____   Wine Captain_____

Dishwasher_____   Disposal_____

FIXTURES (size, finish, and style)

Sink_____   Faucet_____

2nd Sink_____   Water Filter_____

Water Chiller_____   Hot Water Dispenser_____

Soap Dispenser_____   Pot Filler_____

to have it removed or impose a fine. Repercussions also can affect the designer. A designer may be penalized by any organization in which he or she is a member. If any safety issues were to occur as a result of codes not being followed, the designer, along with anybody else involved, could be sued.

Several types of codes may be relevant in the area where a project is located. The major types of codes include the following:

- Building codes
- Plumbing codes
- Electrical codes
- Fire safety codes

The Americans with Disabilities Act (ADA) has a list of guidelines, but they are not official codes. We discuss the ADA further in Chapter 2, which covers space planning for kitchen and bath projects. Codes are created by agencies and are then adopted by municipalities.

Codes vary from municipality to municipality, depending on which they have chosen to adopt. The International Residential Code (IRC) was created by the International Code Council (ICC). These codes are specific to residential construction and design. They were created with the intent that they would replace regional codes in the United States and eventually be used by other countries. The IRC is for one- and two-family dwellings and apartment buildings up to three stories. These codes cover a range of areas for construction and they consider regional differences.

The Uniform Plumbing Code (UPC) covers in detail the standards related to plumbing. These codes are used by most municipalities and therefore are an invaluable source to plumbers. The National Electrical Code (NEC) is the most widely used for electrical systems. Electricians use these codes, which are always being updated. The publication *Life Safety Code* is the most widely used fire safety code and is published by the National Fire Protection Association. We delve more into the specifics of these codes when we discuss planning the kitchen and bath in Chapter 2.

SUMMARY

Working in the kitchen and bath industry is an exciting career. Understanding how to lay the groundwork for a project is essential to a successful project. The designer who fails to ask questions or does not do his or her homework in the beginning is likely to run into problems later. Communication with the client in the early stages is incredibly important. The designer has many factors to think about and consider throughout a project. Having a structure, such as a survey, for the programming phase will greatly benefit the designer.

CHAPTER 1 EXERCISES

I: Estimate how much cabinets would cost for the Sowinskis' kitchen remodel, including the custom hutch in the adjoining dining area. (Figure 1.18). Estimate it in two different ways: vaguely and more accurately. Note: The house is worth $500,000 and the cabinets you sell are typically $200 per linear foot.

II: Measure a room in your home, using the techniques discussed in this chapter.

III: Determine what the finished wall dimensions will be for the following rough-dimensioned stud wall plan that you measured at the job site (Figure 1.19). The installer is using 1/2-inch drywall and there will be 3½-inch casing installed around doors and windows.

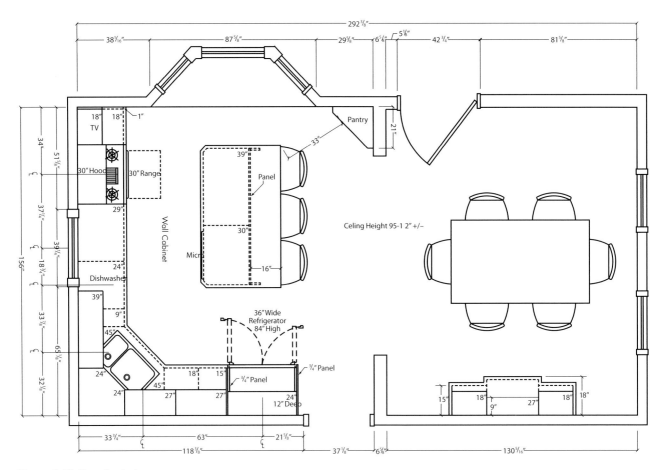

Figure 1.18 Exercise I plan.

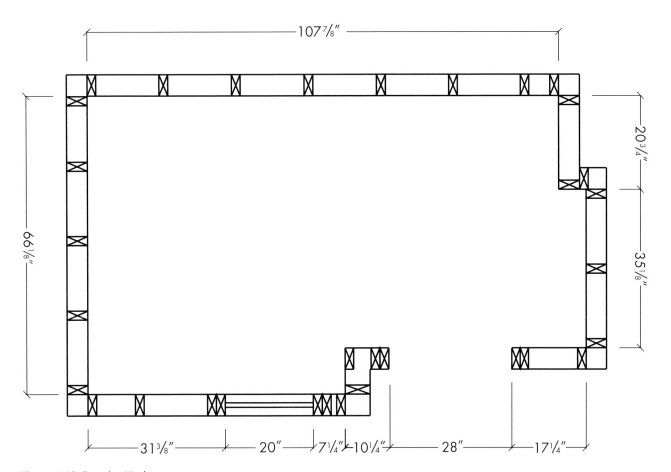

Figure 1.19 Exercise III plan.

CHAPTER 1 DISCUSSION QUESTIONS

1. What type of design firm would you like to work for? Or would you prefer having your own company eventually?
2. If you start your own design business, do you want to have a showroom? If yes, what type?
3. What are the benefits and disadvantages of the client hiring the contractor direct versus through the designer?
4. What items should you bring with you to the initial measure?
5. Name at least three reasons why taking before photos is beneficial to the designer.
6. What is the average length of time between kitchen remodels?

REFERENCE

Miller, Judith. *Period Kitchens: A Practical Guide to Period-Style Decorating*. London: Reed International Books Limited, 1995.

CHAPTER 1: DESIGN CHECKLIST

___ Have you calculated the cost of the kitchen remodel? A kitchen remodel costs roughly 10 percent to 20 percent of the home's value.

___Gather pricing for hypothetical kitchen and bath projects to have a starting point for pricing.

___Obtain a signed retainer, before investing too much time in a project.

___Never round off dimensions when measuring; always use the fraction of the inch to record.

___Take before photographs while measuring.

___Use a survey while interviewing the client, to record all the client's wants and needs for the project.

___Introduce yourself to the contractor if he or she is not employed by you.

___Have professional photographs taken of your completed work to include in your portfolio, if time and budget allow for it.

KEY TERMS

Centerline: The center of an object's location. Normally, the centerline dimension is taken relative to existing walls to ensure accuracy.

Retainer: A lump sum paid by the client to hire, or *retain,* the designer. How the money is applied is specified in the retainer contract between the client and designer.

Rough dimensions: Dimensions of incomplete construction, such as a wall where the drywall has not been hung and the windows and doors may not have been installed.

Walk-ins: People who walk into a showroom without an appointment.

OBJECTIVES

After reading this chapter, you will:

- Identify the elements and principles of design while planning the kitchen or bath space and distinguish specific ways to incorporate them.

- Grasp that space planning initially should be done by hand and technical drawings can be completed after the space layout options have been designed.

- Comprehend and accomplish space planning a kitchen or bath with stock cabinet sizes, because this is the most restrictive of all the various cabinet options.

DESIGN SCENARIO

Your client, the McManus family, is ready for you to space plan their kitchen. They are a family with one young daughter, age 8. The family loves their medium-sized, mixed-breed rescue dog, Jewel. They have filled out and reviewed their project survey with you. They want a kitchen that is both child- and pet-friendly because cooking is a family occasion. You've measured their space and are ready to start working up some different layout options to show them.

1. What can you do spatially to make this kitchen child friendly?

2. What can be done to make it pet friendly?

3. What are the requirements when there are two or more people working in the kitchen at once?

There are many things a designer must keep in mind simultaneously while planning a kitchen or bath layout: the client's needs, standard fixtures and cabinetry available, the elements and principles of design, and codes. Although this may seem like a lot of information to work with, it becomes easier with experience. Let's start out by taking a look at the elements and principles of design.

ELEMENTS AND PRINCIPLES OF DESIGN

Although space planning a kitchen or bath is similar to space planning any space, these rooms have many specific requirements. Because the designer is working with cabinet sizes and fixtures fitting along walls, the design process ends up involving quite a bit of basic math. The elements and principles of design are always important to keep in mind no matter what space is being planned and what stage of the design process is taking place (Table 2.1). These should be considered at every step, from space planning through material selection.

TABLE 2.1 THE ELEMENTS AND PRINCIPLES OF DESIGN	
Elements of Design	Principles of Design
1. Line	1. Proportion
2. Pattern	2. Balance
3. Texture	3. Rhythm
4. Scale	4. Contrast
5. Light	5. Emphasis
6. Color	6. Harmony

The elements and principles of design are important to the designer and should be kept in mind throughout the design process.

ELEMENTS OF DESIGN

The elements of design are what make up the design of a project. They are very important to consider when designing a space. The elements of design are as follows: line, pattern, texture, scale, light, and color.

Line
Two points relating to each other create a line. A line is one-dimensional and gives direction. Lines may be horizontal, vertical, or diagonal. They may be straight or curvilinear. Line can be emphasized in a kitchen or bath in many ways. It can be used architecturally with forms of items or texturally with finishes. (Figure 2.1).

Notice in Figure 2.1 how, above the vanity area, there is a piece of wood (called a *light rail*) housing lights. This piece gives a very horizontal feel to the space. Looking at the vanity cabinets, vertical lines can be seen in the cabinetry's rift-cut oak doors. Line also can be emphasized in other materials and in layout.

Pattern
Pattern is the repetition of a motif. Motifs creating a pattern may be geometric or organic. This, too, is an element that may be used in a design in various ways. For example, a pattern found in the tile may be carried over to the cabinetry or other items.

Texture
Texture is an element that may be both tactile and visual or it may only be visual. The characteristics of a surface are what make the texture. Texture may be used in many ways. Most often, contemporary spaces will have many smooth textures. These may make the space feel cooler. The designer may decide to add rougher textures to make the space feel warmer.

Scale
When a designer talks about scale, it is often in comparison with the human scale. How a ceiling height relates to a person, for example, affects his or her feeling in a space. Lower ceilings feel cozy whereas higher ceilings

Figure 2.1 This bath has used line as a prominent design element. The cabinetry is rift cut oak, with vertical lines. The shower door glass has a vertical line pattern. The light rail creates a horizontal line. *Courtesy of Pamela Polvere Designs and Dennis Jourdan Photography Inc.*

Ambient Lighting Ambient lighting may also be called general lighting. It is the lighting that is provided so people can move about the space safely. In a kitchen or bath, ambient lighting is typically recessed or consists of surface-mounted ceiling light fixtures. It usually is best to incorporate this layer of light after the task and accent lighting have been determined.

Task Lighting Task lighting is lighting used to illuminate an area where a task, or activity, takes place. In a bathroom, task lighting is very important near the mirror, where tasks such as shaving and makeup application will probably be done. Task lighting is also important in task areas such as the tub and shower. In a kitchen, task lighting is important when chopping vegetables on the counter or heating food on the cooking surface. A common example of task lighting in a kitchen is under-cabinet lights. These are lights applied to the underside of the wall cabinets. These lights also may be recessed or surface-mount ceiling lights, but they are directed specifically at a task area.

Accent Lighting Accent lighting emphasizes or highlights an area or item. It is often used to emphasize something, such as a piece of art, that the eye should be drawn to. In a kitchen, some task lights may also be considered accent lights. If decorative pendants are being used over an island, they are both task and accent lights. They are lighting a task, illuminating work at the island, but they also are decorative and therefore act as an accent. Sconces typically are considered accent lighting unless lighting a task area, such as around a vanity mirror. Another option for accent lighting in the kitchen is to have up-lights at the top of the wall cabinets. These lights will create a glow above the wall cabinets that will draw the eye. Another great way to incorporate accent lighting is with a textured wall. Wall washers can be installed to highlight a wall with texture, such as a brick wall.

feel grand. How pieces fit in a space affect the scale. If a small kitchen or bath has very large-scale cabinetry the space may feel wrong. Patterns also affect the scale. Tile creates a pattern when laid. The designer decides if a larger or smaller scale tile is appropriate, based on what is desired.

Light

Light is extremely important, as it is what makes it possible to see the design. Light is varied, depending on the illumination and the color it provides. There are three main types of lighting: ambient, task, and accent. Lighting is discussed in greater detail in Chapter 9.

Color

Color is another important design element. How pure or saturated the color is causes different effects and feelings. How colors work together or contrast each other also creates many various perceptions of a space. A brightly tiled shower enclosure in a bath where everything else is neutral will draw the eye to the shower area. The designer should consider the feel the client would like for the space. A relaxing area should have cool and soothing colors. If a client wants an exciting space, more vibrant, warm, and lively colors should be used.

PRINCIPLES OF DESIGN

The principles of design are considered more complex than the design elements. The elements are what make up the principles of design. The principles of design are as follows: proportion, balance, rhythm, contrast, emphasis, and harmony.

Proportion

The element of scale describes how an object relates to what is expected in terms of size. Proportion describes how an object relates to the whole or to other parts of the whole. The sense of proportion is instinctual. A designer knowing what is considered comfortable for proportion may choose different proportions to add interest to a space. A common trend in the kitchen recently is to have a proportionally large hood to emphasize it as the focal point.

Balance

Balance is the distribution of visual weight in a space. It can be symmetrical, asymmetrical, or radial. Balance is achieved in a kitchen most frequently with the cabinets, appliances, or architecture of the space. Radial balance is the most challenging to incorporate into a kitchen or bath. An example would be a circular kitchen. Perhaps there is a round island in the middle that the room radiates from. This is more challenging to accomplish in a

Figure 2.2 This bathroom's vanity is very much symmetrically balanced. *Courtesy of Drury Design Kitchen and Bath Studio.*

bath, as there is typically limited space. Symmetrical balance is the most common form of balance found. In a kitchen, a hood or other focal point will have a mirror image of cabinetry on either side of the focal point. In a bath, it is common for the sink and mirror area to be the focal point with symmetrical balance on either side (Figure 2.2).

"Symmetry is as essential element in all of my space plans. It is also what the client wants to see. I like to center ranges on walls, and sinks on windows, and make them centerpieces. I then like to mirror what happens from one side of the centerpiece to the other. If I have a 12" wide spice rack to the left of the range, I will place a 12" wide tray divider on the other side. If there is 3" of wall space from the window to the wall cabinet on the right side I will do the same on the left side. I believe the human eye seeks out differences from one side to another and sees them as flaws. By making the design symmetrical, it feels in balance and the end user is more comfortable in the space."
—*Lisa McManus, ASID, Kitchen and Bath Designer*

Rhythm

Rhythm is visual pattern repetition. Elements reoccur in a pattern of repetition. Rhythm may be seen in many aspects of the kitchen or bath; a good example in the bath would be with tile (Figure 2.3). Even if the tile is in different sizes, having the same shape, such as square or rectangular, produces a rhythmic effect.

Contrast

Contrast occurs when design elements are perceived as markedly different. Contrast is essential for adding interest to a space. For example, intentional contrast may be achieved by using multiple finishes: A kitchen

Figure 2.3 This bath is a great example of rhythm. The circle motif can be found in the tile, the vanity mirror, and even the shower doors. *Courtesy of Pamela Polvere Designs and Dennis Jourdan Photography Inc..*

with a perimeter of painted white cabinets and an island made of dark walnut cabinets would be a good example of contrast in finishes. Contrast also can be found within the various elements of design, such as line, color, and so on.

Emphasis

Emphasis describes the presence of a focal point in a design. A focal point draws attention but is still an integral part of the space. A common focal point in a kitchen is the hood. Because hoods are higher up, larger, have many attractive options, and are located above the heart of the kitchen, it becomes a natural focal point. Islands, a large decorative light fixture above an island, appliances built in to resemble an armoire, or a custom buffet are other examples of possible focal points. In the bath, a beautiful tub or vanity can become the focal point, creating emphasis. Art pieces also may be displayed in a manner to make them a focal point.

Harmony

Harmony describes the effect of a design in which the elements in the space work together. Although all the pieces are not the same, there should be a sense of unity or common idea connecting them. Harmony can be accomplished by using other elements of design, such as color or repetition.

CODES, ADA STANDARDS, AND TYPICAL ALLOWANCES

Codes, **Americans with Disabilities Act of 1990 (ADA)** standards, and typical allowances based on anthropometrics are needed when designing a kitchen or bath. Codes and ADA standards can be found in Box 2.1. Additional state and local codes may also be in effect, based on the location of the project. Typical allowances are standard in the industry for the kitchen work triangle, which includes the main sink, cooking surface,

and refrigerator. There are also additional typical allowances for kitchen counter space, traffic, and other areas of the kitchen or bath.

KITCHEN SPACE PLANNING

The following sections present some recommendations on typical allowances for the kitchen. Codes relevant to kitchen space planning can be found in Box 2.1.

Work Triangle

The work triangle consists of the cooking surface, the main sink, and refrigerator. Ideally, no leg of the work triangle should be less than 4' or more than 9'. This also applies to any additional appliances or work areas incorporated. Legs of the work triangle, or travel to additional appliances, are measured from the front center of the appliance or sink. No major traffic should pass through the work triangle. The aisles of the work triangle should be 42" wide for one cook or 48" wide for more than one cook. The path of the work triangle should also not intersect any obstacle by more than 12", as it makes moving between the appliances and sink more difficult.

Countertop Work Space

There are some standard industry allowances for countertop workspace in the kitchen. Countertop space on either side of the cooking surface should be at the same height and between 12" to 15" wide minimum. In addition, a cooking surface located on an island or peninsula should have at least 9" of counter space behind it, if at the same height, for safety. An oven should have, at minimum, a 15"-wide countertop space for landing. A refrigerator's landing space, which should be located next to or up to 48" adjacent, should be at least 15" wide. The main sink should have between 18" and 24" minimum on either side. Any additional sinks should have at least an 18"-wide countertop space on one side. When appliances or sinks share a countertop run, there should be at least a 36" width between them. A microwave should have a countertop space at least 15"

BOX 2.1 SPACE PLANNING CODES AND ADA STANDARDS

KITCHEN

DOOR/ENTRY

- Clear openings of doorways with swinging doors shall be measured between the face of door and stop, with the door open 90 degrees. (**American National Standards Institute [ANSI]** 404.2.3)
- When a passage exceeds 24" in depth, the minimum clear opening increases to 36". (ANSI A117.1 404)

DOOR INTERFERENCE

- For a standard hinged or swinging door, the clearance on the pull side of the door should be the door width plus 18" by 60". (ANSI A 117.1 404.2.3.1)
- The clearance on the push side of the door should be the door width by 48". (ANSI A 117.1 404.2.3.1)

WORK AISLE

Code Reference Regarding ADA
- A clear floor space of at least 30" by 48" should be provided at each kitchen appliance. Clear floor spaces can overlap. (ANSI A 117.1 305.3, 804.6.1)
- In a U-shaped kitchen, plan a minimum clearance of 60" between opposing arms. (ANSI A117.1 804.2.2, 1003.12.1.2)

- Include a wheelchair turning space with a diameter of at least 60", which can include knee* and toe** clearances. (ANSI A117.1 304.3.1)
- A wheelchair turning space could utilize a T-shaped clear space, which is a 60" square with two 12" wide by 24" deep areas removed from the corners of the square. This leaves a minimum 36"-wide base and two 36"-wide arms. T-shaped wheelchair turning spaces can include knee and toe clearances. (ANSI A117.1 304.3.2)

CLEANUP/PREP SINK PLACEMENT

Code Reference Regarding ADA
- The sink should be no more than 34" high or adjustable between 29" and 36". (ANSI 117.1.1002.4.2)
- The sink bowl should be no more than 6½" deep. (ANSI 117.1 1002.12.4.3)
- Exposed water supply and drainpipes under sinks should be insulated or otherwise configured to protect against contact. There should be no sharp or abrasive surfaces under sinks. (ANSI A117.1 606.6)

*Knee clearance must be a minimum 30" wide (36" to use as part of the T-turn) and maintain a 27" clear space under the cabinet, counter, or sink for a depth of 8". The next 3" of depth may slope down to a height of 9", with a clear space of at least 17" extending beneath the element. (ANSI 306.3)

**Toe clearance space under a cabinet or appliance is between the floor and 9" above the floor. Where toe clearance is required as part of a clear floor space, the toe clearance should extend 17" minimum beneath the element. (ANSI A117.1 306.2)

BOX 2.1 SPACE PLANNING CODES AND ADA STANDARDS *(CONTINUED)*

PREPARATION WORK AREA

Code Reference Regarding ADA
In a kitchen, there should be at least one 30"-wide section of counter, 34" high maximum or adjustable from 29" to 36". Cabinetry can be added under the work surface, provided it can be removed or altered without removal or replacement of the work surface, and provided the finished floor extends under the cabinet. (ANSI A 117.1 8.04.6.3, 1003.12.6.3)

DISHWASHER PLACEMENT

Code Reference Regarding ADA
A clear floor space of at least 30" by 48" should be positioned adjacent to the dishwasher door. The dishwasher door in the open position should not obstruct the clear floor space for the dishwasher or the sink. (ANSI A 117.1 804.6.3, 1003.12.6.3)

REFRIGERATOR LANDING AREA

Code Reference Regarding ADA
A clear floor space of 30" by 48" should be positioned for a parallel approach to the refrigerator/freezer with the centerline of the clear floor space offset 24" maximum from the centerline of the appliance. (ANSI A 117.1 804.6.6, 1003.12.6.6)

COOK SURFACE LANDING AREA

Code Reference Regarding ADA
- When a forward-approach clear floor space is provided at the cooktop, it should provide

knee and toe clearance and the underside of the cooktop should be insulated or otherwise configured to prevent burns, abrasions, or electric shock. (ANSI 1002.12.6.4)
- The location of cooktop controls should not require reaching across burners. (ANSI 1003.12.6.4)

COOKING SURFACE CLEARANCE

Code Requirement
- At least 30" of clearance is required between the cooking surface and an unprotected/combustible surface above it. (**International Residential Code [IRC]** M 1901.1)
- If a microwave hood combination is used above the cooking surface, then the manufacturer's specifications should be followed. (IRC M 1504.1)

COOKING SURFACE VENTILATION

Code Requirement
- Manufacturer's specifications must be followed. (IRC G 2407.1, IRC G 2447.1)
- The minimum required exhaust rate for a ducted hood is 100 cubic feet per minute (cfm) and must be ducted to the outside. (IRC M 1507.3)
- Make-up air may need to be provided. Refer to local codes. (IRC G 2407.4)

Code Reference Regarding ADA
- Operable parts should be operable with one hand and not require tight grasping, pinching, or twisting of the wrist. The force

BOX 2.1 SPACE PLANNING CODES AND ADA STANDARDS *(CONTINUED)*

required to activate operable parts should be 5 pounds maximum. (ANSI A117.1 309.4)

- Where a forward or side reach is unobstructed, the high reach should be 48" maximum and the low reach should be 15" minimum above the floor. (ANSI A117.1 308.2.1 and 308.3.1)
- Where a forward or side reach is obstructed by a 20" to 25" deep counter, the high reach should be 44" maximum. (ANSI A117.1 308.2.2)

OVEN LANDING AREA

Code Reference Regarding ADA

For side-opening ovens, the door latch side should be next to a countertop. (ANSI A 117.1 804.6.5.1)

STORAGE

Code Reference Regarding ADA

- Where a forward or side reach is unobstructed, the high reach should be 48" maximum and the low reach should be 15" minimum above the floor. (ANSI A117.1 308.2.1 and 308.3.1)
- Where a 20" to 25" deep counter obstructs a forward or side reach, the high reach should be 44" maximum. (ANSI A117.1 308.2.2)

ELECTRICAL RECEPTACLES

Code Requirement

GFCI (ground fault circuit interrupter) protection is required on all receptacles servicing countertop surfaces within the kitchen (IRC E 3802.6). Refer to IRC E 3801.4.1 through E 3801.4.5 for receptacle placement and locations.

LIGHTING

Code Requirement

- At least one wall switch–controlled light must be provided. Switch must be placed at the entrance. (IRC E 3803.2)
- Window/skylight area, equal to at least 8% of the total square footage of the kitchen, or a total living space that includes a kitchen, is required. (IRC R 303.1, IRC R 303.2)

BATHROOM

DOOR/ENTRY

Code Reference

- Clear openings of doorways with swinging doors shall be measured between the face of door and stop, with the door open 90 degrees. (ANSI 404.2.3)
- When a passage exceeds 24" in depth, the minimum clear opening increases to 36". (ANSI A 117.1 404)

BOX 2.1 SPACE PLANNING CODES AND ADA STANDARDS *(CONTINUED)*

DOOR INTERFERENCE

Code Requirement
No entry or fixture doors should interfere with one another and/or the safe use of the fixtures or cabinets. (IRC P 2705.1.6)

Code Reference Regarding ADA
For a standard hinged door or a swinging door, the minimum clearance on the pull side of the door should be the width of the door plus 18" by 60". (ANSI A 117.1 404.2.3.1)
The minimum clearance on the push side of the door should be the width of the door by 48". (ANSI A 117.1 404.2.3.1)

CEILING HEIGHT

Code Requirement
Bathrooms shall have a minimum floor to ceiling height of 80" over the fixture and at the front clearance area for fixtures. (IRC R305.1.4)
A shower or tub equipped with a showerhead shall have a minimum floor-to-ceiling height of 80" above a minimum area 30" by 30" at the showerhead. (IRC R305.1.4)

CLEAR SPACE

Code Requirement
A minimum space of at least 21" must be planned in front of lavatory, toilet, bidet, and tub. (IRC P 2705.1.5)
A minimum space of at least 24" must be planned in front of a shower entry. (IRC R 307.1)

Code Reference Regarding ADA
- A clear floor space of at least 30" (762 mm) by 48" (1,219 mm) should be provided at each fixture (ANSI 305.3). Clear spaces can overlap. (ANSI 1002.11.2)
- Include a wheelchair turning space with a diameter of at least 60" (1,524 mm), which can include knee* and toe* clearances. (ANSI 304.3.1)
- A wheelchair turning space could use a T-shaped space, which is a 60" square with two 12" wide by 24" deep areas removed from two corners of the square. This leaves a minimum 36"-wide base and two 36"-wide arms. T-shaped wheelchair turning spaces can include knee* and toe** clearances. (ANSI 304.3.2)

Grooming
The clear floor space should be centered on the lavatory. (ANSI 1002.10.1)

Bathing and Showering
Clearance in front of bathtubs should extend the length of the bathtub and be at least 30" wide. (ANSI 607.2)

*Knee clearance must be a minimum 30" wide (36" to use as part of the T-turn) and maintain a 27" clear space under the cabinet, counter, or sink for a depth of 8". The next 3" of depth may slope down to a height of 9", with a clear space of at least 17" extending beneath the element. (ANSI 306.3)

**Toe clearance space under a cabinet or fixture is between the floor and 9" above the floor. Where toe clearance is required as part of a clear floor space, the toe clearance should extend 17" minimum beneath the element. (ANSI 306.2)

BOX 2.1 SPACE PLANNING CODES AND ADA STANDARDS *(CONTINUED)*

Code Reference Regarding ADA
Bathing and Showering.
- When a permanent seat is provided at the head of the bathtub, the clearance should extend a minimum of 12" beyond the wall at the head end of the bathtub. (ANSI 607.2)
- The clearance in front of the transfer-type shower* compartment should be at least 48" long measured from the control wall and 36" wide. (ANSI 608.2)
- The clearance in front of a roll-in–type shower** compartment should be at least 60" long next to the open face of the shower compartment and 30" wide. (ANSI 608.2)

Toileting. When both parallel and forward approaches to the toilet are provided, the clearance should be at least 56" measured perpendicular from the rear wall, and 60" measured perpendicular from the sidewall. No other fixture or obstruction should be within the clearance area. (ANSI 604.3.1, 1002.11.5.2.3)

LAVATORY PLACEMENT

Code Requirement
- The minimum distance from the centerline of the lavatory to a wall is 15". (International Plumbing Code [IPC] 405.3.1)
- The minimum distance between a wall and the edge of a freestanding or wall-hung lavatory is 4". (IRC R 307.1)

*A transfer shower (36" by 36") provides support to a standing person or one who can stand to transfer.

**A roll-in shower is a waterproof area large enough for a person in a wheelchair to remain in the chair to shower. The preferred minimum size for a roll-in shower is 36" by 42" by 60".

DOUBLE LAVATORY PLACEMENT

Code Requirement
- The minimum distance between the centerlines of two lavatories should be at least 30". (IPC 405.3.1)
- The minimum distance between the edges of two freestanding or wall-hung lavatories is 4". (IRC R 307.1)

LAVATORY VANITY HEIGHT

Code Reference Regarding ADA
- The front of the lavatory sink should be no more than 34" above the floor, measured to the higher of the fixture or counter surface. (ANSI 606.3)
- Lavatory controls should be operable with one hand and not require tight grasping, pinching, or twisting of the wrist. (ANSI 309.4)

SHOWER SIZE

Code Requirement
The minimum interior shower size is 30" by 30" or 900 square inches, in which a disc 30" in diameter must fit. (IRC P 2708.1, IPC 417.4)

Code Reference Regarding ADA
- Transfer-type shower compartments should have an inside finished dimension of 36" by 36", and have a minimum 36"-wide entry on the face of the shower compartment. A seat must be provided within the 36" by 36" area. (ANSI 608)

BOX 2.1 SPACE PLANNING CODES AND ADA STANDARDS *(CONTINUED)*

- Roll-in-type shower compartments should have a minimum inside finished dimension of at least 30" wide by 60" deep, and have at minimum a 60"-wide entry on the face of the shower compartment. (ANSI 608.2.2)

TUB/SHOWER CONTROLS

Code Reference Regarding ADA
- Tub/shower controls should be operable with one hand and not require tight grasping. (ANSI 309.4)
- Controls should be on an end wall of the bathtub, between the rim and grab bar, and between the open side of the bathtub and the mid-point of the width of the tub. (ANSI 607.5)
- Controls in roll-in showers should be above the grab bar, but no higher than 48" above the shower floor. In transfer-type shower compartments, controls, faucets, and the shower unit should be on the sidewall opposite the seat, between 38" and 48" above the shower floor. (ANSI 608.5)
- A handheld spray unit should be provided with a hose at least 59" long that can be used as a fixed showerhead and as a handheld shower. In transfer-type showers, the controls and shower unit should be on the control wall within 15" of the centerline of the seat. In roll-in–type showers, shower spray units mounted on the back wall should be no more than 27" from the sidewall. If an adjustable-height showerhead mounted on a vertical bar is used, the bar should not obstruct the use of the grab bars. (ANSI 608.6)

SHOWER/TUB CONTROL VALVES

Code Requirement
Shower and tub/shower control valves must be one of the following: pressure balanced, thermostatic mixing, or combination pressure balance/thermostatic mixing valve types. (IRC P2708.3)

SHOWER/TUB SEAT

Code Requirement
Shower seat must not infringe on the minimum interior size of the shower (900 square inches). (IRC P 2708.1)

Code Reference Regarding ADA
- A removable in-tub seat should be at least 15" to 16" deep and capable of secure placement. (ANSI 610.2)
- A permanent tub seat should be at least 15" deep and positioned at the head end of the bathtub. The top of the seat should be between 17" and 19" above the bathroom floor. (ANSI 610.2)
- Where a seat is provided in a roll-in shower, it should be a folding type and on the wall adjacent to the controls. The top of the seat should be between 17" and 19" above the bathroom floor.
- In a transfer-type shower, the seat should be a folding type and extend from the back wall to a point within 3" of the shower entry. (ANSI 610.3)
- The materials and installation of the shower and/or bathtub seat must support a minimum of 250 pounds of pressure. (ANSI 610.4)

BOX 2.1 SPACE PLANNING CODES AND ADA STANDARDS *(CONTINUED)*

TUB/SHOWER SURROUND

Code Requirement
The wall area above a tub or shower pan must be covered in a waterproof material to a height not less than 72" above the finished floor. (IPC 417.4.1, IRC R 307.2)

GRAB BARS

Code Reference Regarding ADA
Grab bars should be installed at the tub, shower, and toilet according to the following:

- Bathtubs with permanent seats: Two horizontal grab bars should be provided on the back wall, one between 33" and 36" above the floor and the other 9" above the rim of the bathtub. Each grab bar should be no more than 15" from the head end wall or 12" from the foot end wall. A grab bar 24" long should be provided on the foot end wall at the front edge of the bathtub. (ANSI 607.4.1)
- Bathtubs without permanent seats: Two horizontal grab bars should be provided on the back wall, one between 33" and 36" above the floor and the other 9" above the rim of the bathtub. Each grab bar should be at least 24" long and no more than 24" from the head end wall or 12" from the foot end wall. A grab bar 24" long should be provided on the foot end wall at the front edge of the bathtub. A grab bar 12" long should be provided on the head end wall at the front edge of the bathtub. (ANSI 607.4.2)
- Transfer-type showers: Grab bars should be mounted in a horizontal position, between 33" and 36" above the floor, across the control wall and across the back wall to a point 18" from the control wall. (ANSI 608.3.1)
- Roll-in type shower: Grab bars should be mounted in a horizontal position, between 33" and 36" above the floor, on all three walls of the shower, but not behind a seat. Grab bars should be no more than 6" from each adjacent wall. (ANSI 608.3.2)
- Toilet: Grab bars should be provided on the rear wall and on the sidewall closest to the toilet. The sidewall grab bar should be at least 42" long and located between 12" and 54" from the rear wall. The rear grab bar should be at least 24" long, centered on the toilet. Where space permits, the bar should be at least 36" long, with the additional length provided on the transfer side of the toilet. (ANSI 604.5)

GLAZING

Code Requirement
- Glass used in tub or shower enclosures (i.e., tub or shower door) or partitions must be tempered or an approved equal and must be permanently marked as such. (IRC R 308.1)
- If the tub or shower surround has glass windows or walls, the glazing must be tempered glass or approved equal when the bottom edge of glazing is less than 60" above any standing or walking surface. (IRC R 308.4.5)
- Any glazing (i.e., windows or doors) whose bottom edge is less than 18" above the floor must be tempered glass or approved equal. (IRC R 308.4.7.2)

BOX 2.1 SPACE PLANNING CODES AND ADA STANDARDS *(CONTINUED)*

TUB/SHOWER DOOR

Code Requirement
Hinged shower doors shall open outward. (IRC P 2708.1)

Code Reference Regarding ADA
Shower compartment thresholds should be no more than 1/2" high. Changes in level of no more than 1/4" high are permitted, but changes in level between 1/4" high and 1/2" high should be beveled with a slope not steeper than 1:2. (ANSI 608.7.303)

FLOORING

Code Reference Regarding ADA
Plan a slope for the bathtub or shower drain with a maximum slope of 1:48 pitch 1/4 inch per foot. (ratio 1:48) (ANSI 403.3)

EQUIPMENT ACCESS

Code Requirement
- All equipment, including access panels, must be installed as per manufacturers' specifications. (IRC P 2720.1)
- All manufacturers' instructions must be available for installers and inspectors and left for homeowners. (IRC M 1307.1)

TOILET/BIDET PLACEMENT

Code Requirement
A minimum distance of 15" is required from the centerline of toilet and/or bidet to any bath fixture, wall, or other obstacle. (IRC R 307.1, IRC P 2705.1.5, IPC 405.3.1)

Code Reference Regarding ADA
- The toilet should be centered 16" to 18" from a sidewall. (ANSI 1002.11.5)
- The toilet seat should be between 15" and 19" from the floor. (ANSI 1002.11.5.3)

TOILET COMPARTMENT

Code Requirement
The minimum size for a separate toilet compartment is 30" by 60". (IPC 405.3.1)

Code Reference Regarding ADA
Wheelchair-accessible compartments should be at least 60" wide, measured perpendicular to the sidewall, and 56" deep for a wall hung toilet and at least 59" deep for a floor-mounted toilet measured perpendicular to the rear wall. (ANSI 604.8.1.1)

STORAGE

Code Reference Regarding ADA
- Where a forward or side reach is unobstructed, the high reach should be 48" maximum and the low reach should be 15" minimum above the floor. (ANSI 308.2.1, 308.3.1)
- Where a forward or side reach is obstructed by a 20" to 25" deep counter, the high reach should be 44" maximum. (ANSI 308.2.2, 308.3.2)
- Door/drawer pulls should be operable with one hand, require only a minimal amount of strength for operation, and should not require tight grasping. (ANSI 309.4)

BOX 2.1 SPACE PLANNING CODES AND ADA STANDARDS *(CONTINUED)*

ACCESSORIES

Code Reference Regarding ADA
- Mirrors above lavatories should have the bottom edge of the reflecting surface no more than 40" above the floor. (ANSI 603.3)
- The toilet paper holder should be 7" to 9" in front of the toilet bowl and between 15" and 48" above the floor. There should be a clearance of at least 1½" below or 12" above the grab bar. (ANSI 604.7)

ELECTRICAL RECEPTACLES

Code Requirement
- At least one GFCI protected receptacle must be installed within 36" of the outside edge of the lavatory. (IRC E 3801.6)
- All receptacles must be protected by GFCIs. (IRC 3802.1)
- A receptacle shall not be installed within a shower or bathtub space. (IRC E 3902.11)
- Switches shall not be installed within wet locations in tub or shower spaces or within reach while standing in the tub or shower unless installed as part of the listed tub or shower assembly. (IRC E 3901.7)

LIGHTING

Code Requirement
- At least one wall switch–controlled light must be provided. Switch must be placed at the entrance of the bathroom. (IRC E 3901.6, IRC E 3803.2)

- All light fixtures installed within tub and shower spaces should be marked "suitable for damp/wet locations." (IRC E 3903.8)
- Hanging fixtures cannot be located within a zone of 3' horizontally and 8' vertically from the top of the bathtub rim or shower stall threshold. (IRC E 3903.10)

Code Reference Regarding ADA
Operable parts should be operable with one hand and not require tight grasping, pinching, or twisting of the wrist. The force required to activate operable parts should be 5 pounds maximum. (ANSI A117.1 309.4)

VENTILATION

Code Requirement
Minimum ventilation for the bathroom is to be a window of at least 3 square feet of which 50% is operable, or a mechanical ventilation system of at least 50 cubic feet per minute (cfm) ducted to the outside. (IRC R 303.3, IRC M 1507.3)

HEAT

Code Requirement
All bathrooms should have an appropriate heat source to maintain a minimum room temperature of 68 degrees Fahrenheit. (IRC R 303.8)

Source: Courtesy of American National Standards Institute (ANSI), Americans with Disabilities Act (ADA), International Residential Code (IRC), and International Plumbing Code (IPC).

wide, ideally located on the handle side. The accessible kitchen should have multiple countertop heights.

Breaking up Work Centers
A full-height item, such as a pantry cabinet, refrigerator, or tall oven cabinet, should avoid interrupting continuous counter space as much as possible.

Cooking Surface Considerations
At minimum, there should be 24" between the cooking surface and a protected noncombustible surface above it. It also should not have flammable window treatments above it, and a fire extinguisher should be near the exit.

Dishwasher Placement
It typically makes sense for the dishwasher to be next to the main sink to make the dishwashing process easiest. The farthest away the dishwasher should be from the main sink is 36" from the sink edge. If a main sink is located in a diagonal corner cabinet, there needs to be a minimum 9"-width cabinet between the sink cabinet and the dishwasher. If this is not done, the dishwasher will not open while the user is at the sink.

Microwave Oven Placement
When planning the location of a microwave, it is most important to consider the main user to select the appropriate height. However, it should not be located more than 54" above the floor.

Seating Clearance
When planning seating at an island or peninsula, it is important to consider the height the countertop will be at to decide what its depth should be for the users. Basically, the closer to the ground the user is seated, the deeper the knee space should be for the best comfort. When the countertop is 30" high, table height, the knee space should be 18" deep. When the countertop is 36" high, standard work countertop height, the knee space should be 15" deep. When the countertop is 42" high, bar height, it should be 12" deep, minimum. No matter what the height of the countertop, each seated user needs a minimum of 24" in width. When planning for accessible seating, it should be between 28" and 34" high, 30" and 36" wide, and 19" deep.

Knee Spaces for the Accessible Kitchen
In the accessible kitchen, there should be at least a 30"-wide portion of countertop that has a permanent or adjustable knee space. There should also be knee space at or adjacent to the main sink and any additional sinks. It is also important that exposed pipes be insulated at the sink. There should be knee space at the cooking surface, which is lowered to 34" above the finished floor.

BATHROOM SPACE PLANNING

The following sections present standard industry allowances for space planning a bathroom. Codes relevant to space planning the bath can be found in Box 2.1.

Clearance
When planning a bathroom, it is best if there is at least 30" of clear floor space between fixtures or between fixtures and a wall or obstacle. In the accessible bathroom, it is best to account for extra clearance space for maneuvering.

Lavatory Placement
Ideally, the length of the centerline of the lavatory to the sidewall or obstacle should be at least 20". When a double lavatory is used, the distance between the centerlines of the two lavatories should be at minimum 36". When planning an accessible bathroom, it is best to have knee space at the lavatory. Keep in mind, any exposed pipes need to be insulated to prevent scalding.

Toilet/Bidet Placement
Although 15" is the code minimum for a toilet or bidet centerline from any bath fixture, wall, or obstacle, it is recommended that it be 18" if space allows. If a wall-mounted toilet is being used, it is best that the seat height be between 15" and 19" high. When a water

closet, that is, a separate room for the toilet, is used it should be at least 36" by 66", with a door that does not infringe on that space.

Shower Size

Although code requires a minimum 30" by 30" floor space for a shower, the ideal minimum is 36" by 36". When planning an accessible bathroom, a transfer or roll-in shower is best used. A transfer shower is used when the user can stand or at least stand to transfer. A roll-in shower is large enough so that a person in a wheelchair may remain in the chair to shower. For specific code requirements regarding these accessible showers, see Box 2.1.

Tub/Shower Controls

It is best if shower or tub controls are accessible from both inside and outside the water spray. This helps the user select the water temperature before entering the shower or tub. Shower controls should be located between 38" and 48" above the floor. Bathtub controls should be located between the rim of the tub and 33" above the floor. A hand-held spray is a great fixture to recommend for a couple reasons. It is nice for the user to have flexibility with the water spray location. It is also nice to have as it makes cleaning easier.

Shower/Tub Seat

A shower or tub seat is a smart thing to incorporate. When used, it is best if it is between 17" and 19" above the shower floor and 15" deep.

Grab Bars

Grab bars are needed in the accessible bathroom. They are located in the toilet, tub, and shower areas. Their location should be based on the height and needs of the user. It is important that the contractor be aware ahead of time that grab bars need to be installed, so that the walls can be properly prepared to handle the weight. The grab bars themselves are not heavy, but they must be able to support 250 pounds of pressure from a person leaning for support. Grab bars should be

located between 33" and 36" above the finished floor. They should also be 1¼" to 2" in diameter and have a 1½" clearance from the wall.

Steps at the Tub

Tubs should not have steps leading to the entrance. In the event that steps are used, for some reason, there must be a grab bar or hand rail.

Accessories Placement

Locations for accessories should also be decided when planning the bathroom layout. The toilet tissue holder is best positioned between 7" and 9" in front of the toilet bowl and 15"–48" above the finished floor. If a grab bar is also being used, the toilet tissue holder should be at least 1–½" below or 12" above the grab bar to avoid interference. Mirrors placed at a vanity should be hung with the bottom no more than 40" above the finished floor. This is a general rule, and the height of the user should be considered in deciding the best height. It's most important that the mirror is located at eye level based on the user's height. Towel bars, towel rings, and hooks are additional accessories that need to be located. Consider the use when deciding placement of these items. Towel rings are usually located near the sink for hand towels. Towel bars or hooks should be placed where they can be easily accessed when exiting the shower or tub area. The generic standard height for these items is 48" above the finished floor. Again, it is best to decide these placements based on the actual user's height. Many designers will even stand in the space with the client and measure what the most comfortable height is for the user. Another popular accessory that can be considered is one or multiple alcoves in the shower or tub area. Alcoves, sometimes referred to as niches, are openings in the wall that create a little shelf. Typically, alcoves should not be installed on exterior walls. They are also not ideally located on the shower plumbing wall. Not only will the wall already have many pipes within it, but it's not the most convenient for the user to have to reach past the water to grab soap or shampoo. While alcoves are most often used for additional storage while not encroaching on the space, there is also the option to include a small alcove for shaving in a shower situation. This is simply a smaller alcove located closer to the floor and allowing a step to make shaving ones legs easier. Since alcoves are a custom feature built on site, their sizes can vary. Like the other accessories, 15"–48" above the finished floor is a good standard range to locate them. Now that we've discussed planning specific to bathrooms, let's take a look at the allowances relevant to both the kitchen and bath.

SPACE PLANNING ALLOWANCES FOR BOTH THE KITCHEN AND BATH

Some standard allowances are relevant to both the kitchen and bath. The following section covers these typical dimensions.

Traffic for a Kitchen or Bath

Walkways, outside of the work area in the kitchen, should be at least 36" wide. When designing for accessibility and there are two perpendicular walkways, one should be at least 42" wide. A door opening should have a 34"-wide door, at minimum, to allow for sufficient space. If designing an accessible space, the door should be at least 36" wide. In the kitchen, a door should not interfere with appliance doors. Appliance doors should also not interfere with one another.

When traffic needs to pass behind a counter or table, 44" is needed for the walkway. If edging past is acceptable behind the counter or table, 36" is needed in width. A width of 32" is the minimum space for the seated user between the counter or table and wall or other obstruction, which does not allow for any traffic behind.

When planning for an accessible kitchen, 36" is the minimum space between the counter or table and wall or other obstruction. A width of 60" is required if a person in a wheelchair needs to pass by.

Reachable Items in a Kitchen or Bath

Anything that needs to be accessed frequently should be located between 15" and 48" above the finished floor to minimize bending and reaching. This applies to storage and controls. When designing an accessible space, everything should be planned at this height for the user. Any controls used for an accessible space should be easy to manipulate and read.

SPACE PLANNING THE KITCHEN OR BATH

We will first take a look at planning the kitchen. For either kitchen or bath, once measurements have been taken the designer can start working on space planning. Design firms use a range of different systems for drafting plans. Regardless of how the final completed plans are drafted, it is best to work on the initial design layout by hand. The following example is based on the assumption that the designer is using AutoCAD (computer-aided design), but can be applied to almost any system for completing final drawings.

PLAN BY HAND

The first step for space planning the kitchen is to draft only the shell of the space. Once the shell is drafted copies can be made to sketch on, or tracing paper can be laid on top. As mentioned previously, the designer should always space plan by hand initially: Focus only on how to lay out the space, rather than on what the final drafted plans need to be. For example, if space planning in AutoCAD, it would be a waste of time to draft something with all the necessary details only to realize the solution does not work. Many novice designers may be tempted by these newer technologies to think that they can skip the planning-by-hand stage, but it is crucial to good design not to omit this step.

KITCHEN EXAMPLE

Now let's take a look at an example for a way to space plan a kitchen. We start out with a blank shell and the list of requirements that we need to fit in the space (Figure 2.4).

In our examples, we will assume that we are working with a stock cabinet company because this is the most restrictive type of cabinet manufacturer. Once you are able to design with stock cabinetry, you can design with any type of cabinetry, including semicustom and custom. Many designers, who work with semicustom or custom cabinet companies, still try to design within standard sizes to keep the price of the kitchen from rising needlessly.

When space planning a kitchen it is easiest to start by considering the base and tall cabinets. Once these items are in place, the wall cabinets are inserted.

Sink Placement

The first item to be placed is the sink. The sink is to be placed under the window so the user can look outside while working. This sample kitchen will have a 33"-wide sink, which fits inside a 36"-wide cabinet (Figure 2.5). The sink cabinet must be larger than the sink or the sides of the cabinet will have to be cut, which is not ideal. Notice in the example that the image has dimensions showing how much space is remaining on either side of the sink. Keeping notes of the space remaining helps with space planning.

DESIGNER'S DIALOGUE 2.2

"I always start a design with the placement of the sink, because it is the most used appliance in the kitchen. It is used for both prep and cleanup. The sink usually gets placed between the refrigerator and the range, and typically under a window or possibly in a corner. To me, this is a good start to a good working kitchen."
—*Pamela Polvere, CKD, Kitchen and Bath Designer*

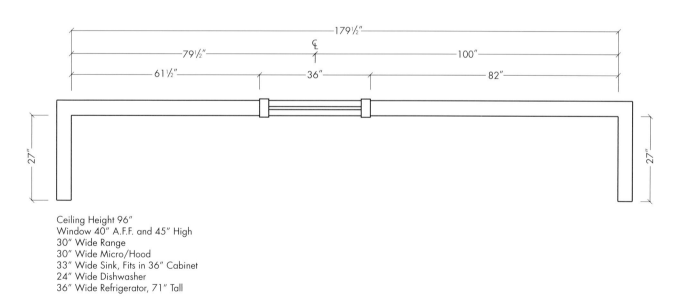

Ceiling Height 96"
Window 40" A.F.F. and 45" High
30" Wide Range
30" Wide Micro/Hood
33" Wide Sink, Fits in 36" Cabinet
24" Wide Dishwasher
36" Wide Refrigerator, 71" Tall

Figure 2.4 Here is the blank kitchen shell with some basic requirements.

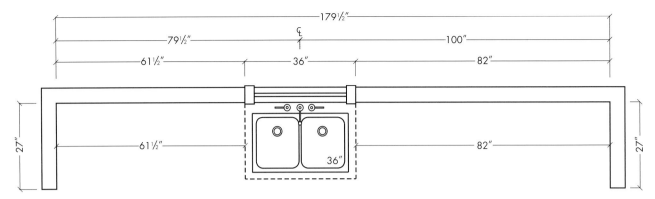

Figure 2.5 The kitchen sink is placed under the window.

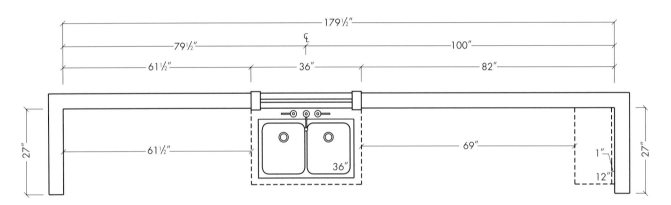

Figure 2.6 A 12"-wide base is placed to allow a landing area for the range.

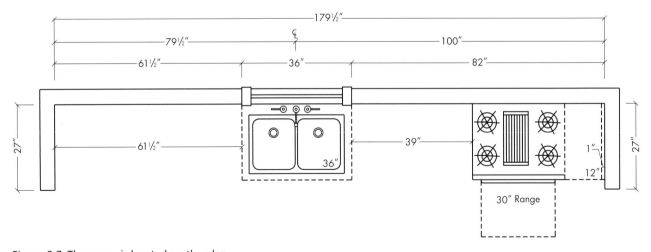

Figure 2.7 The range is located on the plan.

Cooking Surface Placement

Because the appliances making up the work triangle are what's most important for the work area, I will now place another piece of this triangle: the range (Figure 2.6). I decide that, because I have more space to the right of the sink, I will place the range on that side. I remember that my guidelines suggest allowing 12" on one side and 15" on the other side of the range. I decide to place a 12" cabinet to the right of where I want to put my range. Notice I have allowed an inch away from the wall. As we discuss in Chapter 5, walls are never plumb and even. I allow 1", so a filler piece can be cut to follow the wall, leaving no gap between the cabinet and the wall. I then place my range directly next to the 12" base cabinet (Figure 2.7).

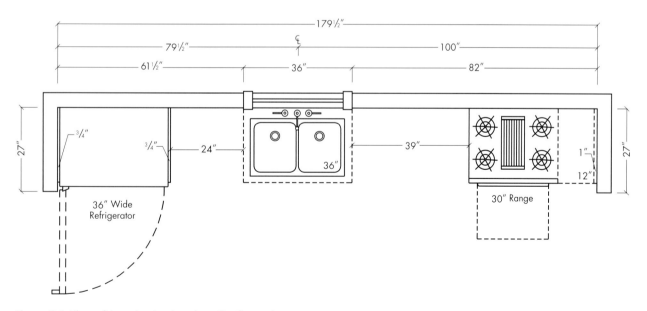

Figure 2.8 The refrigerator is placed on the floor plan.

Refrigerator Placement

Next, I decide to place my refrigerator, as this will complete my work triangle. Because the refrigerator is tall and I do not want a tall item to break up my counter space, I decide to place my refrigerator close to the wall on the other side of the sink (Figure 2.8).

When I place my refrigerator, I also put 3/4" panels on either side of it. Most refrigerators are sold with unfinished sides, so placing tall wood panels will hide these unfinished sides.

Dishwasher Placement

I now have 24" remaining between the refrigerator and sink cabinet. Although I have a 24" dishwasher to place, I would rather leave that space as a cabinet. A dishwasher cannot support the weight of the countertop. It is always necessary to have either a cabinet or panel next to the dishwasher to support the countertops. I turn the space into a cabinet and place the dishwasher directly to the right of the sink cabinet (Figure 2.9).

DESIGNER'S DIALOGUE 2.4

"For kitchens that have a blank slate that allow you to place appliances and plumbing anywhere I will take into account the adjacent room or rooms. This is especially important if it is an open floor plan. It's important to think how the user will work in the space and interact with family and friends who will be watching or helping cook. People spend most of their time at the sink and so I start with that as the main point of the room. It is central to everything you do, so it should be located within reach of the other appliances and work areas. I then move through the space and place the refrigerator in the best spot that can be accessed by the cook and also those not cooking in a way that they will not interfere with the cook. The placement of the ovens and cooking surface are dependent on the type of cook."

—Amy Bodell-Hersch, CKD, Allied ASID, Instructor

Remaining Cabinetry

I have 16" remaining between the dishwasher and the range. Because I am designing with stock cabinetry my cabinets must be in 3" increment widths. I decide to move 1" to my filler on the right wall, which will leave me with 15", an increment of 3". This now completes my base cabinet layout (Figure 2.10).

If I were using custom cabinetry, two things would be different. The filler would become an extended stile on the 12" base cabinet. (Cabinet details such as this one will be discussed further in Chapter 5.) I also would specify that the cabinets on either side of the range and dishwasher have finished sides. The 12" cabinet would be finished left, the 15" cabinet would be finished on both sides, and the sink cabinet would be finished right. This is good practice for cabinets next to appliances because the cabinet sides many be slightly exposed and it is better to see a finished side peeking out than an unfinished side.

Wall Cabinets

Now I am ready to figure out my wall cabinets. Because I need to place a microwave/hood it is best to situate that right away, over the range. The microwave/hood will be attached to a wall cabinet above it. After I place these items my only option to the right of the microwave/hood is a 12" wall cabinet with a 2" filler, which matches up with the base cabinet (Figure 2.11).

It is easy to place wall cabinets in the remaining space. I decide to use a 21" wall cabinet to the right of the refrigerator. I do not go with a 24" cabinet because I do not want my wall cabinet to be right against the window casing. To the right of the window, I use a 36"-wide wall cabinet. This cabinet is also 3" away from the window. It is best to try to have wall cabinets on either side of the window the same distance away from the window. The only wall space still open is above the refrigerator. Because we have panels on either side of the refrigerator we have a 36" wide space above the refrigerator (Figure 2.12). If possible, it is best to use a 24" deep wall cabinet above a refrigerator versus the standard 12" depth.

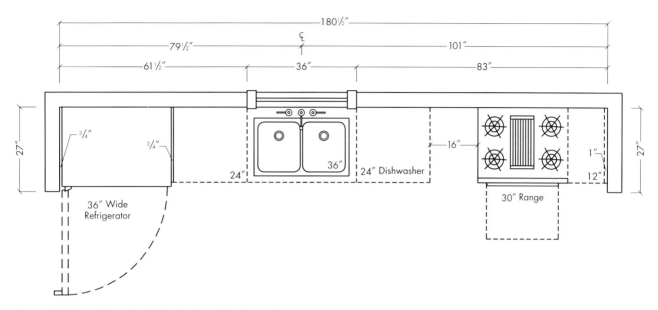

Figure 2.9 The dishwasher is located next to the sink.

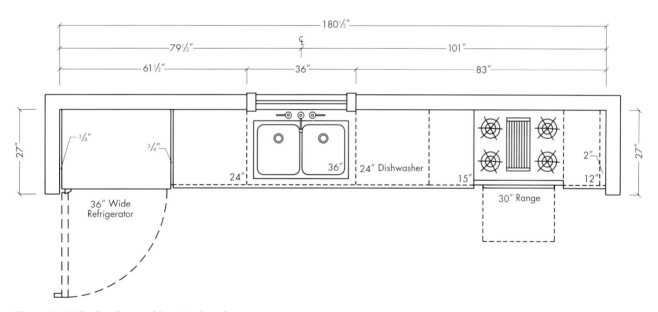

Figure 2.10 The last base cabinet is placed.

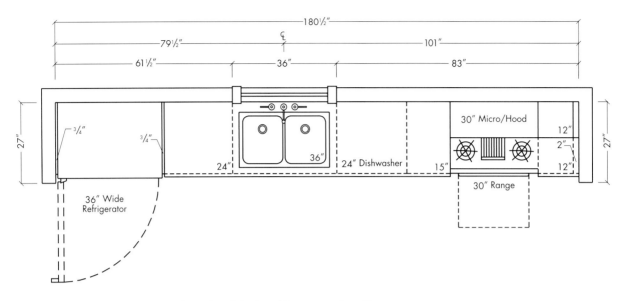

Figure 2.11 The wall cabinet to the right of the hood is easy to place first.

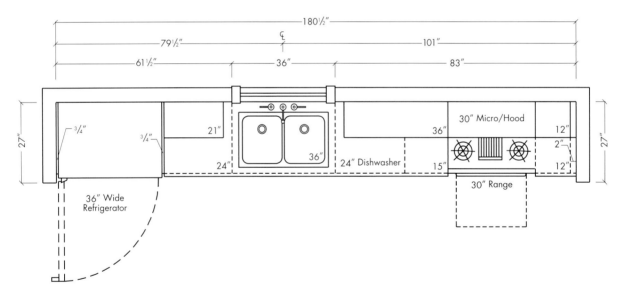

Figure 2.12 The wall cabinets on either side of the window have equal reveals.

Wall and Tall Cabinet Heights

Next, I need to decide on the height of my wall cabinets. Because my ceiling is 96" high I have a few options. I could take the cabinets to the ceiling for a 96" overall height or to another standard tall cabinet height such as 84" or 90" tall. I should also consider the height and projection of any crown molding I plan to use, and specifically how it would affect the cabinetry.

Double-Check Space Plan

I can always double-check that my space planning will actually work, by taking the total length of the wall and subtracting the items I have placed along the wall. If the numbers do not add up it is best to check each section of wall. In our example, I would check each side of the window because I centered my sink on the window.

DESIGNER'S DIALOGUE 2.5

"When considering storage, all items should be placed at the point of first use or last use. Pots and pans can be by the dishwasher or range since they end up in both places. Most people like storage based by first use, so usually pots and pans would be stored by the range. If there is not enough space by the range, it's OK to locate them by the dishwasher since this is still a step in their use. Dishes can be stored by the dishwasher or the table. The dishes get carried to the table to be used, but get carried to the dishwasher as well to be cleaned."

—*Gail Drury, CMKBD, Kitchen and Bath Designer*

BATH EXAMPLE

Now let's take a look at a sample space plan for a bath. We will start out with a blank shell and the list of requirements we need to fit in the space (Figures 2.13 and 2.14).

This shell has an existing toilet location. Although anything can be done for a price, moving a toilet is an expensive endeavor that is often best avoided. Sometimes a toilet can be rotated or moved along a wall fairly easily if the joists are running in the proper direction, but this is not commonly the case. For our example, we are going to assume the worst, that the toilet needs to remain in the same location. Adding a half wall to partially hide the toilet is nice for bathroom ambiance if the space allows it (Figure 2.15).

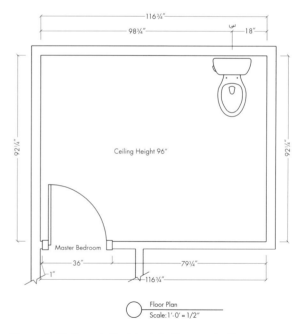

Figure 2.13 Here is the blank bathroom shell.

BATH SURVEY

Date: *9/10/12*   Client Name: *Heather and Jason Morris*

HOUSE INFORMATION

1. When was the house built? *1961*

2. What type of house is it architecturally? *Ranch*

3. What type of architectural details do you love about the house? *Large open areas*

PROJECT INFORMATION

4. When do you want to start the project and when would you like it completed? *As soon as possible*

5. Do you plan on using an interior designer or architect on the project? *No*

6. Do you have a contractor, or do you need a recommendation? *Need recommendation*

7. What is your budget? *$30,000*

8. How many people are in your household? *2 adults and 3 children ages 13-18*

9. What family members will share in the decision making process? *Heather and Jason*

BATH INFORMATION

10. Is this a master *X* , children   , or guest   bath project?

11. How many bathrooms are in the home? *3*

12. Who will use the bathroom? *Primarily Heather and Jason, occasionally the children*

13. How many family members will use the bathroom at one time? *2*

14. Have you considered privacy zoning to allow several users to occupy the space at one time? *Yes, would like.*

15. Do you prefer separate showering and bathing areas? *Yes, but don't think have space*

Figure 2.14 Here are the clients' requirements for the bathroom.

16. Do you prefer that the toilet and/or bidet be separated from the other fixtures, and placed in its own compartment?
_No_

17. Do you want a make-up area?   _No_

18. What type of feeling would you like your new bathroom space to have?   _Spa feeling_

19. Are there any special storage requirements?   _Lots of storage_

PLUMBING FIXTURES:

20. Toilet (one piece, two piece, round seat, elongated seat, etc.)   _Elongated_

21. Bidet   _No_

22. Tub (free-standing, whirlpool, air, drop-in)

23. Tub/shower combination   _Yes_

24. Shower (tile base, built-in bench, steam, clear or obscure glass doors, body sprays, hand-held spray)
Glass doors and hand-held

25. Sinks (undermount, vessel)   _1 is fine, undermount_

26. Faucets   _Want with two handles_

ACCESSORIES:

Phone:	Towel rack:
TV:	Towel warmer:
Stereo:	Medicine cabinet:
Grab bar:	Laundry hamper:
Tissue holder:	Pull-out waste basket:
Towel bar:	Wall mounted shelves:
Towel ring:	Shampoo niche:
Towel hooks:	Robe hooks:

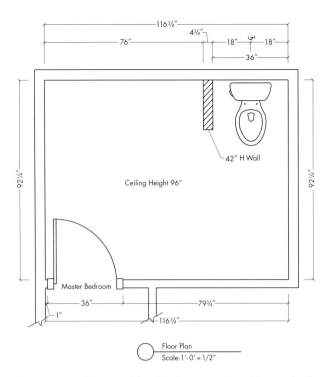

Figure 2.15 A knee wall is added next to the toilet to give it a little privacy.

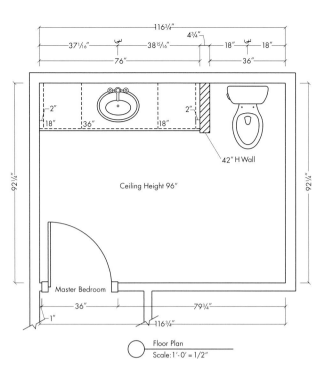

Figure 2.17 As an alternative, the sink can be centered, allowing for two 18" base cabinets on either side.

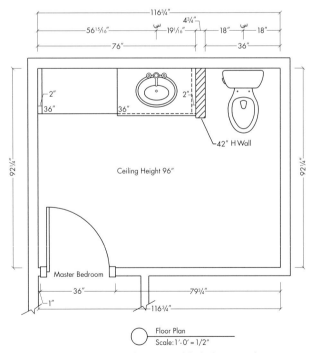

Figure 2.16 A 36" sink cabinet is added along with a 36" tall cabinet.

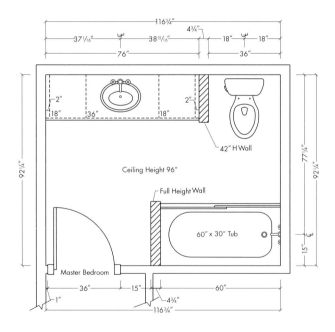

Figure 2.18 The combination tub and shower fits nicely on the opposite wall.

Next, I decide with the space remaining on the toilet wall to have two equal cabinets that are 36" wide each. The extra 4" of wall space I divide equally into two fillers. I used two 36" cabinets because this is a standard cabinet size. A 36"-wide sink cabinet is also a generous size for this use. If I had less space or needed more storage I might go as small as a 33"-wide cabinet for the sink. I decided to make the cabinet to the left of the sink a tall storage cabinet because the client asked for as much storage as possible. If storage was not a priority, the cabinet in that space could become a second sink, or even a lowered makeup drawer to allow for a seated makeup area (Figure 2.16).

I also consider an alternative, in which the 36" sink base cabinet is centered between two 18" base cabinets. Although this option looks more balanced it does not provide as much storage. I could make the 18" cabinets tall instead, but then would need to make my toilet knee-high wall full height. This would make the space not feel as open (Figure 2.17).

I now decide to locate my combination tub and shower on the opposite wall. I select a 60" by 30" tub as this is a standard size and it fits perfectly within the space. I place a new full-height wall to enclose the tub into an alcove (Figure 2.18). I now have a bath option.

SUMMARY

There are many things the designer needs to keep in mind while designing a kitchen or bath, including the client's needs, the elements and principles of design, standard allowances, and codes. Although this may seem like a lot, it is necessary to achieve a beautiful and functional kitchen or bath for the client. Space planning a kitchen can seem like a daunting task to the designer starting out, but with practice becomes easier. Design within standard cabinet sizes as much as possible to avoid needless increases in pricing.

CHAPTER 2 EXERCISES

I: Review the survey form the McManus family filled out for you and space plan their kitchen. Provide two sketched options that are completely figured out and ready to be formally drafted (Figures 2.19 and 2.20).

II: Your client, Mr. Amezquita, is ready for you to space plan his bathroom design. He lives alone in an urban suburb, but frequently has his sons stay with him. You have already measured and gone through the bath survey with him to get an understanding of his needs. Now you need to prepare options to present to him. Review the survey form Mr. Amezquita filled out for you and space plan his bathroom. Provide two sketched options that are completely figured out and ready to be formally drafted (Figures 2.21, 2.22, 2.23, and 2.24).

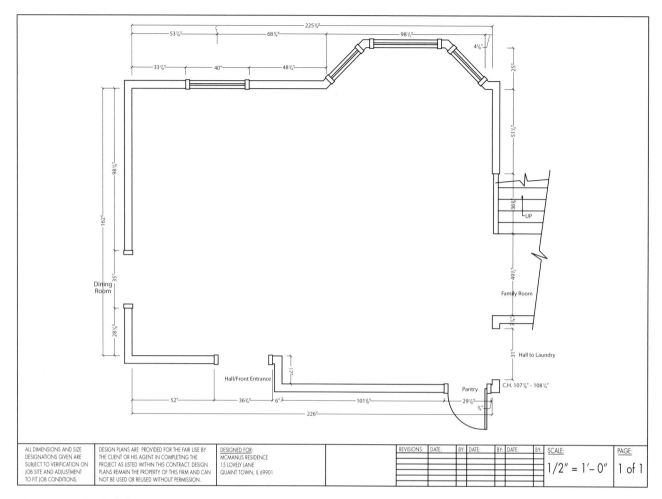

DESIGNED FOR:
MCMANUS RESIDENCE
15 LOVELY LANE
QUAINT TOWN, IL 69901

REVISIONS: DATE: BY: DATE: BY: DATE: BY:

SCALE: 1/2" = 1'-0"

PAGE: 1 of 1

Figure 2.19 The shell for the McManus family's kitchen.

Kitchen Survey

Date: 2/19/2012   **Client Name:** Mr. and Mrs. McManus

HOUSE INFORMATION

1. When was the house built? 1950

2. What type of house is it architecturally? _____

3. What type of architectural details do you like about the house? _____
The large windows

PROJECT INFORMATION

4. When do you want to start the project and when would you like it completed? _____
As soon as possible

5. Do you plan on using an interior designer or architect on the project? No

_____

6. Do you have a contractor, or do you need a recommendation? _____

7. What is your budget? $90,000

8. How many people are in your household? 3, but soon to be 4

9. What family members will share in the decision making process? _____
Mr. and Mrs. McManus

KITCHEN INFORMATION

10. What do you like about your present kitchen? _____
The natural lighting

11. What do you dislike about your present kitchen? _____
Lack of space

    Have you gathered any images of kitchens or features you like? Yes

12. Who is the primary cook? How many household members cook? _____
Mrs. McManus

Figure 2.20 The survey of requirements for the McManus family's kitchen.

13. Are you right or left handed?   Primary Cook _Right_   Secondary _Right_

14. How tall are you?   Primary Cook _5'7"_   Secondary _5'10"_

15. Do you frequently bake or specialty cook?   _No_

16. Do you sit while preparing food?   _No_

17. Would you like a desk or message center?   _Yes, desk_

18. Approximately how many cookbooks do you have? _15-20_
Would you like them hidden or in view? _Hidden_

19. How many sets of dishes do you have in the kitchen? _2_

20. How much glassware do you have? _Standard glassware_

21. How much silverware do you have in the kitchen? _2 sets_

22. Are meals served in the kitchen? _Yes_

23. How frequently do you entertain and for how many? _4 times a year for 50_

24. Do you store liquor or wine in the kitchen? If yes, do you require a lock?
_No_

25. Is there anything you want to display? (wine, pottery, china, etc.)
Tea sets

26. Do you have pets?   _Yes, a dog named Jewel_

27. Do you store any medications or vitamins in the kitchen?
_No_

28. How often do you go grocery shopping? Do you buy any food in bulk?
Weekly. Buy large bags of dog food

29. Do you need a cabinet for brooms, mops and cleaning supplies?
Yes

30. Do you have a preference between cabinets with drawers or doors?
_No_

31. Would you like any cabinets that are open or have glass doors?
Yes, to display tea sets

32. Would you like a TV in the kitchen? If yes, would you like the ability to hide it?
Yes and hide when not in use

ACCESSORIES

_____ Spice rack	__X__ Roll out shelves
__X__ Spice drawer	__X__ Cutlery dividers
_____ Appliance garage	__X__ Utensil dividers
_____ Plate rack	__X__ Knife block
_____ Swing-out pantry system	_____ Plate storage in drawer
_____ Pull-out pantry	_____ Bread box
__X__ Tray dividers	__X__ Waste basket/Recycle bin
_____ Door can racks	__X__ Tilt out sink front
_____ Pull out can racks	__X__ Pull-out towel bar
__X__ Base lazy susan	_____ Swing-up mixer

APPLIANCES (size, finish, gas, electric or dual fuel, wood panels and style).

Free Standing Range 36"W _____   Cooktop _____

Single/Double Ovens _____   Microwave Open to where it's located _____

Warming Drawer _____   Ventilation Decorative hood _____

Refrigerator French door w/panels, 36"W ___   Under counter Refrigerator _____

Ice Maker _____   Wine Captain _____

Dishwasher Fully integrated, w/wood panel ___   Disposal _____

FIXTURES (size, finish, and style)

Sink Bowl and half, undermount _____   Faucet Single handle w/pull-out spray ___

2nd Sink If possible _____   Water Filter Yes _____

Water Chiller _____   Hot Water Dispenser_____

Soap Dispenser _____   Pot Filler_____

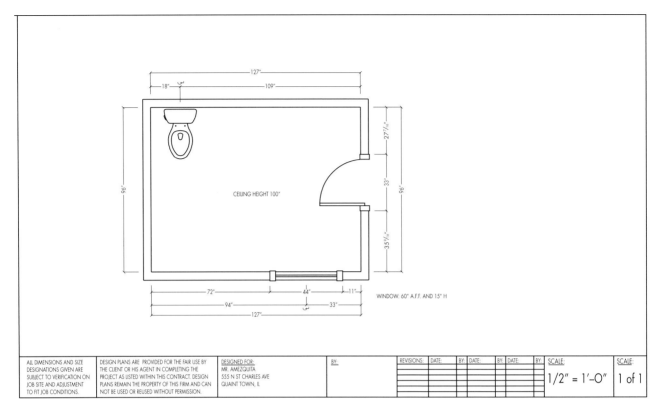

CEILING HEIGHT 100″

127″
18″
109″
96″
27 7/16″
33″
96″
3-5 5/16″
72″
44″
11″
94″
33″
127″

WINDOW: 60″ A.F.F. AND 15″ H

ALL DIMENSIONS AND SIZE DESIGNATIONS GIVEN ARE SUBJECT TO VERIFICATION ON JOB SITE AND ADJUSTMENT TO FIT JOB CONDITIONS.

DESIGN PLANS ARE PROVIDED FOR THE FAIR USE BY THE CLIENT OR HIS AGENT IN COMPLETING THE PROJECT AS LISTED WITHIN THIS CONTRACT. DESIGN PLANS REMAIN THE PROPERTY OF THIS FIRM AND CAN NOT BE USED OR REUSED WITHOUT PERMISSION.

DESIGNED FOR:
MR. AMEZQUITA
555 N ST CHARLES AVE
QUAINT TOWN, IL

BY:

REVISIONS: DATE: BY: DATE: BY: DATE: BY:

SCALE:
1/2″ = 1′–0″

SCALE:
1 of 1

Figure 2.21 The shell for Mr. Amezquita's bathroom.

Bath Survey

Date: 9/12/11   **Client Name:** R. Amezquita

HOUSE INFORMATION

1. When was the house built? 1990

2. What type of house is it architecturally? Simple contemporary condo

3. What type of architectural details do you like about the house?
Nothing in paticular

PROJECT INFORMATION

4. When do you want to start the project and when would you like it completed?
No rush

5. Do you plan on using an interior designer or architect on the project?
No

6. Do you have a contractor, or do you need a recommendation?
I have one

7. What is your budget? Undecided, need advice

8. How many people are in your household? 1 all the time, occasionally 3

9. What family members will share in the decision making process? Just me

BATH INFORMATION

10. Is this a master   X   children _____ or guest _____ bath project?

11. How many bathrooms are in the home? 2

12. Who will use the bathroom? Me and occasionally my sons

13. How many family members will use the bathroom at one time? Maybe 2

Figure 2.22 The survey of requirements for Mr. Amezquita's bathroom.

14. Have you considered privacy zoning to allow several users to occupy the space at one time? _I would like that_

15. Do you prefer separate showering and bathing areas? _If the space allows_

16. Do you prefer that the toilet and/or bidet be separated from the other fixtures, and placed in its own compartment? _That would be nice_

17. Do you want a make-up area? _No_

18. What type of feeling would you like your new bathroom space to have?
Relaxing

19. Are there any special storage requirements?
Would like as much storage space as possible

PLUMBING FIXTURES:

20. Toilet (one piece, two piece, round seat, elongated seat, etc.): _Elongated seat_

21. Bidet: _No_

22. Tub (free-standing, whirlpool, air, drop-in): _Drop in if it fits_

23. Tub/shower combination: _This would be ok_

24. Shower (tile base, built-in bench, steam, clear or obscure glass doors, body sprays, hand-held spray): _Tile base if it works_

25. Sinks (undermount, vessel): _Undermount_

26. Faucets: _Two handles_

ACCESSORIES:

Phone: _____   Towel rack: _X_____

TV: _____   Towel warmer: _____

Stereo: _____   Medicine cabinet: _____

Grab bar: _____   Laundry hamper: _____

Tissue holder :_____   Pull-out waste basket: _____

Towel bar: _____   Wall mounted shelves: _____

Towel ring: _____   Shampoo niche: _X_____

Towel hooks :_____   Robe hooks: _____

Bath Survey

Date: _____ **Client Name:** _____

HOUSE INFORMATION

1. When was the house built?_____

2. What type of house is it architecturally?_____

3. What type of architectural details do you like about the house?_____
_____

PROJECT INFORMATION

4. When do you want to start the project and when would you like it completed?
_____

5. Do you plan on using an interior designer or architect on the project?
_____

6. Do you have a contractor, or do you need a recommendation?_____
_____

7. What is your budget?_____

8. How many people are in your household?_____

9. What family members will share in the decision making process?_____

BATH INFORMATION

10. Is this a master _____children _____or guest _____ bath project?

11. How many bathrooms are in the home? _____

12. Who will use the bathroom? _____

13. How many family members will use the bathroom at one time? _____

Figure 2.23 A blank bath survey.

14. Have you considered privacy zoning to allow several users to occupy the space at one time?_____

15. Do you prefer separate showering and bathing areas? _____

16. Do you prefer that the toilet and/or bidet be separated from the other fixtures, and placed in its own compartment? _____

17. Do you want a make-up area? _____

18. What type of feeling would you like your new bathroom space to have?
_____

19. Are there any special storage requirements?
_____

PLUMBING FIXTURES:

20. Toilet (one piece, two piece, round seat, elongated seat, etc.): _____

21. Bidet: _____

22. Tub (free-standing, whirlpool, air, drop-in): _____

23. Tub/shower combination: _____

24. Shower (tile base, built-in bench, steam, clear or obscure glass doors, body sprays, hand-held spray): _____

25. Sinks (undermount, vessel): _____

26. Faucets: _____

ACCESSORIES:

Phone: _____

TV: _____

Stereo: _____

Grab bar: _____

Tissue holder :_____

Towel bar: _____

Towel ring: _____

Towel hooks :_____

Towel rack: _____

Towel warmer: _____

Medicine cabinet: _____

Laundry hamper: _____

Pull-out waste basket: _____

Wall mounted shelves: _____

Shampoo niche: _____

Robe hooks: _____

Kitchen Survey

Date: _____   **Client Name:** _____

HOUSE INFORMATION

1. When was the house built? _____

2. What type of house is it architecturally? _____

3. What type of architectural details do you like about the house? _____
_____

PROJECT INFORMATION

4. When do you want to start the project and when would you like it completed? _____
_____

5. Do you plan on using an interior designer or architect on the project? _____
_____

6. Do you have a contractor, or do you need a recommendation? _____

7. What is your budget? _____

8. How many people are in your household? _____

9. What family members will share in the decision making process? _____
_____

KITCHEN INFORMATION

10. What do you like about your present kitchen? _____
_____

11. What do you dislike about your present kitchen? _____
_____

    Have you gathered any images of kitchens or features you like? _____

12. Who is the primary cook? How many household members cook? _____
_____

Figure 2.24 A blank kitchen survey.

13. Are you right or left handed?   Primary Cook_____ Secondary_____

14. How tall are you?   Primary Cook _____ Secondary_____

15. Do you frequently bake or specialty cook?   _____

16. Do you sit while preparing food?   _____

17. Would you like a desk or message center?   _____

18. Approximately how many cookbooks do you have? _____
Would you like them hidden or in view? _____

19. How many sets of dishes do you have in the kitchen? _____

20. How much glassware do you have? _____

21. How much silverware do you have in the kitchen? _____

22. Are meals served in the kitchen? _____

23. How frequently do you entertain and for how many? _____

24. Do you store liquor or wine in the kitchen? If yes, do you require a lock?

_____

25. Is there anything you want to display? (wine, pottery, china, etc.)

_____

26. Do you have pets?   _____

27. Do you store any medications or vitamins in the kitchen?

_____

28. How often do you go grocery shopping? Do you buy any food in bulk?

_____

29. Do you need a cabinet for brooms, mops and cleaning supplies?

_____

30. Do you have a preference between cabinets with drawers or doors?

_____

31. Would you like any cabinets that are open or have glass doors?

_____

32. Would you like a TV in the kitchen? If yes, would you like the ability to hide it?

_____

ACCESSORIES (circle)

Spice rack   Roll out shelves

Spice drawer   Cutlery dividers

Appliance garage   Utensil dividers

Plate rack   Knife block

Swing-out pantry system   Plate storage in drawer

Pull-out pantry   Bread box

Tray dividers   Waste basket/Recycle bin

Door can racks   Tilt out sink front

Pull out can racks   Pull-out towel bar

Base lazy susan   Swing-up mixer

APPLIANCES (size, finish, gas, electric or dual fuel, wood panels and style).

Free Standing Range_____   Cooktop_____

Single/Double Ovens_____   Microwave_____

Warming Drawer_____   Ventilation_____

Refrigerator_____   Under counter Refrigerator_____

Ice Maker_____   Wine Captain_____

Dishwasher_____   Disposal_____

FIXTURES (size, finish, and style)

Sink_____   Faucet_____

2nd Sink_____   Water Filter_____

Water Chiller_____   Hot Water Dispenser_____

Soap Dispenser_____   Pot Filler_____

CHAPTER 2 DISCUSSION QUESTIONS

1. What are the elements of design? What are some examples in the kitchen or bath?
2. What are the principles of design? What are some examples in the kitchen or bath?
3. How much landing space does a refrigerator need?
4. How much wall space is recommended for a toilet?
5. Why is it best to try to design within standard cabinet sizes?

REFERENCE

Slotkis, Susan J. *Foundations of Interior Design*. New York, NY: Fairchild Publications, 2006.

CHAPTER 2: DESIGN CHECKLIST

___The first step to space planning a kitchen or bath is to draft the shell of the space.

___Always complete the initial space planning by hand.

___Work up two or three suitable space-planning options to present to your client.

___Remember to keep the elements and principles of design in mind while space planning.

___In the bathroom, move the toilet only if budget allows.

___Stay within standard cabinet sizes as much as possible.

KEY TERMS

ADA: The Americans with Disabilities Act of 1990 is a federal law. The Architectural and Transportation Barriers Compliance Board (ATBCB) administers the accessibility guidelines. ADA requirements are incorporated in many state housing codes.

ANSI: The American National Standards Institute is a body that produces technical standards and design guidelines for new buildings and remodeling so that they are accessible to all people.

IRC: The International Residential Code consists of codes that have been created by the International Code Council (ICC), which is a non-profit based in the U.S. that is dedicated to developing codes. It establishes minimum regulations for one and two-family dwellings of three stories or less that are required for the public health and safety. Although the IRC is widely accepted throughout North America, some jurisdictions may not recognize it.

CHAPTER 3 UNIVERSAL AND SUSTAINABLE DESIGNS FOR KITCHEN AND BATH

OBJECTIVES

After reading this chapter, you will:

- Grasp how to incorporate universal and sustainable design elements into projects.

- Understand and research products that truly are sustainable.

- Recognize that the interior design industry is constantly changing, so it is important to stay up to date on advancements for universal and sustainable design.

DESIGN SCENARIO

You recently have started working with a new client, Ms. Craig. She is a baby boomer and has had surgeries for treating her rheumatoid arthritis. Even with the surgeries, grasping objects can be challenging for her. She also is very passionate about sustainable design and wants her project to be as "green" as possible. She wants your advice for the best way to accomplish a kitchen and a bath design that is easy for her to use while making it sustainable.

1. What can you incorporate to make working in her kitchen as easy as possible for her?

2. What can be done in the bath for it to be the most comfortable?

3. What materials can you incorporate that would be considered sustainable?

4. What other things can you do other than just using sustainable materials?

UNIVERSAL DESIGN

Universal design and **sustainable design** are two concerns of great importance for the kitchen and bath designer. These issues are becoming so well known that many clients ask their designers to incorporate these methods in their project. For a kitchen and bath designer, it is beneficial to have an understanding of universal and sustainable design in the event of being approached by a knowledgeable client, not to mention it is just good design practice.

Universal design is an issue that will become more prevalent as the baby-boomer generation ages. It is not uncommon to hear universal design referred to as **"barrier-free design"** or **"accessible design."** When designing a kitchen or bath for a homeowner who plans on remaining in his or her home through the elder years, this should be considered while space planning and selecting the materials. Life expectancy has risen over time. The current life expectancy for people living in the United States is 78 years. The homeowner(s) may or may not have already given some thought to whether they will continue to live in their home as they age. As the designer, it is best to discuss this with the client. For example, although concrete may make a nice contemporary flooring option, standing on it for long periods can cause the user's feet or legs to hurt. What if the user has arthritis? Arthritis worsens over time and, in addition to softer flooring, it is better to use fixtures that will not require gripping and grasping. There are many products available and planning tips that we will cover, and that the designer can recommend to aid in a space that will remain functional as the user ages.

Not only is universal design beneficial for clients planning to remain in their home through the elder years; it is good design for everyone. At first, universal design was used primarily for people with disabilities, such as wheelchair users or people with arthritis. As mentioned above, universal design has really grown with the increased need for this type of design. It should be kept in mind that it is referred to as *universal design*

for a reason. It is design that universally works for everyone. It is not uncommon for people to have a temporary disability that would benefit from a home with universal design. Unfortunately, many people are injured temporarily at some point in their lives, such as breaking an arm or leg. Women who are pregnant are, in a sense, temporarily disabled. These people too would benefit from the design elements discussed below.

DESIGNER'S DIALOGUE 3.1

"I had a couple who didn't need ADA clearances, but they plan to stay in their home. It was designed with grab bars and a no-threshold entrance into the shower. It's great to incorporate universal design anyway, if not cumbersome. You have to think about resale and other family members potentially using the space."
—*Gladys Schanstra, CKD, CBD, Allied ASID, Kitchen and Bath Designer*

CERTIFIED AGING-IN-PLACE SPECIALIST (CAPS)

The National Association of Home Builders (NAHB) has a program available for becoming a Certified Aging-in-Place Specialist (CAPS). Their program covers technical, business management, and customer service skills relevant to home planning for aging-in-place. This is a nice option by which to learn more about universal design and to earn certification to prove your knowledge on the topic.

BASIC PRINCIPLES OF UNIVERSAL DESIGN

When designing a space to be universal, there are several basic principles to consider. It should be equally usable by any person, have flexibility, be simple and intuitive, require little physical effort, and have easy-to-perceive information. The main goal of universal design is that environments be usable by all people, to the greatest extent possible. People of any age, size, ability, gender, or culture should be able to use the space.

IN THE KITCHEN

There are many ways to accomplish universal design in the kitchen, from the space planning stage through the material selection stage. Let's look at some specific ways to incorporate this type of design.

Adjusting Appliance, Countertops, and Toe-Kick Heights

An important consideration for the universal kitchen is the heights of the appliances, countertops, and toe kick.

As people age, become physically challenged, or both, it becomes more difficult and painful to bend down. It is ideal to locate an appliance at a height that does not require too much bending. One way to accomplish this is to raise undercounter appliances. Ovens and dishwashers can be raised off the ground for easier accessibility by installing them on top of a platform or on a custom cabinet. Microwaves can be located at the top of a base cabinet or at eye level in a tall or wall cabinet (Figure 3.1).

Figure 3.1 Locating a microwave drawer, which is accessed from the top, at the top of a base cabinet is a good location for universal design. *Courtesy of Pamela Polvere Designs and Dennis Jourdan Photography Inc.*

Countertops also are an item that can be adjusted, based on the needs of the client. Countertops can be lowered to allow wheelchair users to easily work at the countertop. Once the countertop is lowered, a cooktop, sink, or other appliance can easily be installed at the lower height for ease of use. It is even possible to design a sink with an adjustable height for added flexibility. Toe kicks may also be adjusted for the wheelchair user. When planning a kitchen for a wheelchair user a 9-inch-high toe kick should be used instead of the standard 4-inch height. Specific allowances for wheelchair users are discussed further in space planning in Chapter 2.

DESIGNER'S DIALOGUE 3.2

"I have designed several kitchens for wheelchair users. It is important to have storage in base cabinets, low counter heights, and lower appliances for wheelchair use. Having shelves that pull out below appliances is also helpful to set down items."
—*Gail Drury, CMKBD, Kitchen and Bath Designer*

Opportunity to Sit

Another consideration is the option to sit while working. No matter what age the person, standing for long periods can be uncomfortable or even painful. It is best to plan for a place for the cook to sit, even if it is just a small area with a stool. This allows the cook to sit while preparing ingredients.

Remote Exhaust Fans

Some exhaust fan companies now offer the option of exhaust fans with a remote control, as is discussed in Chapter 6. This is a great feature for those who are unable or do not wish to stretch to reach the power switch to turn on the exhaust.

Simplify and Consolidate

Simplify and consolidate the work area as much as possible. Keep the work triangle legs shorter so that cooking does not become more work with extra walking.

Appliances are best located where easily accessed from multiple sides. Dining should be located close by, so that meals are easy to serve and eat.

Roll-out Shelving

Roll-out shelving on full-extension glides is a great feature to incorporate in the kitchen for universal design. This allows the user to easily roll out shelving to access everything stored in the cabinet. This helps avoid having to bend for long periods to locate items in the back of the cabinet.

Pull-down and Pop-up Shelving

There are companies now that make accessories for cabinetry that include a pull-down shelf mechanism. This brings down items stored higher up, so the user can easily reach the contents. There also are pop-up shelves available that raise the base cabinet shelf for easy access. These pop-up shelves are great for stand mixers or other countertop appliances that are not stored on the countertop.

Magnetic Latches

Magnetic latches on cabinets instead of standard pulls and knobs is a nice feature for opening cabinets easier. These latches require little strength to activate for opening the cabinets.

Smooth and Nonslip Walkway Surfaces

Smooth and nonslip flooring is another design detail that would be ideal for universal design. Uneven surfaces give the opportunity for people in the space to trip or have trouble using a walker or wheelchair. Having a smooth and nonslip floor eliminates this potential problem.

Cushioned Floor Mat

It is beneficial for a cushioned, nonslip mat to be provided by the sink and the food-prep areas. Standing for long periods of time on hard surfaces is wearing to one's legs; floor mats will help alleviate this problem.

Wide Interior Doors and Walkways

Having wide, extended interior doors and walkways also is ideal for the universal space. As with smooth flooring, this allows all users to move about the space without interference.

Lever Handles for Doors and Faucets

Specifying hardware and fixtures that do not require gripping and grasping also is important for universal design. As people age they may develop arthritis, which limits grasping capabilities. Lever handles are much easier to operate for all types of users.

Reachable Controls and Switches

Switches and controls located between 42 and 48 inches above the finished floor will be accessible to anyone, including those in a wheelchair. If a range is used, it would be better to specify one that has controls on the front, if there are no children in the household or if it has safety features.

Pot Fillers

Pot fillers are a consideration for the universal kitchen that the designer should offer to the client. Providing a pot filler by the cooking surface eliminates the need to carry a full pot of water from the sink to the cooking surface, making the task a bit easier.

Lighting

Lighting is very important for any space and even more so for the universally designed space. Lighting should be increased for tasks at the sink, cooking surfaces, and other areas where tasks are done. It is best to use the highest wattage bulb possible for the fixture.

IN THE BATH

As in the kitchen, there are a number of ways to achieve the goal of a universally designed bathroom. Some of the ways to accomplish universal design in the bath are the same as in the kitchen. Smooth walkway surfaces, wide interior doors and walkways, and lever handles also are good design considerations for the bathroom. There are a few things to consider in addition to these that are specific to the bathroom.

Touch Faucets and Automatic Faucets

As in the kitchen, specifying a touch faucet is a great option for the bathroom. Chapter 4 discusses materials, such as these faucets, that the user simply touches to control. With this type of faucet, hands do not even need to be used; it can be turned on just as easily with an arm. This will avoid gripping and grasping by the user, which is beneficial for those with arthritis. Another option is an automatic faucet. These faucets are similar to those found in public restrooms. Some companies are now making these for the residential market. The temperature is set below the counter so it can be adjusted if needed. The person using the faucet simply moves his or her hands as he or she would if in a public restroom.

Toilet

The best type of toilet to use for the universally designed bath is one with a seat that is higher than usual. This style of toilet is called different names by different manufacturers, but simply has a seat that is typically about 2 inches higher than in other models. The difference in height makes it easier for users to lower and raise themselves from the toilet. Such a toilet, combined with grab bars, makes an ideal situation for the universally designed bath.

Vanity Height

When planning for universal design in the bath, one aspect to consider is the vanity height. It is helpful to have varied vanity heights that are suitable to the user. Commonly, more homes are using a 36-inch-high vanity instead of the former, frequently used 32-inch height. This height allows the user not to bend as far when at the sink. If the user is in a wheelchair, or will likely be in a wheelchair later, a wheelchair height vanity should certainly be included. Clients often worry about resale when they remodel a kitchen or bath in their home. Clients should be reminded that they will be using the space and their quality of living is well worth the remodel compared with the value of the resale.

Shower Area

There are a few ways to make sure the specific shower area is accessible for all users. Let's take a look at the different ways to make the shower barrier free.

No-Threshold Shower. For the universal bath, consider a no-threshold shower. There are companies now that are making drains that are long and flat, spanning the entire length of the shower. This is a great option for a person who uses a wheelchair. They can roll into the shower and maneuver much more easily onto a bench.

Shower Seating. A bench or seat is ideal in the shower area. A bench can be a built-in if space allows. If the room lacks space, a fold-down bench may be used. These benches simply attach to a wall that has blocking behind it and can be folded down for use and folded up when not in use to allow for more shower space.

Grab Bars. Like the toilet area, the bathing area also should have grab bars. Some companies have gotten smart and realize the demand for universal design and therefore are making more aesthetically pleasing grab bars. These companies are making grab bars that are not the standard, commercial-looking ones. They have more decorative brackets and are available in various

finishes. Finishes such as polished chrome, brushed nickel, and antique brass are available in addition to many more.

Watch Out for Hot Water. Hot water can quickly become scalding. It is important to consider this when designing a universal bath. If pipes are exposed underneath a sink, they should be insulated. A panel can be placed to cover the pipes yet still allow open space below the counter. This is particularly important for the wheelchair user, as his or her legs can easily come into contact with pipes below a counter. It is also a good idea to set the home water heater to 120 degrees to avoid scalding. Installing a pressure balance valve will also help to avoid scalding in the shower. This fixture makes sure the water temperature doesn't change by more than 3 degrees in the event of a change in water pressure from the hot or cold water supply line.

Shower Heights. Once again, height is important for universal design. A handheld sprayer or an adjustable showerhead is a great way to provide a shower that is flexible for the users. Handheld sprayers are especially great with bench seating, so users can remain seated for bathing if necessary.

Bathtubs

Bathtubs share most of the same goals as the shower area. They should have grab bars, have a bench for seating, avoid scalding water, and have heights for fixtures that are easy to access. In addition to the standard tubs available, walk-in bathtubs also are an option. These tubs have a door and typically have a bench built into them. The disadvantage of these tubs is that the user must stay in the tub until the water drains out completely. Some manufacturers are adjusting these tubs to drain faster to avoid this problem.

Technology Connecting to Hospitals

As technology advances, there are more and more features that can be incorporated into the bath design to make life easier for the users. One advancement that is making life easier is an automated system that allows clients to determine their blood pressure, blood oxygen saturation level, and other vital signs and send the information to their health care provider directly from their home. One example is the Cleveland Clinic Heart Care at Home monitoring program, which allows patients to provide Cleveland Clinic heart specialists with vital signs from the patient's home for a period of time. Once a day, the patient sends his or her vital signs by means of a wireless monitoring box that is installed in the home. The box is connected to a digital scale, blood pressure cuff, and other items to track vital signs. We may start to see more of this technology with the increased needs of the baby-boomer generation.

SUSTAINABLE DESIGN

Another major design issue that has become popular recently concerns sustainability. Sustainable design, sometimes called "green" design, is intended to keep the care of the environment in mind. It involves making decisions that will have a neutral or positive effect on the environment. There are many different ways to create a sustainably designed project. The main considerations are water and energy conservation, the use of recycled materials, and low toxicity. Before these new items can be installed in the space, some consideration may also be given to the existing items.

RECYCLING EXISTING SPACES

When an original kitchen or bath is being torn out for a remodel, consider the pieces that are being torn out. Is it possible that the countertops or cabinets might be reused or repurposed? Is there a way to recycle any materials that are past their shelf-life? The answer to both of these questions is *yes*. As a kitchen and bath designer, it is beneficial to be familiar with your local options for these items. Pieces in reasonably good condition can be sold on auction websites or donated to organizations. Major appliances are a great source of metal and can be recycled. Some power companies will actually pay to pick up old appliances that squander energy. A very large percentage of an old refrigerator can be recycled. Because energy standards have changed it is more beneficial for the environment to recycle it than to keep it in the garage or basement, eating up large amounts of energy. A great Internet resource to find local recycling is Earth911 (http://earth911.org). Solid countertop material can be repurposed for use in a new space. For example, an old granite or solid surface kitchen countertop can be cut down and used for a bathroom vanity top or a tabletop. As a designer, it is a very responsible habit to have this information prepared to offer to your clients as they get ready to start their project (Figure 3.2).

SMALLER IS BETTER

In general, the most sustainably planned space is a smaller space, which uses fewer resources. A smaller space means smaller appliances, which use less energy. In addition, a smaller footprint, in terms of square footage, means less material is being used. A smaller space design is likely to produce a more efficient kitchen or bath.

Figure 3.2 This bathroom has bamboo cabinetry, which some argue is not truly sustainable due to the costs of shipment from Asia. It also has a dual-flush toilet, a repurposed sink countertop, and recycled paper countertop for a make-up area. *Courtesy of Pamela Polvere Designs and Dennis Jourdan Photography Inc.*

SAVING ENERGY

Saving energy is an essential, important part of accomplishing a sustainable design. Wherever energy is used in a project, the following question should be considered: "How can energy use be minimized?" It should not be surprising that the kitchen is the room in the home that uses the most energy. Not only does it need to be well lit for all the tasks that occur, but the appliances use substantial energy to run.

APPLIANCES

Appliances use much energy and therefore specifying those that are the most energy efficient is very important. California and New York have been the leading states in pushing energy efficiency. Energy Star is a program run by the U.S. Department of Energy (DOE) and the U.S. Environmental Protection Agency (EPA). It is possible that some Energy Star–rated appliances will cost 10 to 15 percent more initially than those that are not. The advantage is that energy and money will be saved over the life of the product. Another thing to consider when selecting appliances is what sizes to use. It is better to use smaller appliances than large, commercial-type appliances.

LIGHTING

To light any space in an energy-efficient and environmentally friendly way, the two key things to think about are how to use daylight and what energy-efficient fixtures to specify.

Daylighting

Daylighting describes the use of natural light to illuminate a space. It is great to maximize the use of daylight because this means fewer powered lights will need to be used. Besides energy savings, daylight is beneficial because it helps the users of the space feel connected to the outside and its changes.

Light Fixtures

The three major types of lighting, which are discussed further in Chapter 9, are ambient, task, and accent lighting. Ambient lighting is general lighting for a space, task lighting illuminates a specific task area, and accent lighting creates an accent. Fluorescent lights and light-emitting diode (**LED**) lights are good, energy-efficient options to light a space. Both fluorescent and LED lights are now available as dimmable and in various sizes. As for energy-efficient appliances, these types of fixtures will cost more initially, but will provide energy savings over time. Also as for appliances, these light fixtures may be Energy Star rated. Fluorescent and LED lights are available in practically every type of fixture, such as under-cabinet, recessed ceiling, or flush mount to name a few. Incandescent lights are rather inefficient and should be avoided as much as possible for the sustainable kitchen or bath. Low-voltage halogen lights are also not low-energy, and therefore are not the most energy-efficient option to use, either. Fluorescent and LED lights are being made in various color temperatures,

so that incandescents will not be required to achieve a warm, glowing light level. Fluorescent and LED lights will be marked as warm or cool, so that warmer color renditions may be selected.

SAVING WATER

Another important thing to keep in mind for saving is water. Using less water will help protect the fresh water available and put less stress on the wastewater treatment systems (Table 3.1). It is easy to reduce water use, by installing the appropriate fixtures and appliances.

Faucets

Faucets are an important fixture when considering water conservation. Faucets that use less water typically have an **aerator** inside. This aerator pushes air in with the water flow, making it feel like a typical water flow, but using less water in the process. This is available not only for lavatory faucets, but also for shower and tub faucets as well.

TABLE 3.1 AVERAGE WATER USE IN A HOME	
Task	Average Water Use
Toilet	1.6 GPF with standard fixture. With water-conserving technology: 1.28 or as low as 0.9 GPF
Shower	2.5 gallons per minute
Bath (tub)	28–50 gallons
Teeth brushing	1 gallon
Washing hands and face	1 gallon
Shaving (face or legs)	1 gallon
Dishwasher	4–6 gallons per use
Hand-washing dishes	3 gallons per minute

Abbreviation: GPF, gallons per flush.
Source: http://ga.water.usgs.gov/edu/sq3.html

Dishwashers

Washing dishes by hand actually uses more water than running a load in the dishwasher. It makes sense if you think about it; dishwashers are made to get dishes clean with the least amount of water. If space permits, it is ideal to design the sustainable kitchen with an energy-efficient dishwasher.

Toilets

In bathrooms, toilets are a great place where water can be saved. It seems that toilet manufacturers are constantly coming out with new products that are getting the gallons per flush (GPF) rate lower and lower. The standard requirement for toilets in the United States is 1.6 GPF. Some companies make a 1.28 GPF toilet. There are also dual-flush toilets available. Dual-flush toilets have two buttons for flushing: one button will flush the toilet at the 1.6 GPF rate, and the other will flush at a 0.9 GPF rate.

MATERIALS

It is best to use materials that are manufactured not more than 500 miles from the project. Materials should also be used that will last over time. It is not very sustainable to use a material that will need to be replaced within a few years.

Wood

When wood is used for a sustainable project, it is best to use reclaimed or Forest Stewardship Council (FSC)–certified wood. The FSC is an independent organization that produces standards for responsible forestry management. If neither of these options is available it is best to use species from the region of the project, or an abundant species. To learn more about the various species of woods, see Chapter 5.

Bamboo

Bamboo is often marketed as being a sustainable material. There is some debate about whether it is truly sustainable because of the distance it needs to travel. Most bamboo comes from Asia, which is a long way from the

United States. Because of the popularity of bamboo, some companies have started growing it in the United States.

FLOORING

Although wood is a good option for sustainable flooring, other materials will also work nicely. Tile is a good option, as it is typically a material that will last a long time. Many tiles available now are made up partially or 100 percent of recycled materials.

Linoleum

Another sustainable option for flooring is linoleum. Linoleum is made from linseed oil and is available in many colors. Linoleum has recently become popular again, probably because of increased interest in sustainable design. A disadvantage of this material is that it does **outgas** volatile organic compounds **(VOCs),** but this will decrease over time. The advantage is it actually gets harder and grows stronger over time as well.

Cork

Cork flooring has also become popular again with the popularity of the sustainable movement. It is a durable material that is comparable in traits to hardwood. Cork flooring can scratch but is rather resistant to staining and moisture. Because cork has some cushion to it, this material is also easier on the feet of the cook. Cork flooring is typically available in tiles or as tongue-and-groove engineered flooring.

Concrete

Concrete can be considered a sustainable product because it is inert and so does not outgas any chemicals. It is very durable and should last an exceptionally long time. Concrete will acquire cracks over time, so clients should be informed of this before they make their decision. Concrete floors are cold and will be hard to stand on for long periods of time. Some people argue that concrete is not really the most sustainable option because of the energy needed to make it.

CABINETRY

When selecting cabinetry with sustainability in mind, the first thought should be for its durability. Durability is important because replacing products frequently is not sustainable. A sustainable cabinet will ideally be composed of woods that were reclaimed or are FSC certified. They will be constructed with glues low in toxins. The construction may not be plywood but medium-density fiberboard (MDF), which maximizes the use of wood scraps. This MDF will be faced with melamine or real wood veneer that is not finished with a toxic finish.

DESIGNER'S DIALOGUE 3.4

"Most cabinet lines are feeling the need to put out cabinets that are sustainable. If they don't, they're eliminating themselves from a potential market. The client may go elsewhere."
—*Lisa McManus, ASID, Kitchen and Bath Designer*

COUNTERTOPS

As with the other materials discussed thus far, countertop material is another item that is best if it is durable, recycled, or recyclable. It is also better if it does not outgas and is manufactured within 500 miles of the project location. Wood and bamboo are good sustainable countertop options. Reclaimed wood countertops have become a very popular option. There also are manufacturers that create countertops that consist of recycled glass or recycled glass in cement. These materials are discussed further in Chapter 4.

WALL FINISHES

Paint is easily the most popular finish used for walls. There are paints available with low or no VOCs. These are the best types of paint to use for a sustainable project.

TOXICITY AND HEALTH

Another sustainability issue concerns toxicity, or designing for a healthy space. If toxicity is an issue for the client, then clean air will be very important. It is best to avoid toxins that will be breathed in by the users. Items that outgas VOCs should be avoided or minimized. Low- or no-VOC options are available for glues, paints, and stains. Polyvinyl chloride (PVC) products also should be avoided. Older homes may need to be tested for lead or asbestos. Ventilation is very important for the circulation of fresh air for a healthy space. Exhaust fans should be installed in the kitchen and bath to remove moisture and odors to the outside.

DESIGNER'S DIALOGUE 3.5

"More clients have been coming to me with toxicity issues. A lot of people want water-based finishes instead of oil-based. More and more people are becoming conscious of the outgassing. I have had clients sleep with a door sample next to their bed to see if they get a headache."
—*Gail Drury, CMKBD, Kitchen and Bath Designer*

GREENWASHING

With sustainability becoming a popular topic, many companies have started claiming to be sustainable. When a product is advertised as being "green," but after some research it becomes clear it is not really green, this is an example of **greenwashing.** The designer must learn to ask questions: Just because a manufacturer states that a product is sustainable doesn't mean that it truly is.

DESIGNER'S DIALOGUE 3.6

"Watch out for greenwashing. Many companies will advertise themselves as green, but they may not be. There is also controversy about green products. Bamboo, for example, grows fast but comes from China, so may not still be considered green."
—*Gail Drury, CMKBD, Kitchen and Bath Designer*

SUMMARY

With the aging baby-boomer generation, universal design will continue to grow in importance. It is crucial that the kitchen and bath designer understand ways to accomplish universal design and to stay aware of advancements. Sustainable design is another consideration that is very important. More clients are becoming savvy and actually requesting that their projects be sustainable. Again, the designer must stay up to date on what can be done and specify what best serves their clients.

CHAPTER 3 EXERCISES

I: What are the key things you can do or specify for your client Ms. Craig to best suit her needs for universal and sustainable design? List as many as you can.

II: Find a manufacturer that states that its product is sustainable. Research further to determine whether this company's product truly is sustainable. Is there anything about the product or how it's made or shipped that makes it not sustainable? Explain.

CHAPTER 3 DISCUSSION QUESTIONS

1.   What is an aerator?
2.   When designing with sustainability in mind, products should be used that were manufactured within how many miles of the project?
3.   What traits should sustainable cabinets have?
4.   How high should the toe kick be for a wheelchair user?
5.   What are some things that should be incorporated into a universal shower?

REFERENCES

National Association of Home Builders. http://www.nahb.org (home page; accessed 13 June 2012).

Roberts, Jennifer. *Good Green Kitchens*. Layton, UT: Gibbs Smith, 2006.

ADDITIONAL RESOURCES

AARP. http://www.aarp.org (home page). AARP's website has many articles covering various topics, issues, and technologies on aging.

Bakker, Rosemary. *Revitalizing Your Home: Beautiful Living for the Second Half of Life*. New York, NY: Lark Books, 2010

Earth911. http://www.earth911.org (home page). Earth911 provides recycling information for across the United States. According to their website: "Our Earth911 Recycling Directory is the most accurate and comprehensive directory of its kind and contains recycling information for over 300 materials."

National Association of Home Builders. http://www.nahb.org (home page). The National Association of Home Builders has a program available for becoming a Certified Aging-in-Place Specialist (CAPS). Their website has more information about this program.

___Include adjustable appliance heights, which are helpful when possible.

___Provide a place to sit.

___Use roll-out shelving.

___Allow for larger doorways and walkways.

___Locate controls and switches within a reachable distance.

___Select nonslip surfaces for flooring materials.

___Specify faucets with levers or touch technology for ease of use.

___Provide sufficient task lighting to avoid eye strain.

___Use daylighting as much as possible to save energy.

___Incorporate LED lighting as well, to save on energy.

___Provide seating, grab bars, and a handheld sprayer in the shower space.

___Consider a no-threshold shower.

___Recycle existing materials as much as possible.

___Are the products you are specifying really sustainable? You may need to do further research.

___Specify faucets with aerators, Energy Star–rated dishwashers, and dual-flush toilets to help conserve water.

___Recommend Energy Star–rated appliances to conserve energy.

___Choose low- or no-VOC paint to lower toxicity in the space.

___Smaller is better for sustainable design.

KEY TERMS

Accessible design: A phrase used in reference to universal design.

Aerator: A part that is installed in a faucet to add air to the water stream, causing less water to be used.

Barrier-free design: A phrase used in reference to universal design.

Greenwashing: When a manufacturer tries to make their product sound "green" when it really is not.

LED: Light-emitting diode; a type of lighting that uses energy very efficiently.

Outgas: When a material releases toxins that potentially may be inhaled by people.

Sustainable design: Designing spaces with the goal of sustaining the environment.

Universal design: Design to make environments usable by all people, to the greatest extent possible.

VOC: Volatile organic compound.

OBJECTIVES

After reading this chapter, you will:

- Examine specific kitchen and bathroom materials to educate clients.

- Formulate sensible decisions when making selections with and for your client.

- Recognize the unique traits of countertop materials for each client's specific needs.

- Identify various types of tiles and decide which would be best for performance, aesthetic, and budget for backsplashes and/or flooring.

- Determine the best choice for flooring, wall coverings, and hardware for a project.

DESIGN SCENARIO

You've been working with your client, the Mowats, for more than a month now. The layout has been finalized and the clients are eager to select materials for their kitchen The Mowats are a young couple with two small boys, ages 3 and 5. They want to select materials that are beautiful but still durable enough to hold up to the everyday wear and tear of a family with young children. As their designer, they look to you for information and advice on what materials make the most sense to suit their family's needs and lifestyle.

1. What is the most durable countertop material?

2. What kind of flooring would make the most sense to recommend?

3. What materials have the easiest maintenance for this busy family?

Although material codes for residential sites are not as strict as for commercial properties, materials are still a very important aspect of the kitchen or bath project. There are a variety of options for every surface in these rooms. This chapter discusses distinctive materials available for the kitchen or bath and explains the benefits and drawbacks to these choices. By the end of this chapter, you will have an understanding of the various materials that can be installed in a kitchen or a bath and their traits.

COUNTERTOPS

Countertops in a kitchen or a bathroom are a significant detail of each room. In the kitchen, countertops can end up being the third largest surface area. Whichever countertop material is selected, this choice is significant to the overall aesthetic of the space. Another important aspect of a countertop is the seaming. After the material has been selected and the area has been measured, the fabricator will establish how many seams are needed and where to place them. The designer can ask the fabricator for a seam diagram to determine whether the proposed seams are acceptable. In most cases, unless it is a small project, seams will be necessary.

Countertops can be natural or man-made. Both options offer many colors and patterns to choose from. When natural materials are used, slabs of the material are selected. Materials, such as **quartz** and **solid surfacing,** do not require slab selection because they are man-made and relatively consistent. We will look more closely at the specific types of natural and man-made materials to learn the benefits and disadvantages of each.

NATURAL MATERIALS

Natural countertops are made of materials, such as stone or wood, that come straight from the earth and undergo minimum manufacturing to become countertop material. These types of material have been dominant for some time. Amongst the various stones and woods, it is very likely that you will find something that will work for the project, whether it is contemporary or traditional. An important trait of natural materials to consider is that they will require more maintenance than man-made materials. This, among other positive and negative aspects, is important to consider when suggesting natural materials for a project.

STONE

Since approximately the mid- to late 1990s, granite has been a popular countertop material. Stone has been used for centuries as a building material. In kitchens, granite and slate quarried locally were the preferred materials for flooring and wall covering during the Tudor (1485–1603) and Jacobean (1567–1625) periods. Granite and slate were favored materials because they are not flammable, such as wood. There are many different types of stone that have slightly different qualities. Although all stone is considered porous, some types are more porous and, therefore, more delicate than others. These are important qualities to consider when discussing stone as an option with the client. Because stone is natural, there are no two pieces that will be exactly the same.

Selecting and Laying Out the Slab
If a natural stone is being used, the slabs must be selected in person. This is important because each slab is unique. Once the slabs are selected the area on the slab that should be used needs to be marked. Laying out the slab is an important step in countertop selection. Because no two slabs are the same, some may have more or less movement or markings. The color of a material also can change over time as the stone **quarry** is dug deeper. You may show your client a stone sample in a meeting only to find the slabs available

are not the same color you have shown. To be sure the installation has the desired results it is best to view slabs and be clear exactly what portion of the slab should be used.

Stone Care

The client also should be informed that he or she will need to seal stone countertops at least once a year. Depending on the use, they may even need to do so twice or more a year. The way to test whether a stone countertop needs to be sealed is very easy. Water should be spilled on the countertop and left to sit for a minute. If water remains beaded on the top, the sealer is still working. If water starts to soak into the countertop, sealer needs to be reapplied. Oftentimes, softer stones, such as marble, will need to be sealed more frequently, such as twice a year or more. Although someone can be hired to reseal the countertops, it is very easy for the homeowner to do this without hiring someone. Sealer can be purchased at home improvement stores for less than $50.00. The instructions from the sealer manufacturer should be followed, but basically the homeowner simply applies it to the countertop surface and allows it to dry.

Marble

Marble is a metamorphic rock formed from carbonate rocks, often limestone. Although marble is a beautiful material it requires a lot of maintenance, and it is often suggested that it be sealed more frequently than once a year. Marble is softer than granite and sensitive to acids. Because it is soft and porous, marble will soak up oils and any spills, and also will show etching. Marble countertops can be chipped and scratched by normal everyday use. Because it is sensitive, the users need to be diligent about immediately cleaning any spills or marks. Marble countertops are usually **polished** or **honed.** Polished marble is slightly more durable than honed marble because the polish acts as extra protection. Although protected, a polished marble may still become etched

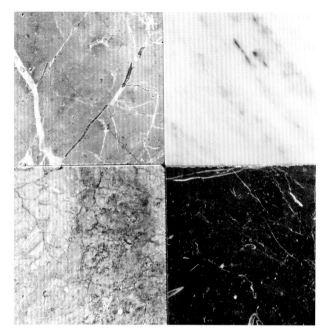

Figure 4.1 Marble is known for its movement. *Courtesy of Pamela Polvere Designs and Brad Wilkening.*

and possibly stained. Although marble requires a bit of maintenance, it is still a very popular stone. Marble is the second most commonly used stone countertop material, after granite (Figure 4.1).

DESIGNER'S DIALOGUE 4.1

"Marble seems to be used on countertops a lot in kitchen application lately, but we always learned to not use marble on the countertop. The fabricator will also tell you to not use marble in a kitchen. Everyone really wants it until they have their first party and someone spills wine. Fashion sometimes seems to supersede good design."
—*Lisa McManus, ASID, Kitchen and Bath Designer*

Granite

Granite is an igneous rock. It is a very hard and dense stone. Granites may appear uniform and consistent, but there also are many with more movement. Some granite colors are so consistent that laying out the slab may not be necessary. An advantage of granite is that it does not scratch easily. Of the various stones, granite is the best at fighting bacterial contamination. Although granite is considered more durable than marble, limestone, and other stones, it is still porous and can etch or stain (Figure 4.2).

Quartzite

Quartzite is a hard metamorphic sandstone that has been converted through heat and pressure. This material is not the same as man-made quartz, although sometimes the two are confused. Quartzite is a very hard stone and therefore fabricators may have a more challenging time working with it. It is also commonly available in smaller slabs. The difficulty in fabrication and smaller slab sizes may lead to labor being more costly when this material is used (Figure 4.3).

Travertine

Travertine is oftentimes characterized as a marble. Its characteristics are very similar to marble. Some travertine has holes and pits that are filled with a resin for a more finished look and easier maintenance. Like marble, it is a higher maintenance material and will etch and stain, easily shows scratches, and also absorbs liquids more easily than other stones.

Limestone

Limestone is a sedimentary rock composed mostly of the mineral calcite. It is a soft stone and is also susceptible to acid etching and scratching, just like marble and travertine. Limestone is normally too soft to be polished and therefore is typically honed or flamed. Some limestone has little shells visible and hence may be called a shell stone. Shell stone is a more porous limestone. Because limestone is so porous and soft it is not ideal

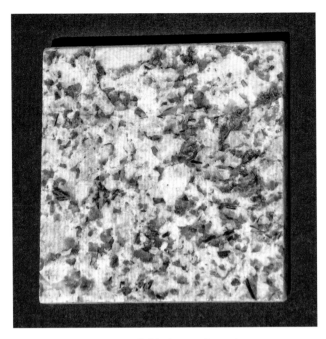

Figure 4.2 Granite is available in a variety of movements.
Courtesy of Pamela Polvere Designs and Brad Wilkening.

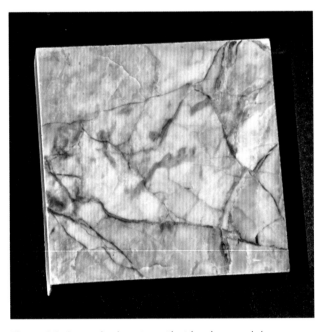

Figure 4.3 Quartzite is a stone that has been gaining popularity. This sample looks very much like marble.
Courtesy of Pamela Polvere Designs and Brad Wilkening.

for use in kitchens. It can, however, make a nice surface material for bathrooms (Figure 4.4).

Sandstone

Sandstone is made mostly of quartz, which is a very hard surface. It consists of sand masses created by moving water or by wind. It has a very distinct and unique look. Sandstone absorbs liquids easily, and is not a good choice for countertop use.

Soapstone

Soapstone is a stone with quartz and talc, along with other minerals. It is a softer stone and will patina over time, which the client should be informed of before choosing this for a countertop. Although it patinas, it is actually a nonporous stone. Soapstone is rather tolerant of heat and is fairly impervious. It is typically treated with mineral oil to speed the patina process, but this is not required. If using mineral oil, it needs to be reapplied every week for a couple of months. Over time, the soapstone will darken and reapplication will be needed only about once a month. As water spots begin to appear and the mineral oil evaporates, the surface must be cleaned and fresh mineral oil applied. Typically soapstone is available in smaller slabs, and is an expensive stone compared with the other options.

Onyx

Onyx is a microcrystalline quartz, which has a glossy and reflective surface. Other stones sometimes are referred to as onyx because of their translucency but are not true onyx. Onyx has bands of contrasting lines running through it and contrasts within itself. Like marble, onyx is very soft and porous. Onyx, unlike marble, will even absorb water. Onyx is not an ideal countertop material and is not best for any heavy use area. Stains are extremely hard to remove from onyx and it also is prone to etching. Although not the best countertop option,

Figure 4.4 Limestone is a softer stone and is not an ideal kitchen counter material. *Courtesy of Pamela Polvere Designs and Brad Wilkening.*

onyx still can be used vertically to make a design statement in a space.

Slate

Slate is typically known for its cleft face or irregular surface. The majority of slates will have this characteristic. Slate does not etch or burn; is nonporous, durable, and waterproof; and requires very little maintenance. One disadvantage of slate is that it will scratch. In addition, its unevenness causes it not to be a good countertop material choice.

WOOD

Wood is another popular natural option for countertops. Although wood is not as hard as granite, its durability depends on the species of wood being used.

Wooden countertops will show scratches and dents, but some homeowners prefer this rustic look. The maintenance for wood countertops involves reoiling approximately once a year. Surprisingly, wood makes for a rather hygienic surface, and is simple to clean: on a regular basis, simply wash a wooden countertop with mild soap and water. Once the countertop is dried from the washing, vinegar can then be used as a disinfectant. Wood does not harbor bacteria more than any other countertop materials available. Although the wood will be assembled by a tradesperson to create a large surface area, it is still considered natural (Figure 4.5).

MAN-MADE MATERIALS

In addition to natural countertop materials, numerous man-made options are available. The most common of

Figure 4.5 Wood countertops are available with a plank or end grain pattern. *Courtesy of Pamela Polvere Designs.*

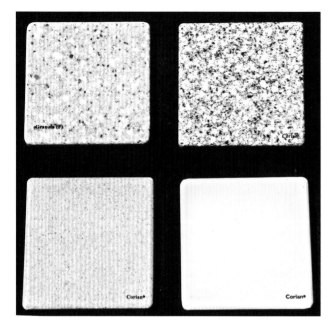

Figure 4.6 Solid surfacing is available in many colors and patterns. *Courtesy of Pamela Polvere Designs and Brad Wilkening.*

these are solid surfacing, quartz, terrazzo, glass, concrete, and stainless steel. Of these materials, solid surfacing was very popular for a while, and some designers think it may be returning as a trend. Quartz has been prevalent, because of its durability and similar look to stone. Although terrazzo, glass, concrete, and stainless steel are being used, they still are not the top choice for most designers and homeowners.

Solid Surfacing

Solid surfacing has not been as dominant recently, but some designers think it may return as a trend. What the material is composed of varies between manufacturers and is proprietary. Because of this, performance also varies between manufacturers. The materials most commonly used are polyester and acrylic. Acrylic is more expensive than polyester and has chemically bonded seams. Chemically bonded seams are more durable than polyester's mechanical seams. All solid surface materials have color that is consistent throughout its thickness. The

advantage to solid surface having its color throughout is that scratches and stains can be buffed out. Another advantage of solid surfacing is the option to also have an integrated sink bowl. These are sinks that are integrated into the countertop. This makes cleaning very easy as there is not much of a seam. Solid surface countertops are generally less expensive than other options, natural or man-made (Figures 4.6 and 4.7).

Quartz

Several large companies manufacture engineered quartz countertop material. Quartz is a man-made material composed of natural stone and resin. Quartz is twice as strong as granite, resists stains, does not require sealing, and is safe for food preparation. Of all the countertop materials available, quartz is the strongest and most durable option available. Because it is so strong, repairs are difficult to make once it is installed. One drawback is that it also will dull knives. Because quartz is man-made, the color options are typically more consistent and look similar to a granite with little movement. The companies making quartz have also been working to produce colors that replicate the look of marble, but it is still possible to distinguish man-made quartz from natural stone. Some quartz companies also offer colors that look similar to concrete, which

Figure 4.7 Integrated sink bowls can be made from solid surfacing material. *Courtesy of Pamela Polvere Designs and Brad Wilkening.*

have been trendy. Like stone, it is available polished or honed. Also like stone, the honed version of this material is more susceptible to stains and scratching. A honed quartz top will absorb oil, spots will remain, and fingerprints will show. These are very important details to share with clients so they will not be dissatisfied once the material is installed (Figure 4.8).

Terrazzo

Terrazzo has become a popular countertop material with the movement toward sustainable design, which is discussed in further detail in Chapter 3. Several companies now make countertops that are essentially a form of terrazzo. These companies take recycled glass and mix it with concrete to create countertop material. The result is a very strong countertop material. The look of these products is certainly more contemporary than traditional, although designers tend to use them in both styles of space. Because this material is still made with concrete, it risks developing hairline cracks, and is susceptible to chipping at very sharp edges. Terrazzo is similar to granite in strength, durability, heat resistance, and maintenance. Although it is strong, acids will still etch this material as well. If a spill is not wiped up immediately, it can stain. A terrazzo countertop requires waxing a few times a year and should be sealed once every 1 to 2 years (Figure 4.9).

Glass

Glass is yet another option available in countertop materials. Glass has a smooth and glossy finish, giving it a contemporary feel. Glass countertops can be textured, etched, sandblasted, grooved, or patterned, and come in a wide range of colors. Because glass is non-porous, it is rather hygienic and extremely heat resistant. However, a glass countertop can be difficult to

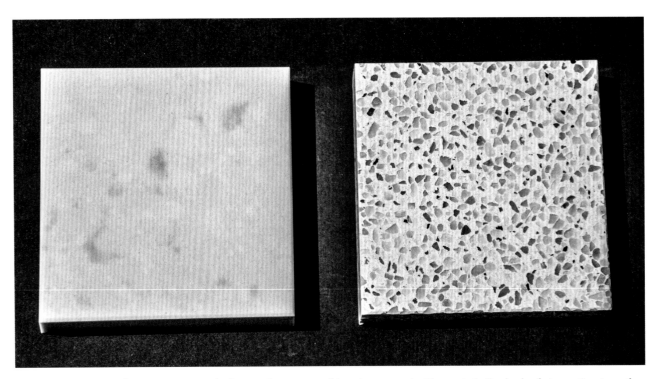

Figure 4.8 Quartz surfaces are composed of stone, but are considered man-made. They mimic the look of stone. *Courtesy of Pamela Polvere Designs and Brad Wilkening.*

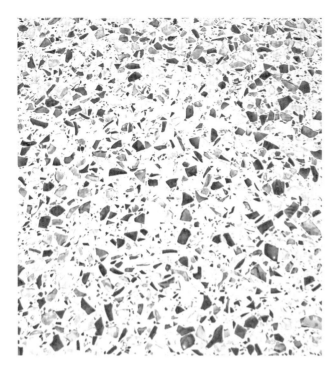

Figure 4.9 Terrazzo countertops may be gaining in popularity because of the many companies now offering these with recycled glass as a sustainable option. *Courtesy of Pamela Polvere Designs and Brad Wilkening.*

care should be taken when placing heated items on concrete. Too much heat can damage the sealer. Sharp edges can chip and the surface will develop hairline cracks. Concrete ordinarily does not stain, but can stain if the sealer wears off. Although this material has some downfalls, concrete can still be used for countertops as long as the homeowner is made aware of and understands these traits.

Figure 4.10 Glass countertops make a nice contemporary option, but the client should be warned about its characteristics. *Courtesy of Abt Electronics and Brad Wilkening.*

keep clean, as it easily shows fingerprints and smudges. Glass used for kitchen countertops is **tempered** and is relatively durable, but can break if heavy objects are dropped on it. A glass countertop also is not easy to repair if breakage or damage occurs. Each damaged piece would need to be replaced. It should not be cut on and should be cleaned with nonabrasive cleaners. Therefore, glass countertops are not recommended for a high-use kitchen (Figure 4.10).

Concrete

Concrete is a very customizable and newer countertop option, in that it can be sculpted, molded, texturized, or colored. As with most counter materials, cutting is not recommended directly on a concrete surface. Cutting directly on it can lead to scratches and gouges and also will harm knives. Also like most countertop surfaces,

Stainless Steel

Stainless steel countertops frequently are used in commercial kitchen settings, but also may be used in a residential setting. They are not typically seen in bathrooms, but that does not mean they cannot be used there. Stainless steel is nonporous, so staining is not an issue. It will not be damaged by heat, but it is susceptible to scratching and marks will show over time.

DESIGNER'S DIALOGUE 4.2

"Materials are important. They are paying you to know about them, so you need to educate the client. I had a woman who went somewhere else and had been recommended stainless steel countertops. It is very soft and shows scratches. A month later it will look worn and it's not like a granite or wood that you can buff out. The client needs to know that. This client was not happy and decided to replace all the tops. When you educate them about the materials, it becomes their choice, based on the traits."

—Joanne Giesel, Kitchen and Bath Designer

Recycled Paper

Recycled paper is a newer option available for countertops. This material is considered sustainable because it is composed of recycled paper. This material is composed of 50 percent to 100 percent recycled postconsumer recycled paper, depending on the color. It is also made with petroleum-free resin, and is supposed to absorb almost no water, but clients should still be warned of this possibility (Figure 4.11).

LAMINATE

Laminate is another option in countertops. Laminate consists of layers of paper bonded with resin. The decorative visible layer of paper is available in many prints and colors. These papers are covered by a protective, transparent overlay. Laminates are bonded to a substrate, such as particle board, medium density fiberboard, or plywood with a smooth surface. Water can be a problem for the substrate, so the substrate must be

Figure 4.11 Recycled paper countertops are a newer material being offered that is sustainable. *Courtesy of Pamela Polvere Designs and Brad Wilkening.*

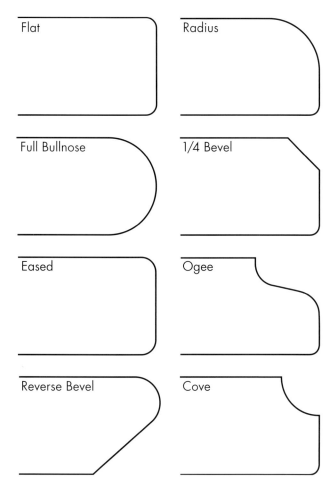

Flat

Radius

Full Bullnose

1/4 Bevel

Eased

Ogee

Reverse Bevel

Cove

Figure 4.12 There are many different options for countertop edges.

Most often, clients hiring a kitchen and bath designer do not typically select this material for their project (Table 4.1).

COUNTERTOP EDGES

Not only are there many options for countertop materials, but also for the edges. The most commonly used edge is the simple flat square edge. Another popular, more decorative edge is the ogee style. Typically a more decorative edge such as the ogee will be more expensive than the standard square. What edges are available depends on the material being used and the fabricator. A material such as concrete will have limited edge options, whereas granite and marble generally have many options. The thickness of the countertop also contributes to the possible edges available. A thicker edge usually allows for more variety in possible edges if the material allows (Figure 4.12).

TILE

Tile is a versatile material that can be used outside and inside. Tiles can be placed vertically or horizontally and are decorative and functional. Like countertops, tile may be made of natural materials or man-made materials. Either of these options can be used in a project to make it look traditional or contemporary. In kitchens, tile often is used for a backsplash or as flooring material. In the past, tile was used for countertops; however, its popularity has decreased immensely because **grout** lines become dirty over time. Tile also is occasionally used with custom hood designs. In the bathroom, tile is installed on the floors, walls, and even ceilings. Many different options are available when choosing tile. No matter what type is used, there are many factors that should be kept in mind when working with tile.

Selecting what type of tile to use for a project is only a portion of the thought process that is necessary.

protected from water penetration. If water reaches the substrate, it will swell and break the bond between the substrate and laminate. Only overmount sinks should be used with laminate countertops, to help seal the edge to avoid water getting to the substrate. Seams are noticeable with laminate, and so the layout of the seams is important for the designer to consider. Laminate is perhaps the least expensive option available for countertops. Laminate countertops as an option have diminished in popularity among designers and their clients.

TABLE 4.1 COUNTERTOP MATERIAL COMPARISON			
Material	Pros	Cons	Sustainability
Natural materials			
• Marble	Aesthetically beautiful option	Soft material, susceptible to etching, scratching, and staining Needs to be sealed regularly Typically expensive	Can be sustainable if reusing marble from a tear-down
• Granite	Available in a variety of colors and patterns Reasonable amount of hardness	Needs to be sealed regularly Not the most durable option available	Can be sustainable if reusing from a tear-down Can also be sustainable if quarry is located within 500 miles of project
• Quartzite	One of the stronger stones available Aesthetically attractive option	Typically expensive Needs to be sealed regularly	Can be sustainable if reusing or if the quarry is located within 500 miles of project It is a strong material and can last decades
• Travertine	Aesthetically attractive option	Susceptible to etching, scratching, and staining Needs to be sealed regularly	Can be sustainable if quarry is located within 500 miles of project
• Limestone	Aesthetically attractive material	Soft material, susceptible to etching, scratching, and staining	Can be sustainable if quarry is located within 500 miles of project Can possibly be reused
• Sandstone	Aesthetically attractive and has a unique look	Not a good choice for countertops	Can be sustainable if quarry is located within 500 miles of project
• Soapstone	Aesthetically beautiful option Tolerant of heat	Involves considerable initial maintenance if choosing to oil the stone Material patinas over time, which some clients will not like	Can be sustainable if quarry is located within 500 miles of project
• Onyx	Aesthetically attractive material	Soft material, really not ideal for countertop use	Can be sustainable if quarry is located within 500 miles of project
• Slate	Aesthetically attractive option	Not a good countertop material because of its unevenness	Can be sustainable if quarry is located within 500 miles of project
• Wood	Aesthetically beautiful option Wood is a hygienic surface Can be sanded down if scratches occur Easy to clean	Typically expensive	A reusable material that should last a long time Can be sustainable if manufactured within 500 miles of the project

TABLE 4.1 COUNTERTOP MATERIAL COMPARISON			
Material	Pros	Cons	Sustainability
Man-made materials			
• Quartz	The most durable countertop material currently available Does not need to be sealed Available in many different colors and patterns	Typically one of the most expensive countertop options Repairs can be difficult because it is so strong	A durable material that will last a long time Can be sustainable if manufactured within 500 miles of project
• Terrazzo	Aesthetically attractive option A rather hard surface, with durability comparable to granite	Susceptible to cracks on sharp edges Prone to hairline cracks because it is made from concrete	Generally does not outgas and will last a long time Many countertop terrazzo companies offer recycled glass as the aggregate
• Glass	Hygienic and rather heat resistant	Not easy to repair Can be difficult to keep clean Not recommended for a high-use kitchen	Can be considered sustainable if manufactured within 500 miles of project Recyclable. Does not outgas.
• Concrete	Will not outgas Unique aesthetic option	Sharp edges can chip Concrete will crack over time; this is generally considered part of its beauty, but some do not like this fact	Can be considered sustainable if manufactured within 500 miles of project
• Stainless steel	Beautiful product Can be cleaned very easily	Stainless steel will scratch Can be an expensive option	Can possibly be recycled later Can also be sustainable if manufactured within 500 miles of project
• Recycled paper	A unique option for countertops	Although it isn't supposed to absorb water, clients should still be warned that it is possible	Made from recycled material
• Laminate	Inexpensive material	Seams are noticeable Edges can be susceptible to moisture Not popular aesthetically	Can be somewhat sustainable if manufactured within 500 miles of project.

There are several details that should be kept in mind when designing a tile layout, such as accounting for **overage,** what size or thickness to use, maintenance, and how the tile will work with other elements in the space.

TILE OVERAGE

When calculating how much tile is needed, the designer must account for overage. The designer should first calculate the area of the space to be tiled. When accounting for floor quantity, keep in mind that the tile will be installed under any cabinets, appliances, toilets, and freestanding tubs. If the floor is not even underneath all of these items, problems arise later. A lower floor beneath a dishwasher will trap the dishwasher in the space, making it impossible to replace without tearing out the floor.

If a tile pattern is to be installed straight, 10 percent overage should be ordered to account for cuts made. If a tile pattern is to be installed on a diagonal or in a shaped space that will require more cuts, 15 percent overage should be ordered. Sometimes, if a tile has a very long lead time, it is a good idea to order 15 percent overage: If the tile installer ends up running short, it would be very inconvenient to have to wait 8 or more weeks to receive the needed tiles to complete the project. Be sure to ask the tile provider how the tile is sold, as sometimes full cartons must be purchased. The designer also needs to be careful not to overorder the tile. Many tiles that have long lead times are considered a special order and are therefore not returnable. If the client sees an unopened box full of unused tiles, he or she may expect a credit from the designer, even though the designer will have to keep the tile and still pay for it. Always calculate tile quantities carefully and double-check the math.

INSTALLATION

One of the most important things regarding tile is for the installer to read the manufacturer's installation instructions. It is best if the designer reminds the

installer of this, as some installers who have experience with a certain type of material may think they already know how to work with it. If the installer installs the tile incorrectly, it makes for a very expensive and possibly time-consuming repair (Figure 4.13).

GROUT

There are two main types of grout: sanded and unsanded. Sanded grout is more commonly used because it cleans up easily. It is also less likely to crack. When used with polished tiles the installer will need to take care as to avoid scratching the tile. Unsanded grout is used for very tight joints no wider than 1/8 inch. Any larger and cracks will appear, the result of shrinkage. Grout is available in many different colors. The designer can select a color that blends or contrasts with the tile, based on the aesthetic desired. Grout also will have to be sealed by the installer. When selecting a grout shade, it is important for the designer to keep in mind that even with sealer, a light grout will become dirty over time. Alternatively, darker grouts may lighten.

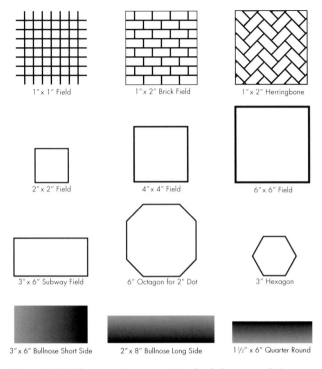

1" x 1" Field	1" x 2" Brick Field	1" x 2" Herringbone
2" x 2" Field	4" x 4" Field	6" x 6" Field
3" x 6" Subway Field	6" Octagon for 2" Dot	3" Hexagon
3" x 6" Bullnose Short Side	2" x 8" Bullnose Long Side	1½" x 6" Quarter Round

Figure 4.13 Tile comes in many standard shapes and sizes. Here are just a few that are commonly found.

SIZING

Tile is available in many different sizes. Some of the standard sizes that are seen are 1 by 1, 2 by 2, 4 by 4, 6 by 6, 12 by 12, 18 by 18, 24 by 24, and 3 by 6 inches. Tile sizes are not limited to these by any means. When selecting tile, the manufacturer will have information on all sizes available within different colors or series. Another point to be aware of is that sometimes the size stated is **nominal.** For example, you may order a 4 by 4 inch tile for your client, only to find when you receive it that the tiles are 3¾ by 3¾ inches in size. It is helpful to be aware of this before ordering the tile so that adjustments can be made in the quantity ordered if necessary.

What sizes are used in a design is determined by the nature of the overall design goal for the space. Larger tiles are usually considered to look more contemporary. A 3 by 6 inch tile is considered a traditional size because

this is the standard size for subway tile. Because 12 by 12 inches or larger may be used for flooring, it is important to consider the use intended for the tile. In a bathroom, where the floor will become wet, it is important to inform the client that a larger tile could become slippery. When specifying a custom-tiled shower floor, it is best to use tiles that are 2 by 2 inches or smaller. The smaller tiles end up having more grout lines, which adds texture and minimizes floor slipperiness.

CONSIDERATIONS FOR LARGER FORMAT TILE

Other issues to consider regarding tile size have to do with incidents that may arise. When larger format tiles are installed, the floor must be perfectly level, or the tile could crack or break as a result of the uneven floor. Large format tile, such as a 20 by 12 inches, often will have a bow in it. If this type of tile is used for an offset pattern, it should not be offset more than 30 percent or there will be too much variation in the height between the tiles.

WORKING WITH DIFFERENT TILE THICKNESSES

In general, the thickness of the tiles being used should be monitored. It is possible to use tiles of different thicknesses together, but more labor will be required. The installer will need to build up the wall behind the thinner tile so that they are all on the same plane. This happens frequently with glass tile, which is typically thinner compared with all other types of tile.

TILE MAINTENANCE

We discuss tile maintenance in Stone Tile Maintenance (below), and in the following descriptions of the different types of tile. Keep in mind that it is important to talk with the client about the sort of maintenance he or she is envisioning. If clients tell you they prefer minimal, worry-free maintenance, the options are automatically narrowed down as to what they should be shown. Although this may seem like common sense, many designers tend to get caught up in the overall aesthetic they are trying to achieve, and may end up suggesting a material that is not appropriate for the client.

WHEN TO SELECT THE TILE

Although there are always exceptions, it is generally best to select the tile after the cabinet and countertop finishes have been selected. Once these two items are selected, they, like the desired level of maintenance, will help narrow down what the appropriate tile options will be. Because the cabinets and countertops account for such a large surface area, it is likely they will have a larger effect on the aesthetic of the space. Of course, this is not always the case and there is nothing wrong with starting with a tile if the client is in love with something in particular. But, for the most part, it is best to start with the larger surface area items.

HOW CABINETS AND COUNTERTOPS AFFECT TILE SELECTION

Imagine you have already helped a client select cabinet and countertop finishes. Together, you have selected "Absolute Black" polished granite, which is a very solid black selection. You also are using a cherrywood cabinet with a medium-range stain on a flat-door style. These are rather clean and simple finishes to have selected. Although a simple tile could be selected to keep with the overall minimal look, there is also the option to use a tile with more movement. The appearance of movement can be inherent to the tile itself, or result from a pattern created with the tile. Oftentimes, it is nice to have contrast within a design. If the cabinets and countertops are more elaborate, then it may be best to stick with a simpler tile and pattern so that the whole space does not look too busy. All finishes and items selected should always be done so with consideration to the home. An ultracontemporary home will not usually

have a traditional kitchen and bath. Although we offer these suggestions as designers, it is ultimately the clients' decision as they are the ones paying for it and will be living in the space.

It is also important that both the designer and client see the tile and approve it before it is installed. This is especially important for tile that will have variation, such as stone tile.

TILE MATERIALS

Selecting the type of tile material is an important and hopefully initial step. The first question to ask the client is what their expectations are regarding maintenance. If minimal maintenance is a primary concern this should alert the designer to avoid certain materials. Other clients may not be as concerned but simply want to achieve a certain look. Let's now take a look at the different types of tile available and what their strengths and weaknesses are.

Stone Tile

Although stone tile would usually be considered more traditional, it can still be used in a way that makes it look more contemporary. Typically simple, large, clean tiles made of stone can be found in modern spaces. More ornate stone tile, with elaborate moldings, will be more traditional. Not only do the size and shape of the stone tile affect the aesthetic, but also the movement of the stone selected. As discussed earlier in this chapter, there are many types of stone, which have different appearances. Because it is from nature, stone will always have variation and be unique. Each tile piece will be different, no two will be the same, but this is the source of its beauty and adds richness to the overall tile design (Figure 4.14).

The advantage of stone tile is that it can be slightly sanded down on site if needed. This is useful when pieces such as **corner** or **bullnose** end pieces are not available. The installer can simply sand down the tiles to give a finished edge, because the color extends throughout the stone.

Stone Tile Maintenance. Stone tile requires the most maintenance of any tile option because it is soft and can scratch. Like stone countertops, stone tiles need to be sealed and cleaned with an appropriate cleanser suitable for the specific stone.

When stone tile is being used, all the tiles ordered should first be removed from their boxes. They should be laid out to be viewed together. Because stone is natural and has variation, this gives the opportunity to create a desirable blend of the various movements and colors before installation. For the same reason it also makes sense to order extra tile to allow the best tiles to be selected for use. Less attractive tiles can be installed in areas, such as under cabinets or in closets, where they will not be as visible.

Ceramic Tile

Ceramic tile is also known as clay tile. It is not a very dense tile, and therefore smaller tiles will withstand pressure better than larger tiles. Tiles 4 by 4 inches or smaller should be used on floors to best withstand pressure. Larger ceramic tiles risk becoming cracked because they are not so dense. These tiles can be machine-made or hand-crafted. Machine-made ceramic tile is the least expensive tile available (Figure 4.15).

Figure 4.14 This shower is covered in limestone tile of different sizes. *Courtesy of Crossville, Inc.*

Figure 4.15 Machine-made ceramic tile is very consistent and economical. *Courtesy of Brad Wilkening.*

Hand-Crafted Ceramic Tile

When ceramic tile is hand-crafted it becomes expensive and is usually found in high-end residential projects. Many hand-crafted tiles are made in the United States by artisans in smaller factories. Hand-crafted ceramic tile is more expensive, but it also has great color and size range. Companies making these tiles are capable of making custom colors and will have numerous options for trim pieces, which give a much more tailored look. Because these tiles are made by hand, the edges will not be perfectly even and will result in wider grout lines than machine-made ceramic tiles. In addition, because of the process required to make these tiles, lead times will be longer as it will always be a special order for these pieces. This is something to consider when planning the schedule for a project. Ceramic tiles are offered in matte, gloss, and crackle finishes. Keep in mind that a crackle finish is more porous and must be sealed (Figure 4.16).

Figure 4.16 Hand-crafted ceramic tile will not be as consistent as machine-made tile, which adds to its beauty. *Courtesy of Brad Wilkening.*

Porcelain Tile

Porcelain tile also consists of a clay body. It differs from ceramic tile in that it has pigment throughout the clay so that the color is also throughout the body. This is useful because it does not show wear as easily. Of all the tiles, porcelain is the most durable. It is used inside and outside for residential and commercial projects. If chipped or scratched, a porcelain tile does not show the damage as much as a ceramic tile. Porcelain tile is also hard and will not chip as easily. Unlike some of the other tiles mentioned earlier in this chapter, porcelain is dense, does not need to be sealed, and is maintenance free. The surface of porcelain can be polished, matte, or textured, and is available glazed or unglazed. Porcelain is a great option because of its durability. Many manufacturers are even making it to replicate stone rather well and also in very nice contemporary options (Figure 4.17).

Glass Tile

Glass tile has been very fashionable for the past 10 to 15 years. It is more expensive compared with the other options, but it makes a great accent among field tile. Glass tile is typically considered contemporary, but some designers still use it as an accent in a traditional space. It is a tile that is very exciting and vibrant. Manufacturers are constantly evolving with new patterns, sizes, and colors. Not only are there many field size options, but also coordinating trim pieces. A benefit of glass tile is that it can be cut, which helps make installation a little easier. Some glass tiles are intended for use only on walls whereas others may be used on either walls or floors. Not only does glass tile come in an array of colors, but it is also available in different finishes. Some of the distinctive finishes that can be found are matte, iridescent, and noniridescent, which would also be clear. More benefits of glass tile are that it works well with other materials and is very low maintenance. Glass tile does not need to be sealed, as does stone tile and even some ceramics. One thing to remember about glass tile: As with any other tile, consider the roughness

Figure 4.17 Porcelain tile often looks very similar to stone. *Courtesy of Crossville, Inc.*

Figure 4.18 Glass tile has become very popular. *Courtesy of Crossville, Inc.*

of the edges. If a glass tile has uneven edges the grout lines will be larger when it is installed. Also as for other tiles, it is very important that the installer carefully follow the manufacturer's instructions for installation. Some installers may think they have experience with glass tile, so they'll know how to install it, but many a glass tile has been installed incorrectly because of this assumption, leading to higher costs and longer installation times (Figure 4.18).

Metal Tile

Metal tiles have become popular recently. They work well as an accent piece, and that is how they are mostly being used. Some metal tiles are actually made of metal and other metallic tiles are made of resin. There are also ceramic tiles that have a metallic glaze applied. Metal tiles can be cut. True metal tiles will acquire a patina as they are exposed to water, but can be cleaned. This change in the tile's color over time is considered part of its beauty. What type of patina it acquires depends on the type of metal, and a further description will be provided by the manufacturer (Figure 4.19).

Figure 4.19 Most metal tiles have a contemporary look to them. *Courtesy of Crossville, Inc.*

FLOORING

Flooring typically consists of materials such as tile, wood, cork, bamboo, concrete, or linoleum. The common tile flooring materials are stone, porcelain, and ceramic. Wood flooring is popular and available in many different species, although oak and maple are among the most popular. In addition to the previously described materials linoleum, vinyl, and cork also are possible flooring materials.

LINOLEUM

Linoleum is a natural and biodegradable material. It is created by oxidizing linseed oil to form linoleum cement, which is cooled and mixed with pine resin and wood flour to form sheets on jute backing. It is recyclable, durable, and hygienic. A weakness of linoleum is that it can be damaged by standing water. Linoleum is available in tiles or sheets (Figure 4.20).

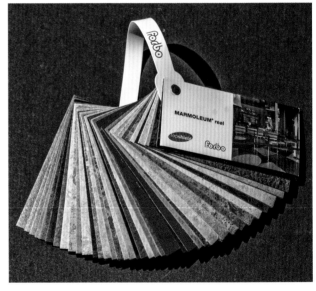

Figure 4.20 Linoleum flooring is available in a wide range of colors. *Courtesy of Pamela Polvere Designs and Brad Wilkening.*

VINYL

Vinyl is available in sheets or tiles and is a very inexpensive flooring material. It can be made of pure vinyl or vinyl composition, both having different degrees of fillers. There are many different patterns and styles to choose from. It can have slip-retardant or static control properties. It can be smooth or embossed. The durability is based on the thickness of the upper, wear layer. Whereas linoleum has been gaining popularity again, due to its being a sustainable material, vinyl has continued to lose popularity for the client hiring a kitchen and bath designer.

CORK

Cork is a popular flooring material. Its traits are similar to wood and it is available in various sizes. Cork flooring can be purchased unfinished or prefinished with wax or polyurethane. It must be sealed, as is susceptible to staining. Cork also may be stained, giving it different appearances. Some benefits of cork are that is helps absorb sound, is insulating, and comfortable to stand on (Figure 4.21).

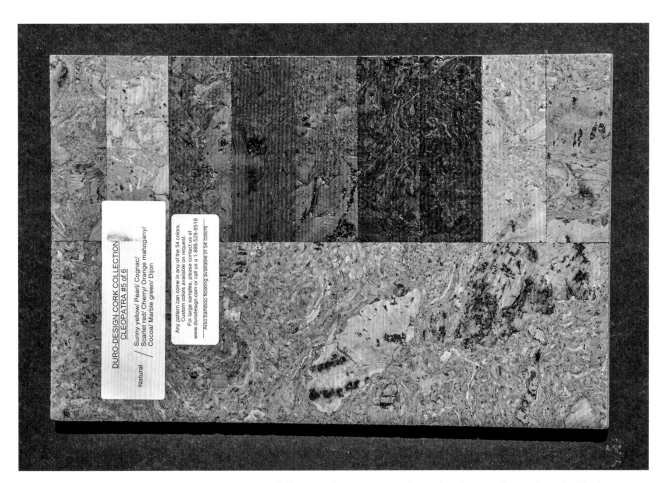

Figure 4.21 Cork flooring is also available in many different colors. *Courtesy of Pamela Polvere Designs and Brad Wilkening.*

WOOD

Wood flooring is frequently used in kitchens, but not commonly in bathrooms. There are various species of wood available, but oak and maple are used most often, due to their durability and pricing. More unusual wood species will be more expensive. Wood flooring is available in a variety of aesthetics. It can look sleek and contemporary, rustic, or traditional depending on the wood species, finish, plank size, and texture selected. When new wood flooring is installed in a space unfinished, the designer can select the exact stain on site. After the unfinished flooring is installed the tradesperson can paint an area with the stain so it can be approved. As an alternative, prefinished boards can be used. Because sustainable design has become a trend, more companies are offering recycled wood for flooring.

BAMBOO

Bamboo flooring is similar to wood. It has become popular with the sustainable movement as well. It is considered sustainable because it grows fast. Some people would argue it is not truly sustainable because it typically ships from Asia, which is a long journey. Bamboo is strong and durable, like wood, and also is available in a variety of finishes.

TILE

Tile is often used for flooring in kitchens and bathrooms because it is generally a durable surface. The various materials available for tile have already been discussed in detail previously in this chapter. Keep in mind that the tile size is also important to consider because it will affect the aesthetic and slip resistance. When aiming for a more slip-resistant floor it is best to use a smaller tile, because the additional grout lines will add texture.

WALL COVERING

Typical wall coverings found in kitchens and baths are paint, wallpaper, and tile. Paint is the most popular, probably because it is easy to change and not very expensive. Wallpaper is not being used as much, although some designers believe wallpaper is returning as a trend. Let's look further at the different traits of these wall covering options.

PAINT

Paint is the most popular wall covering because it is easy to maintain and change. It is also very clean looking, yet works in any style space. There are two main types of paint: latex and oil. Latex is made from a water base whereas oil is made from an oil base. Oil paint dries harder and more evenly than latex paint, but takes longer to dry and eventually can crack and chip. Both types of paint give off fumes, but some latex paints now offer low- or no-**VOC (volatile organic compound)** formulas. VOCs are toxic, so these low- or no-VOC formulas make for a healthier environment.

Gloss Level

When selecting paint for a space, one of the first considerations should be the gloss level. Standard gloss levels that are available include gloss, semigloss, satin, eggshell, and flat. On occasion, manufacturers use their own names for gloss levels, but samples can be seen to decide between them. The higher the gloss level of a paint, the easier it is to clean. The disadvantage of higher gloss levels is that the paint then shows all the surface imperfections. In a kitchen or bath, gloss levels that are commonly used are satin or a washable eggshell. Some paint companies even offer a specific paint sheen called "kitchen and bath."

WALLPAPER

Although wallpaper is not being used as much in kitchens and baths lately, it is still an option. Some designers even believe it is a trend that is resurfacing. Wallpaper is available in residential and commercial grades. Commercial-grade wallpapers are more durable and rated on the basis of fire resistance. The code requirements for wallpaper do not typically apply to residences, due to the nature of the building. The exception to this might be in a high-rise building, but it would then apply to the common corridors acting as a means of egress, not the individual home. The common types of wallpaper found in residential projects are vinyl-coated, cloth-backed vinyl, paper-backed vinyl, foil, and various textiles such as silks, linens, and grass cloth (Figure 4.22).

HARDWARE

The kitchen and bath designer will typically provide, or help their client select, cabinet hardware for the project. Selecting the hardware is based on a few factors: budget, the client's preferences, and the general aesthetic of the space. Because there are so many options for hardware, these three factors help narrow down the search. Hardware is also available in many different materials. They can be seen with glass, stone, or standard metal just to name a few. Usually hardware that incorporates glass or other materials still has a metal base for attaching to the cabinet or appliance. Hardware also is made in a variety of finishes such as polished chrome, brushed nickel, and antique brass. Again, this is just a small sample of the many finishes that can be found.

Figure 4.22 Some people believe wallpaper is becoming a popular trend once again. This bathroom has subtle patterned wallpaper throughout. *Courtesy of Pamela Polvere Designs and McShane Fleming Studios, Chicago.*

KNOBS

Knobs are small, typically round, handles. Knobs also can be found in square or other shapes. There are many manufacturers of both knobs and handles. They are available in many different finishes and custom finishes also are available.

PULLS

Pulls are an alternative hardware option to knobs. The decision to use knobs or pulls is primarily a question of what the client prefers; there are some instances when pulls are preferred. If using custom hardware for appliances, it is better to install longer pulls on dishwashers, refrigerators, and other large appliances; if a small knob were placed on them, they would be more difficult to open. Combining the use of knobs and pulls on a project also occurs frequently for a more interesting look.

SUMMARY

Material selection is a critical step in kitchen and bath design. What materials are used has a huge effect on the aesthetic of the space. Although aesthetic is important, function is even more important. A beautiful countertop that is ruined within a year because it could not withstand the use is a waste of time, money, and resources. It is the designer's responsibility to educate the client so he or she can make an informed decision.

CHAPTER 4 EXERCISES

I: Determine the quantity of tile that should be ordered for the tile layout plan in Figure 4.23.
II: The Mowat family described at the beginning of this chapter is requesting a vintage-style kitchen. They need easy-to-maintain materials because they are busy with their two young boys.
    What would you suggest for walls, backsplash, countertops, flooring, and hardware, and why?

CHAPTER 4 DISCUSSION QUESTIONS

1. What are some of the differences between machine-made and handmade ceramic tile?
2. What type of maintenance do stone countertops require?
3. How do you know it is time to reseal stone countertops?
4. When specifying a custom tile floor for a shower, what is the largest size tile that should be used?
5. What are some sustainable flooring options?

REFERENCES

Godsey, Lisa. *Interior Design Materials and Specifications*. New York, NY: Fairchild Publications, Inc., 2008.

Miller, Judith. *Period Kitchens: A Practical Guide to Period-Style Decorating*. London: Reed International Books Limited, 1995.

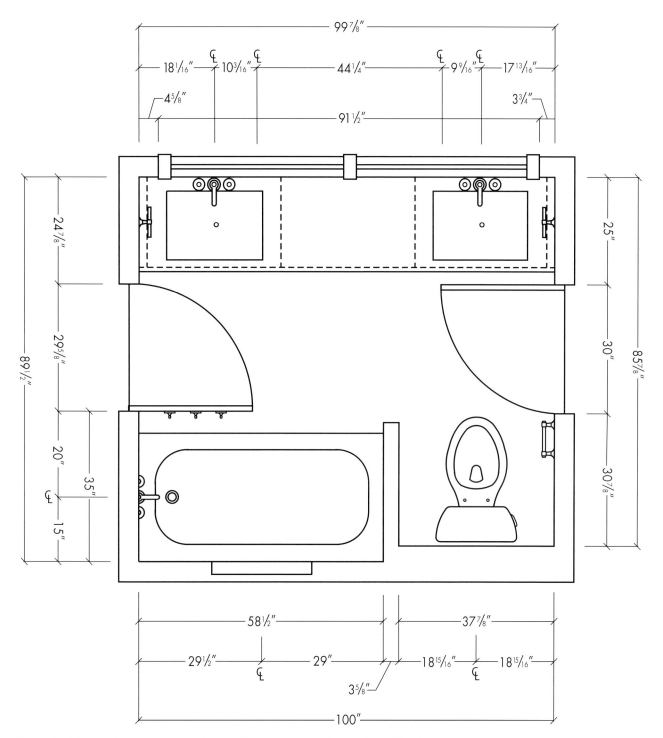

Figure 4.23 Determine the amount of floor tile that needs to be purchased for this space.

___Which countertop material makes the most sense, based on your client's needs?

___ Inform the client about maintenance of the selected countertop.

___Do you need to schedule laying out the countertop slab?

___What type of edge should the countertop have?

___What type of tile should be used, according to your client's needs?

___When determining tile quantities, be sure to add 10 percent overage. Add 15 percent for installations on a diagonal or having a unique shape requiring more cuts. Also be sure to order 15 percent overage if the tile has a particularly long lead time.

___Are different tile materials being used (i.e., different thicknesses)? If so, be sure to inform the installer ahead of time for accurate labor pricing.

___What type of flooring material should you suggest, based on the client's wants and needs?

___How should the walls be finished?

___What type of hardware does the client prefer?

KEY TERMS

Bullnose: A type of tile that has a curved or finished end to be used on the edges of a tile design for a finished look.

Corner: A tile piece shaped so that it can be used in the corner of a tile design to create a finished look.

Grout: A thin mortar used for filling spaces between tile; available as sanded or unsanded and in many colors.

Honed: A smooth, matte finish available for stone and other materials.

Nominal: A theoretical size, but possibly not the actual, accurate size.

Overage: Extra material needed to compensate for wastage that occurs during cutting.

Polished: A smooth shiny finish available for stone and other materials; considered to be the most durable finish.

Quarry: An excavation site where stone is acquired.

Quartz: A mineral consisting of silicon dioxide.

Solid surfacing: Man-made material typically made of bauxite, acrylic, or polyester resins and pigment.

Sustainable design: Designing spaces with the goal of sustaining the environment.

Tempered: Glass treated to prevent shattering; when broken the glass will bead, preventing injury.

Universal design: Design to make environments usable by all people, to the greatest extent possible.

VOC (volatile organic compound): Chemical compounds that have high vapor pressure; they are emitted as gases from certain liquids and solids and are considered unhealthy.

CHAPTER 5 KITCHEN AND BATH DESIGN: CABINETRY

OBJECTIVES

After reading this chapter, you will:

- Comprehend crucial information about selecting cabinetry for a project to accomplish the design goal while staying within budget.

- Distinguish the different types of cabinetry available to help the client select an appropriate type and style for the project.

- Recognize the fine details of cabinets, which can be specific to create a well-designed and finished project.

- Identify the many different accessories available for cabinets and indicate where to obtain them.

DESIGN SCENARIO

Your client, Ms. Hahn, has decided on a space layout for her kitchen and is excited about selecting cabinets. As her designer, you've already asked about the budget in the initial consultation and taken this into consideration while designing the layout. You also have a vision for the style that is the appropriate direction to stay within her budget.

1. Based on the budget for this project, what type of cabinet makes the most sense?

2. What sort of cabinet accessories can you include?

3. What species of wood would you recommend?

As with materials, there are many different types of cabinetry that may be used for a kitchen or bath project. Cabinetry can be generalized into three main categories from least expensive to most expensive: **stock, semicustom,** and **custom**. These three category titles are rather self-explanatory to the basic nature of each type of product. We will discuss further specifics about the differences among these types of cabinetry. Within these three types of cabinetry there are also many styles and options to choose from. We consider these features and options further when selecting the product to use.

CATEGORIES OF CABINETRY

The three main categories of cabinetry are stock, semicustom, and custom. Stock cabinetry is the least expensive option. Semicustom is more expensive but offers more customizable options. Custom is the most expensive, but practically anything can be built for a price. There are benefits and downfalls to each of these types of cabinetry.

STOCK CABINETRY

Stock cabinetry is the least expensive of the three categories. It is referred to as *stock* because these cabinets are typically stocked by the cabinet companies. Because these cabinets are made to maintain inventory in the warehouses, there are no special or custom choices the buyer can make. By limiting the options available, the manufacturer can quickly and easily mass produce cabinets to sell. The advantages of stock cabinetry are that the cabinets are less expensive and available quickly.

Sizes for stock cabinetry are standard throughout the industry. Cabinets are made in widths of 3-inch increments. For example, standard cabinet widths would be 9, 12, 15, 18 inches, and so on until 48 inches. The height and depth of the cabinets also are standard among cabinet companies. Base cabinets are 24 inches deep and 34½ inches high. Wall cabinets are 12 inches deep and have standard heights of 12, 15, 24, 30, 36, and 42 inches. Tall cabinets have depths of 12, 18, 21, and 24 inches and standard heights of 84, 90, and 96 inches (Table 5.1).

Stock cabinets also are limited in the door styles, wood species, and finish options available. Because these cabinets are specifically made to be sold at an affordable price, they usually will not be constructed of the more expensive or exotic woods available. Oak, maple, and birch are a few common woods that could be found in a stock cabinet. It would not be likely to find quarter-sawn oak in a stock cabinet option. The limited selection of woods also will have a limited range of stains. The cabinet manufacturers consider the market and produce those door styles and finishes that are the most popular.

Stock Cabinetry Accessories
Although options are limited for stock cabinetry, manufacturers have become savvy to the trends of the kitchen and bath industry. Consumers watch design television shows and research options online, and want the latest accessories without purchasing the most expensive cabinets. It is fairly easy for the cabinet manufacturers to incorporate standard accessories, such as knife blocks, spice storage, tray dividers, and **lazy Susan** systems for corner cabinets, to name a few.

Stock Cabinetry Construction
The construction of stock cabinetry ranges in quality but typically is the lowest of the three main types of cabinetry. The cabinet box and drawers are typically stapled or simply glued together. The material used for the box is usually a particle board or plywood. The interior most often is a white or a light-wood grain print vinyl.

TABLE 5.1 STANDARD CABINET SIZES

Cabinet Style	Height	Depth	Width	Availability
Kitchen base cabinets	34½ inches high	24 inches deep standard Also, frequently available 12, 15, 18, or 21 inches deep	Widths in increments of 3 inches (12, 15, 18, 21, 24, 27, 30, 33, 36, 39, 42, 45, and 48 inches)	Some companies have cabinets as small as 5, 6, or 9 inches in width for spices or other accessories
Bathroom vanity cabinets	32 or 34½ inches high	21 inches deep standard	Widths in increments of 3 inches (12, 15, 18, 21, 24, 27, 30, 33, 36, 39, 42, 45, and 48 inches)	Also frequently available 24 inches deep
Wall cabinets	30, 36, or 42 inches high	12 inches deep	Widths in increments of 3 inches (12, 15, 18, 21, 24, 27, 30, 33, 36, 39, 42, 45, and 48 inches)	Additional heights are occasionally available for over-refrigerator placement
Tall cabinets	84, 90, or 96 inches high	12, 15, 18, 21, or 24 inches deep	Widths in increments of 3 inches (12, 15, 18, 21, 24, 27, 30, 33, 36, 39, 42, 45, and 48 inches)	

DESIGNER'S DIALOGUE 5.1

"Most people frown at stock and semistock cabinets because they are limited in sizes, accessories, and modification ability. I find this challenge an opportunity to exercise creative skills. I have learned not to let the limitations of the cabinets hinder creativity. Think of them as Legos or building blocks; you can always turn things sideways or make something from several different parts."
–*Gladys Schanstra, CKD, CBD, Allied ASID, Kitchen and Bath Designer*

SEMICUSTOM CABINETRY

The second main type of cabinetry is the semicustom group. The name explains exactly what they are: cabinets that are somewhat customized to the client's specifications. Typically the manufacturer will allow the sizes to be changed within certain limits. Instead of having cabinets only in 3-inch increments it might be possible to order cabinets at almost any whole number width or depth. Semicustom cabinets also typically will offer more accessory options, door styles, wood species, and finishes to choose from. These cabinets are typically made per order, so the lead time will be longer than that of a stock cabinet company. The benefits to this type of cabinetry are that it will have more options and be of better quality than a stock cabinet. The disadvantages are that it will be more expensive than a stock option and still will not be considered fully as custom.

Semicustom Cabinetry Construction

The construction generally is better than that of a stock cabinet. Typically, semicustom cabinets have dovetailed or dado-joint drawers. The cabinet box is made of plywood or medium-density fiberboard (MDF) furniture board. The interior will usually be a light, wood-grain print vinyl. Drawers likely will be **full extension.**

CUSTOM CABINETRY

Custom cabinets are the third category for cabinetry. These are the most expensive cabinets that can be purchased but also allow the most flexibility. Typically,

TABLE 5.2 TYPES OF CABINETRY		
Type and Definition	Pros	Cons
Stock: Cabinetry that is stocked	1. Least expensive option 2. Available quickly because stocked 3. Typically most popular styles and accessories available	1. Quality isn't generally the best 2. Limited to the standard options
Semicustom: Cabinetry that allows for some customizations at a price	1. Midrange pricing 2. While lead time is slightly longer than for stock, still generally not long 3. Quality is generally good 4. Typically there is reasonable variety in the possible styles and finishes 5. Capable of some customizations	1. More expensive than stock 2. Still has some limitations and customizations can be costly
Custom: Cabinetry that is built per order and entirely custom	1. Practically anything that is drawn by the designer can be built within reason, allowing for the most flexibility in design 2. The quality is generally the best available	1. This is the most expensive option in cabinetry 2. Lead times can be long because these cabinets are typically built to order

if the designer can draw what he or she wants, the cabinet company can build it. These cabinets have a wide range of door style and wood species options. They have the best construction available. Drawers will be dovetailed and have full-extension glides. Custom cabinets are made per the submitted order. This means that, of the three categories, they have the longest lead time. It can take anywhere from 4 to 10 weeks, or even longer, to make custom cabinets.

Custom Cabinetry Construction

A common misconception about custom cabinets is that they are made of solid wood. Even the highest end cabinet manufacturers typically use furniture board to construct the cabinet boxes. Although it is mostly the general public's belief that all-wood cabinets are the best, it is not true. Wood expands and contracts because it is susceptible to moisture. Furniture board, on the other hand, does not have that problem and therefore makes a more stable box for the cabinet. Often cabinet manufacturers understand that this is not something the end user will understand or trust. Many high-end manufacturers offer an alternative plywood-box option

for those people who believe solid wood cabinets are the best (Table 5.2).

FRAMED AND FRAMELESS CABINETRY

Not only are there the three main types of cabinetry, but there is also the option of **framed** or **frameless cabinetry.** These two types are exactly as they are worded. Framed cabinetry has a face frame on the front of the cabinet box. Frameless cabinetry has no frame on the cabinet box. Whether a cabinet is framed or frameless does not affect whether the cabinet is traditional or contemporary. A range of door styles can be found in either type. Although these are two different styles of cabinetry, it is hard to call one better than the other. There are advantages to both these types of cabinetry.

Framed Cabinetry

Framed cabinetry allows for additional door style options. There are three types of door that can be used with a framed cabinet: inset, full overlay, and partial overlay.

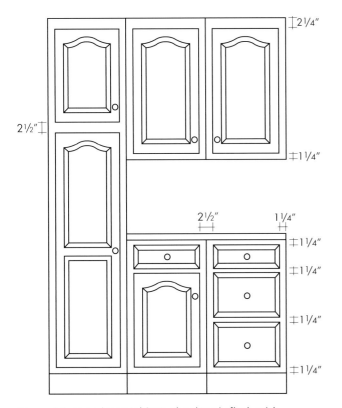

Figure 5.1 In an inset cabinet, the door is flush with the cabinet face frame. This is a traditional style. *Courtesy of Plato Woodwork, Inc.*

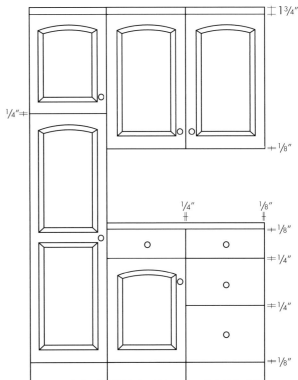

Figure 5.2 In a full overlay cabinet, the door fully overlays the face frame. *Courtesy of Plato Woodwork, Inc.*

Inset. In a cabinet with an inset door style the face frame is visible and is flush with the door. This is generally the most expensive type of door. Hinges can be exposed or fully concealed (Figure 5.1). Exposed hinges will usually have a selection of finish options available so they can match other hardware in the kitchen or bath. There also may be different hinge styles to select from. Although inset doors can have a contemporary door style they are still typically considered traditional. Kitchens from the early 1900s had inset doors. When specifying inset doors for a project, the designer should warn the client about the characteristics. Because the doors are made of wood they will expand and contract. As a result, the gaps between the door and the frame will change and may not be exactly the same from cabinet to cabinet.

This can be a particular issue in climates with high humidity or drastic changes in humidity. As long as the client is made aware, this can still be a great option for the cabinets.

Full Overlay. In a full overlay cabinet the door fully overlays the face frame. This door style gives a very clean look (Figure 5.2). Although the doors overlay the frame, the gaps are rather tight. The doors hide the cabinet box.

Partial Overlay. In a partial overlay cabinet the door partially overlays the face frame so that part of the frame is visible (Figure 5.3). This style is typically found in stock or semicustom cabinetry and is usually the least

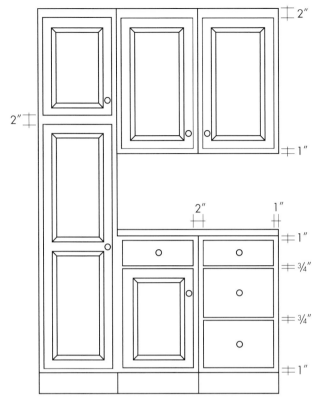

Figure 5.3   In a partial overlay cabinet, the door partially overlays the face frame, exposing some of the frame. This style is usually found in lower end cabinets. *Courtesy of Plato Woodwork, Inc.*

European Cabinetry. The label of "European cabinetry" is one often heard in the cabinet world. These are simply cabinets that are made in Europe. Typically European cabinets are frameless (Figure 5.4). Because Europe uses the metric system, all the cabinet dimensions are in millimeters. Some designers dislike using European cabinetry because they prefer not having to convert the sizes from metric to the imperial system used in the United States. Other designers prefer using European cabinets and like using the metric system; Figure 5.5 presents information allowing quick conversion from millimeters to inches.

Cabinet Nomenclature. Now that the different types of cabinetry have been discussed, let's take a look at cabinet **nomenclature.** Nomenclature is a term commonly used in the kitchen and bath industry. This refers to the abbreviations given to cabinets to specify what type of

expensive of the framed door styles. This style is similar to full overlay, but more of the cabinet box is visible.

Frameless Cabinetry

Frameless cabinetry is most often produced by European companies. It is sometimes referred to as *full access cabinetry* (Figure 5.4). These cabinets have no face frame. Although this type of cabinet can have basically any door style, it typically is seen as more contemporary. Frameless cabinets are known to be more difficult to install than framed cabinets.

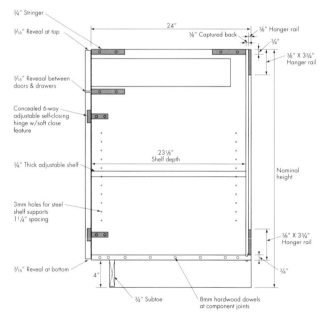

Figure 5.4 This drawing shows the construction of a frameless style cabinet. *Courtesy of Plato Woodwork, Inc.*

Millimeter Conversion Table

MM	Inches	Decimal	MM	Inches	Decimal
.79	1/32	.03125	13.49	17/32	.53125
1.00		.03937	14.00		.55118
1.59	1/16	.06250	14.29	9/16	.56250
2.00		.07874	15.00		.59055
2.38	3/32	.09375	15.08	19/32	.59375
3.00		.11811	15.87	5/8	.62500
3.17	1/8	.12500	16.00		.62990
3.97	5/32	.15625	16.67	21/32	.65625
4.00		.15748	17.00		.66929
4.76	3/16	.18750	17.46	11/16	.68750
5.00		.19685	18.00		.70866
5.56	7/32	.21875	18.26	23/32	.71875
6.00		.23622	19.00		.74803
6.35	1/4	.25000	19.05	3/4	.75000
7.00		.27559	19.84	25/32	.78125
7.14	9/32	.28125	20.00		.78740
7.94	5/16	.31250	20.64	13/16	.81250
8.00		.31496	21.00		.82677
8.73	11/32	.34375	21.43	27/32	.84375
9.00		.35433	22.00		.86614
9.52	3/8	.37500	22.22	7/8	.87500
10.00		.39370	23.00		.90551
10.32	13/32	.40625	23.02	29/32	.90625
11.00		.43307	23.81	15/16	.93750
11.11	7/16	.43750	24.00		.94488
11.91	15/32	.46875	24.61	31/32	.96875
12.00		.47244	25.00		.98425
12.70	1/2	.50000	25.40	1	1.00000
13.00		.51181	26.00		1.02362

Figure 5.5 A table showing the conversion between the metric and imperial systems. *Courtesy of Plato Woodwork, Inc.*

ferent standard cabinet depth it will be noted in their catalog. In this example the first set of numbers refers to the width of the cabinet. This is standard throughout cabinet nomenclature. A base cabinet might be B1D24. This would be a base cabinet with one drawer that is 24 inches wide. Again, the depth is not specified, as it would be a standard 24-inch depth for a kitchen base cabinet. The height also is not specified in this instance because kitchen base cabinet heights also are standard

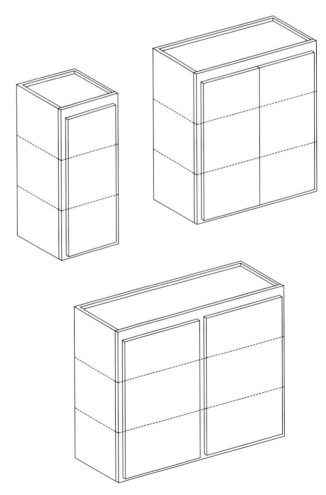

Figure 5.6 These are examples of typical cabinet line drawings that can be found in the cabinet manufacturer's catalog. *Courtesy of Plato Woodwork, Inc.*

cabinet it is. Although every cabinet company is slightly different, there are some basic guidelines that can be followed.

A wall cabinet may have the nomenclature W3630. This means it is a wall cabinet that is 36 inches wide and 30 inches high (Figure 5.6). The depth does not need to be stated because 12 inches is the industry standard for wall cabinet depth. If the cabinet company has a difat 34½ inches high. An example for a tall cabinet would be TU3090. This would be a tall utility cabinet that is 30 inches wide and 90 inches tall. The depth is a standard 24 inches. The height needs to be called out for this cabinet, just like for the wall cabinet, because there is a range of height options.

When a cabinet is 24 inches in width, the specifier typically has the choice for the cabinet to have one door or two doors. The decision is usually based on the design of the room. Cabinets that are larger than 24 inches in width will automatically have two doors and below 24 inches in width will have one door.

The vertical pieces of a door are referred to as the *door stiles*. The horizontal pieces of the door are called the *rails*. In the middle of the door is what is known as the *panel*. The panel can be flat, raised, or textured, such as **beadboard.** The panel also can be omitted to allow for glass or special inserts, such as fabric or metal. Some more contemporary door styles will just be one piece, not having stiles, rails, or a middle panel.

PRICING AND ORDERING CABINETRY

It has become more common for a cabinet manufacturer to have its own software for specifying cabinets. This makes it easier for the person specifying the cabinetry to price the cabinets and place the order. This software generally offers an option to print the order for faxing or even e-mailing it to the cabinet company. Once the order is submitted to the cabinet company, it is acknowledged and returned to the submitter. The acknowledgment then needs to be checked for any errors. If the order meets with approval, it can be confirmed. Many cabinet companies will assume acceptance of the acknowledgment after a certain number of days if they receive no response. It is important to be aware of these procedures when working with cabinet companies. Once the order has been acknowledged the cabinet company will typically provide a ship date or a window for the ship date.

CABINET MATERIALS

Typical cabinet materials for the exposed surfaces include wood, high-pressure laminate, **melamine,** metal laminate, and **Thermofoil** options. Not all cabinet companies will offer all these options. As mentioned previously, the cabinet box may be constructed of MDF furniture board or plywood. The exposed surfaces of the cabinet offer many more options, allowing for a variety of styles.

WOOD

A wide range of woods can be used for cabinetry. Hardwood is generally the type used for cabinets (Figure 5.7). Some of the woods more commonly used are oak, maple, cherry, alder, birch, pine, walnut, mahogany, hickory, and veneers.

Oak
Oak is a very heavy, strong, and hard wood. The two main types of oak are white and red.

The major difference between the two is that red oak is much more porous. The grain is open and therefore very noticeable in this wood. It also has a large variation in color, and this may be seen from cabinet to cabinet. Oak also can be found as quarter sawn from many cabinet manufacturers. *Quarter sawn* is called this simply because of the way the lumber is cut from the log. Standard oak would be plain sawn. Quarter-sawn oak is known for its very visible straight lines of graining.

Maple
Maple wood is a very hard and stiff wood. It is harder than oak and has less grain movement than oak. Maple is capable of taking a high polish and will stain acceptably. Maple is generally straight grained, but can sometimes have a curly or bird's eye grain.

Figure 5.7 Square pieces of different types of wood, including yew, cherry, larch, walnut tree, ash, mahogany, beech, and oak. *Photo by Peter Chadwick.*

Cherry

Cherry is a moderately heavy and hard wood. It is stiff and strong. This wood has a distinctive reddish color to it. Cherry wood's close grain gives it a very smooth appearance and finishes very well. Its color will darken over time and the client should be informed of this.

Alder

Alder has a close, rather straight, grain and readily accepts a stain. It is a fairly soft wood and therefore has lower strength and shock resistance than other woods. Its color ranges from light pinkish brown to almost white. It is often used as an alternative to cherry wood and sometimes even to walnut or mahogany.

Birch

Birch is a heavy and hard wood with a light reddish brown color.

Pine

Pine is a rather light-weight wood. It is known as a soft wood. This wood will not resist shock as well as harder woods. The coloring of pine varies from blond to pink and light brown.

Walnut

Walnut is a heavy and hard wood, which takes and holds paints and stains exceptionally well. Walnut wood also can be polished. Its color ranges, but is typically seen as brown or a dark brown. This wood has a pronounced grain that is usually straight and is one of the more expensive woods in cabinetry.

Mahogany

Mahogany has moderate density and hardness. This wood varies in color from a pale to deep reddish brown. The graining may be straight or wavy. Color variations can be noticeable within a cabinet. Like walnut, mahogany is one of the more expensive woods in cabinetry.

Hickory

Hickory is a heavy and hard wood, which is very strong and stiff. Hickory has a brown to reddish-brown color. When using hickory for cabinetry the designer should keep in mind the variation in color. One cabinet in hickory can show extreme color differences. This also should be considered when showing the client a small wood sample. The client should be informed of the wild variation that will occur.

Lyptus

Lyptus is an environmentally friendly wood that can be used for cabinetry. It is grown on plantations in Brazil. It is a fast-growing wood and is considered a good alternative to mahogany.

Bamboo

Bamboo is actually a grass, not a wood. As a flooring or cabinet material, however, wood is the closest category it would fall into (see Table 5.3). Bamboo can be considered sustainable because it grows so quickly; it takes just 5 years to regenerate. The argument can be made that it is not particularly sustainable because of the long journey it must travel from Asia to North America. Bamboo is light in color but also is available in a darker brown shade.

Distressing

Distressing, as a trend in cabinetry, seems to be losing its popularity. A distressed cabinet has been treated by the manufacturer to give it the look of an aged piece. There are many different types of distressing. The cabinets can literally be hit with items such as chains or pins. They also can be made to look distressed with the stain or paint finish. A distressed paint finish typically will have areas where the paint is chipped or worn away. Distressing is generally found only on solid wood doors. It is not used as much on veneer door styles.

VENEERS

Wood veneers offer a wide variety of options for cabinetry finishes. What the wood is, how it was sliced from the log, and the grade of the veneer all affect the options available.

Cuts

There are various styles of cut veneer (Figure 5.8). Here are the most common types found in cabinetry:

- **Plain cut:** Plain cut produces cathedrals and straight grain.
- **Quarter cut:** Quarter cut produces a straighter grain with flakes. This cut appears striped.
- **Rift cut:** Rift cut produces a straight grain without flakes. Oak is the only wood that is rift cut.
- **Rotary cut:** Rotary cut produces the greatest amount of cathedrals and figuring. The grain is very wide and bold.

Veneer Matching

How the veneer is applied to the substrate results in a pattern effect. These arrangements can cause the same wood to have many different looks (Figure 5.9):

- **Book Match:** This veneer matching is one of the two most often seen in cabinetry. The pieces are laid to create a mirror image.

TABLE 5.3 WOOD SPECIES COMPARISON				
Type of Wood	Rigidity/Firmness	Color	Grain	Other
Oak	Very hard wood species	Large variation in color that can be seen from cabinet to cabinet	Open grain	Available as quarter sawn
Maple	Very hard wood species	It can have yellowish hues over time	Less grain movement than oak	Generally straight-grained
Cherry	Moderately hard wood species	Reddish color	Smooth graining, will darken over time	
Alder	Rather soft wood species	Ranges from light pinkish brown to almost white	Rather close and straight grain	
Birch	Hard wood species	Light reddish brown	Fine and uniform graining	
Pine	A soft wood	Varies from blond to pink and light brown	Can have large knots	
Walnut	Hard wood species	Color ranges but frequently seen as brown or dark brown	Has pronounced grain	Stains exceptionally well; one of the more expensive woods
Mahogany	Moderately hard wood species	Varies from pale to deep reddish brown; variations can be noticeable within cabinet	Graining may be straight or wavy	One of the more expensive woods
Hickory	Very hard wood species	Brown to reddish-brown, has extreme color variation	Closed grain without much figuring	
Lyptus	Moderately hard wood species	Compares in shades with mahogany and cherry	Closed grain	Considered sustainable because it grows quickly
Bamboo	Is comparable to hard wood in hardness (bamboo is actually a grass, but its flooring traits are similar to wood)	Light color, but also available in darker brown	Appears to have a very linear grain due to the way bamboo is assembled into panels	Considered sustainable because it grows quickly; some disagree because of the distance it needs to travel before installation

- **Slip Match:** Slip matching is the other of the two most often used matchings in cabinetry. The veneer is applied sequentially.
- **Diamond Match:** In diamond matching the veneer is laid at an angle in a mirror image that forms a diamond pattern.
- **Reverse Diamond Match:** In reverse diamond matching the veneer is laid at an angle in a mirror image moving away from the center.

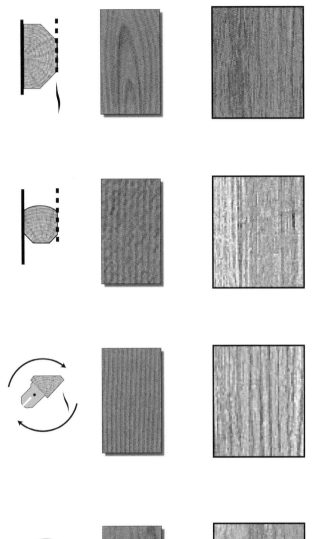

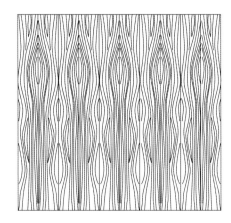

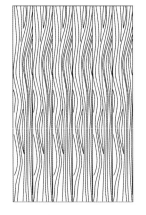

Figure 5.8 The manner by which the wood is cut will affect the grain pattern.

Figure 5.9 The same wood veneer can be laid out in many different ways.

LAMINATE CABINETRY

Laminate cabinetry is made from three layers: a paper layer, a decorative layer, and a protective layer. These three are pressed together under high heat and pressure. High-pressure laminate cabinetry is very durable and easy to clean. Melamine is a laminate that was applied with low pressure. They are less impact resistant than high-pressure laminate, but this can be improved with a better substrate. Wood cabinetry has been the favored trend in recent years. However, cabinet manufacturers offering sleek laminate cabinets are a great option for contemporary spaces.

Metal Cabinetry

Metal cabinetry often falls into the laminate category. When metal laminate is used, the construction is essentially the same; a metal laminate is applied to the same substrates. A wide range of metal laminate is available. It should be kept in mind that the surface will scratch and its color will likely change.

Thermofoil Cabinetry

Thermofoil is a vinyl applied to substrate with heat and pressure. Thermofoil cabinetry gives the appearance of a painted cabinet, mimics the detail of a wood door well, and is easy to clean. Thermofoil cabinets are typically available in white or an off-white. The disadvantage of Thermofoil is that it requires a little more attention. Scratches and dents can allow water to get in and damage the substrate. This can cause swelling and bubbling to occur.

CABINET DETAILS

In addition to the individual cabinets, many details must be considered. Moldings, for example, are available in a wide range of profiles and can enhance the kitchen or bath design. Accessory options are numerous. There

are also finer cabinetry details that may be specified to achieve a well-designed space. Let's look at the various ways to add these fine details.

EXTENDED STILES AND FILLERS

Even if the best installer in the world is working on a project, the walls will never be perfectly plumb and even. One way to overcome this in custom cabinetry is to specify cabinets with an extended stile when they are located in a corner. In stock or frameless cabinetry, fillers will typically need to be specified. A cabinet has an extended stile when the face frame of the cabinet is made to extend past the cabinet box. This stile can be ordered in various widths (Figure 5.10). A standard

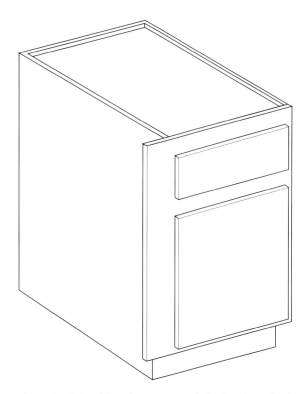

Figure 5.10 A cabinet has an extended stile when the face frame of the cabinet extends past the cabinet box. This allows for cutting on site for a perfect fit. *Courtesy of Plato Woodwork, Inc.*

size width would be 3 inches so that the installer can cut it down on site to fit exactly in the space. It is best to avoid anything longer than 3 inches for the stile or filler width. Once it is more than 3 inches, it will be very noticeable and at that point the next larger standard cabinet width probably should have been ordered. For example, a 21-inch cabinet width with a 4-inch stile probably should have become a 24-inch wide cabinet with a 1-inch stile. A filler serves the same purpose as the extended stile. Most often stock cabinetry will have fillers instead of an extended stile option because these cabinets are not made to order. A filler is a separate piece that is cut down to fill the gap between the cabinet and the wall.

WIDE STILES

Semicustom and custom cabinets often will also have a wide stile available to specify. If a 24-inch cabinet had a 3-inch-wide stile, it would have a door and drawer that would normally fit on a 21-inch cabinet. Unlike an extended stile, a wide stile does not extend past the cabinet dimension. Instead, it makes the face frame on the front of the cabinet wider. A wide stile is typically used either to give space to a corner so the door has no problem opening, or so a decorative piece can be applied. For example, a cabinet with a 3-inch-wide stile could have fluting applied to it (Figure 5.11).

MOLDINGS

There are a variety of cabinet moldings available. Usually cabinet companies will offer some standard moldings

that can be ordered with their cabinets. In addition, there are many companies that specialize only in moldings and applied details for cabinets. When ordered from a source other than the cabinet company, pieces are received unfinished. These pieces can either be sent to the cabinet company to be finished or can be finished on site to match. Which route is taken depends on the cabinet company. It is best if the cabinet company can finish the pieces to match, but sometimes the company may not offer this option (Figure 5.12).

It is also important to consider what wood is being used for the project's door style before ordering these moldings. If designing a kitchen with cherry wood cabinets it is best to order moldings that are also cherry wood. Different woods will take stain differently; it is safest to order moldings and cabinets in the same wood so that when stain is applied they will match.

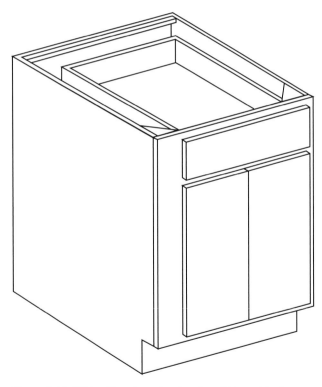

Figure 5.11 Wide stiles do not extend past the cabinet, as do extended stiles. They are often used to allow decorative moldings, such as fluting, to be applied. *Courtesy of Plato Woodwork, Inc.*

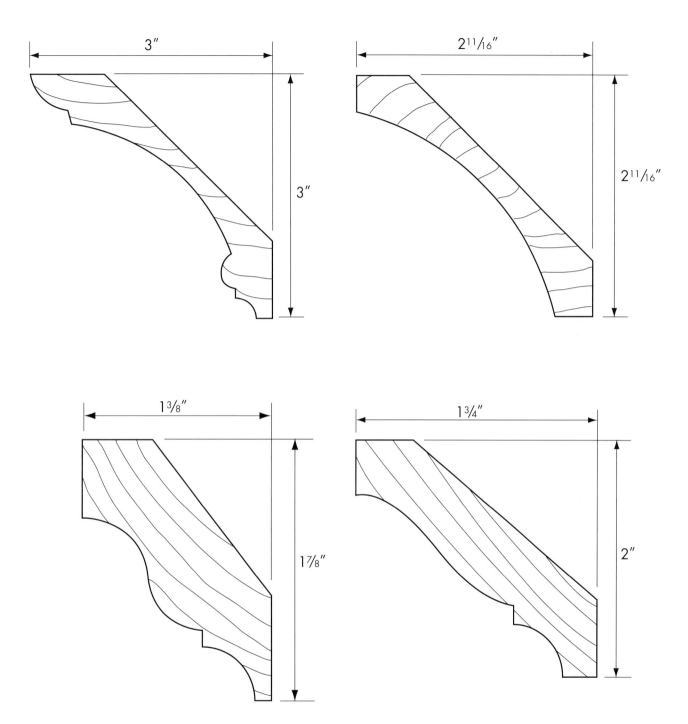

Figure 5.12 Although numerous moldings are available, cabinet manufacturers will have their own standard moldings available. *Courtesy of Plato Woodwork, Inc.*

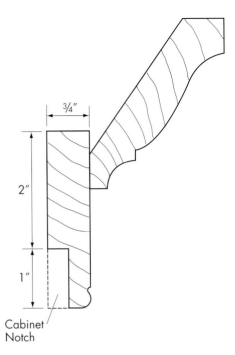

Figure 5.13 Fascia, or frame stock, can be used to build up the height of the crown molding. *Courtesy of Plato Woodwork, Inc.*

Crown Molding

Crown molding is used at the top of wall or tall cabinets. To make the crown look larger or reach higher, it can be installed with a board that is called **fascia** or **frame stock** (Figure 5.13). This piece is attached to the cabinet, and then the crown is attached to the board.

Undercabinet Molding

On the bottom of wall cabinets a molding, sometimes referred to as a *light rail,* can be applied. The benefit of a light rail, other than adding another dimension to the cabinetry, is that it hides lights, and the glare from these lights, that may be installed along the bottom of the wall cabinet. Undercabinet molding is often called a light rail because it is hiding the undercabinet lights. These pieces can be more detailed for a traditional or transitional kitchen or more simplified for a more contemporary space. An alternative, if using a custom cabinet manufacturer, is to order the bottoms of the wall

cabinets flush and finished. This method will not hide the undercabinet lights, but does make the cabinet look finished (Figure 5.14).

FURNITURE BASE

Furniture base, also known as furniture board, is occasionally used to make cabinet pieces look like furniture. It is often used on islands or free-standing tall cabinets. The furniture base can be simple or it can have a cut out, giving it a shaped look (Figure 5.15).

VALANCES

A piece that is very similar to shaped furniture board is a valance. This piece will typically look the same but be used on or between wall or tall cabinets and occasionally on base cabinets. Like furniture base, valances can have a variety of shaped options.

ONLAYS

To make cabinets more decorative and elaborate, onlays can be applied. These can be applied to areas such as flat drawers or wood hoods, just to name a few. Again, a wide range of styles is available. Cabinet companies

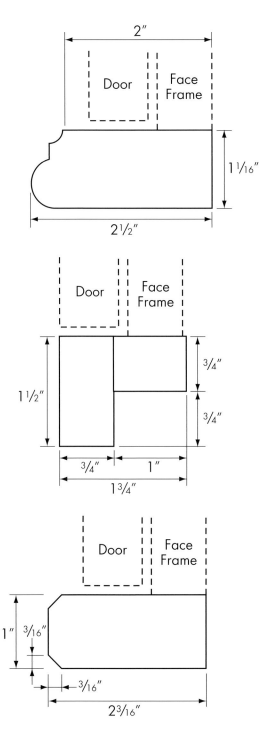

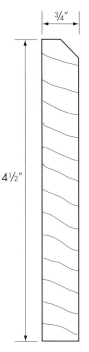

Figure 5.15 Furniture base makes a cabinet look like a piece of furniture. *Courtesy of Plato Woodwork, Inc.*

Figure 5.14 Undercabinet molding is nice to include to help hide any undercabinet lighting. *Courtesy of Plato Woodwork, Inc.*

will generally have limited options for onlays. A larger selection may be offered by a manufacturer that specializes in wood details.

PANELS

Cabinet panels can be found in all types of cabinetry. In stock cabinets the panels will typically be flat and available in standard sizes that can be cut down on site. Semicustom or custom cabinet companies will offer the option to order the panels to almost any size needed. They will also offer the option to order panels that have false doors applied. Sometimes there may be restrictions for panels that are larger. Panels are used for backs and ends of cabinet runs or as support for countertops. They can be used on appliances to disguise the fact that it is an appliance.

End Panels

Panels that are used on ends can be plain or can be made to look like beadboard, doors, or wainscot paneling. A plain panel would be the least expensive of these options. Because the wood used to make the panels comes only in certain lengths and widths, there are usually restrictions on the size that can be ordered. Often, panels over 48 inches wide will require a spline to combine two panels as one. Lengths over 96 inches may also require that two panels be ordered for shipping purposes, if the cabinet company does not have its own trucks or trucking service. Again, the exact restrictions depend on the cabinet company. Always be sure to read the details or ask questions of the specific cabinet company being used.

When planning an undercabinet appliance such as a refrigerator, wine cooler, or dishwasher, the countertop support must be considered. If one of these appliances is at the end of a run it will need a panel on the end to support the countertop. These appliances are not made to hold weight. If one of these appliances is not at the end of a run and has cabinets on either side of it, a panel is not necessary. In this case the cabinets on either side would be supporting the countertop.

Appliance Panels

Custom panels can be made to hide where certain appliances are located. Panels can be ordered for dishwashers, refrigerators, and warming drawers that are made to accept them. Some dishwashers that accept panels will still have the control panel visible. Fully integrated dishwashers will have the controls on the inside edge of the door, so that they will have a fully paneled front and will truly blend in with the cabinetry.

Not only can refrigerators have paneled fronts, but panels can be used on the sides. Most refrigerators have unfinished sides. Although the front may be stainless steel, present a particular color, or accept panels, the sides will most likely be unfinished in appearance. These sides are best hidden as much as possible. Cabinet companies may offer a specific refrigerator cabinet that has sides and a cabinet above, leaving an opening for the refrigerator to slide in. Another option is to use panels on the side of the refrigerator with a deep wall cabinet at the top between them. Let's say we have a refrigerator that is 36 inches wide and 71 inches high. We could put ¾-inch panels on both sides of the refrigerator in standard heights, such as 90 or 96 inches. Then a 24-inch-deep wall cabinet can be installed between the panels above the refrigerator. If we had an overall panel height of 96 inches and needed 71 inches in height for the refrigerator, we could put a standard 24-inch-high or a custom 25-inch-high wall cabinet above it.

Certain warming drawers may also accept panels. When a panel is used the handle or handles to open the drawer can match the hardware on the rest of the cabinets. This really helps hide the fact that it is an appliance.

CUSTOM PIECES

Cabinet companies also typically offer custom pieces, such as hoods or furniture pieces. The options for these would be most limited in a stock cabinet company. Semicustom and custom cabinet lines will offer more variety and ways to make these pieces unique.

FURNITURE PIECES

Furniture pieces are items such as hutches, buffets, and mudroom lockers. Because these pieces have become popular, cabinet companies may offer some standard options to choose from to make specifying and ordering easier. Other companies may have a system to make specifying these pieces easier. For example, they might have a hutch or mudroom program offering options to select each part to build the custom hutch or locker wanted (Figure 5.16).

The mudroom locker has become a popular feature. Many homeowners are fond of having an area where coats, shoes, umbrellas, and other items can be taken off and stored without tracking dirt throughout

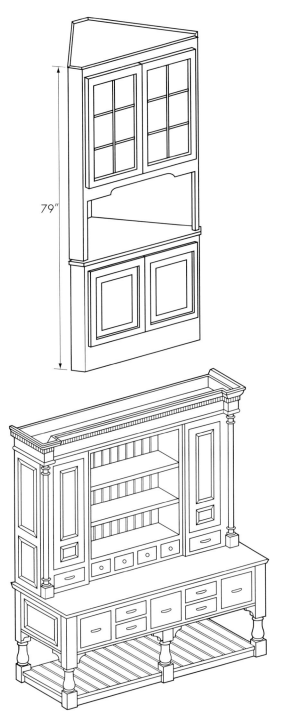

79"

Figure 5.16 Many cabinet companies offer coordinating furniture pieces. *Courtesy of Plato Woodwork, Inc.*

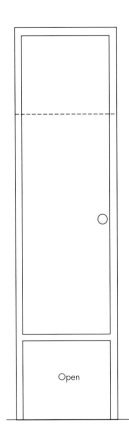

Open

Figure 5.17 Mudroom lockers have become very popular, so many cabinet companies offer them as an option. *Courtesy of Plato Woodwork, Inc.*

the house (Figure 5.17). It is very common for the kitchen and bath designer to design these areas also, since they are familiar with cabinetry in general.

HOODS

Since wood hoods have become popular it is more common for cabinet companies to offer some options. Wood hoods can be chimney, box, or hearth style. Stock or semicustom cabinet companies will again have more limited options to choose from. Custom cabinet companies may offer some standards to build your own hood design, but should again be able to make almost anything the designer can draw. The hearth style of

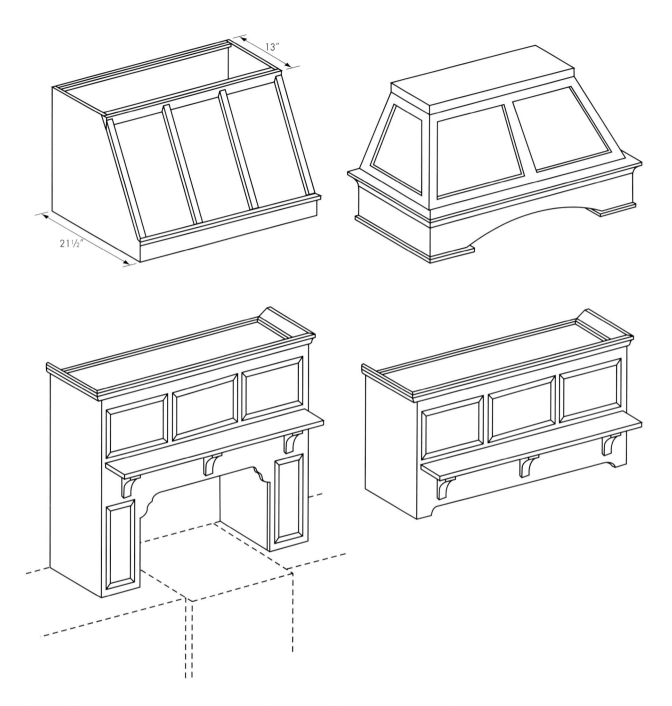

Figure 5.18 Cabinet companies also commonly offer several different standard wood hood options. *Courtesy of Plato Woodwork, Inc.*

hood often includes options for spice storage near the cooking surface. Although this is a nice idea in theory, it should be kept in mind that storing spices close to heat actually causes the spices not to last as long (Figure 5.18).

ACCESSORIES

In addition to everything discussed thus far, cabinets come with a wide range of accessory options (Figure 5.19). If the cabinet company is limited in what it offers, there are companies that specialize in these accessories and can provide the designer with what is not available from the cabinet company. Once an accessory is ordered it can either be sent to the cabinet company to be installed or installed on site. There are several companies that offer many high-quality accessories for cabinets (Figure 5.20).

BATH CABINET CONSIDERATIONS

Although almost any of the cabinets discussed previously can be used in the bathroom, cabinet companies usually have bathroom-specific cabinets. Base cabinets that are 34½ inches high, as in the kitchen, are being used more frequently in bathrooms as they require less bending to use; in the past, 32-inch-high base cabinets were often installed. In addition, bathroom cabinets are usually not as deep as kitchen cabinets: whereas kitchen base cabinets are typically 24 inches deep, bathroom base cabinets are usually 21 inches deep.

In addition to the slight difference in measurements, bathroom cabinets typically offer more variety in sink vanity cabinets. Instead of having to specify three separate cabinets to provide a sink and two banks of drawers, the cabinet manufacturer may make a single bathroom cabinet like this as standard. Availability depends on the cabinetmaker.

ACCESSORIES

Spice rack	Door can racks
Roll out shelves	Tilt out sink front
Spice drawer	Pull out can racks
Cutlery dividers	Pull-out towel bar
Appliance garage	Base lazy susan
Utensil dividers	Swing-up mixer
Plate rack	Hamper
Knife block	Jewelry tray
Swing-out pantry system	Wine rack
	Door lock
Plate storage in drawer	Pull-out chopping block
Pull-out pantry	Pull-out ironing board
Bread box	Pull-out bottle storage
Tray dividers	Pull-out wire baskets
Waste basket/ Recycle bin	Stemware rack
	Paper towel holder

Figure 5.19 Here is a list of some of the accessories available for cabinetry. *Courtesy of Plato Woodwork, Inc.*

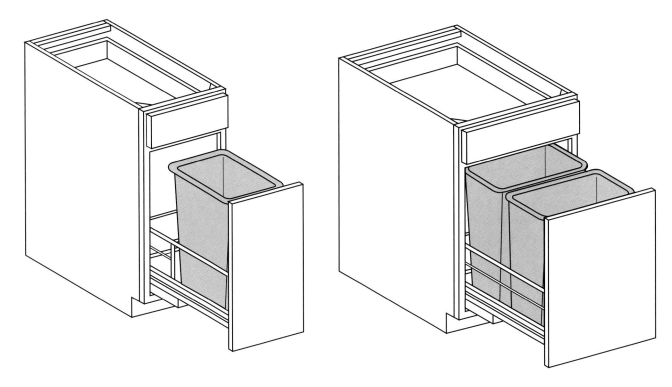

Figure 5.20 Pull-out waste bin cabinets are very popular, as this is a great way to hide the garbage and recycling. *Courtesy of Plato Woodwork, Inc.*

Other cabinet offerings for bathrooms include hamper accessories and appliance garages to allow for hair dryer or razor storage near the sink. Waste bin cabinets are beneficial to incorporate into the bathroom as well. Tall cabinets are useful for towels or toiletry storage.

OTHER AREAS

As mentioned when discussing mudroom lockers, kitchen and bath designers can design any area of the home with cabinetry. The majority of kitchen and bath designers represent one or multiple cabinet lines. The designer becomes familiar with the cabinet company and so can specify cabinets for basically any area. It is common for the kitchen and bath designer to also design home offices, wood fireplace mantels, or built-in bookcases. This allows homeowners to have coordinating cabinetry throughout their homes.

SUMMARY

Because of the many types of cabinetry and features available, it is very important that the designer be educated on these products. The client relies on the designer for guidance in selecting the type of cabinet to use and what accessories should be included. Although the designer may only work with one or a few cabinet lines, it is still beneficial to be aware of how those lines compare with the other options available to the consumer.

CHAPTER 5 EXERCISES

I: Ms. Hahn wants a traditional kitchen, but has a lower budget to work with. What type of cabinetry would you recommend and why? Would the cabinets be framed or frame-less and why? If they are to be framed, what type and why?

II: List 10 different cabinet accessories available and the benefits of each.

CHAPTER 5 DISCUSSION QUESTIONS

1. European cabinetry is typically what type of cabinetry?
2. Why do some designers dislike working with European cabinetry?
3. What type of wood is considered sustainable because it grows fast and is also a good alternative to mahogany?
4. Cabinets come in standard increments of what?
5. What are some other areas the kitchen and bath designer can design with cabinetry?
6. Name three different ways panels can be used.

REFERENCES

Feirer, John L. *Cabinetmaking and Millwork*. Peoria, IL: Glencoe/McGraw-Hill, 1988.

Godsey, Lisa. *Interior Design Materials and Specifications*. New York, NY: Fairchild Publications, Inc., 2008.

ADDITIONAL RESOURCES

Plato Woodwork, Inc. http://www.platowoodwork.com (home page; accessed June 15, 2012).

Rae, Andy. *The Complete Illustrated Guide to Furniture and Cabinet Construction*. Newtown, CT: Taunton Press, 2001.

___Which type of cabinetry would be most appropriate for the client: stock, semicustom, or custom?

___Should the cabinetry be framed or frameless? If framed, should the door be inset, full overlay, or partial overlay?

___What type of wood is most appropriate for the cabinets?

___What accessories should be included, based on the client's needs and wants?

___Should a matching wood hood be used?

___What types of moldings should be used to finish the space?

___Are any of the cabinets meant to look like furniture? Do you need to include furniture base?

___Have you accounted for extended stiles or fillers everywhere a cabinet meets the wall?

___Are there any other areas in the home in which the client would like to have coordinating cabinetry?

___Are you going to include any custom pieces that will require a price quote?

___What are some of the key specialty pieces your cabinet manufacturer offers?

KEY TERMS

Beadboard: A type of paneling that has interlocking tongue-and-groove wood elements; the recessed strips create a bead effect.

Custom cabinetry: Cabinetry that can be fully customized.

Fascia/frame stock: A board applied to the top of wall cabinets and to which crown molding is then applied. It aids in assisting crown molding to reach the ceiling.

Framed cabinetry: Cabinetry that has a frame on the face of the cabinet to which the door is attached.

Frameless cabinetry: Cabinetry that has no face frame.

Full-extension glides/drawers: Full-extension glides allow the drawers of a cabinet to slide open far enough that the entire drawer can be accessed; full-extension drawers are equipped with such glides.

Lazy Susan: Accessory, available for corner base cabinets, that rotates so all the storage space can be accessed.

Melamine: A laminate applied with low pressure to cover a substrate.

Nomenclature: The abbreviations used in the cabinet industry to refer to specific types of cabinets.

Semicustom cabinetry: Cabinetry that has limited options that can be customized.

Soft-close: A feature available for cabinets that causes doors and drawers to close softly, even if slammed shut.

Stock cabinetry: Cabinetry that is available in standard sizes and shapes, and is kept in stock.

Thermofoil: A vinyl applied to substrate, using heat and pressure.

CHAPTER 6 KITCHEN AND BATH DESIGN: APPLIANCES

OBJECTIVES

After reading this chapter, you will:

- Distinguish the various types of appliances available to help the clients decide which would be best to use for their project.

- Understand the features and options available within the various types of appliances to assist the clients in deciding which features would be best for their situation.

- Know what information you need from the appliance specifications and what information the contractor needs.

DESIGN SCENARIO

You have a newer client, the Benners, whom you need to assist with selecting appliances for their kitchen. The Benners are a couple living in a house located in a large city with a kitchen that has limited space. They love to cook and entertain. Sustainable design is very important to them and they would like the most energy-efficient appliances. You meet with them to discuss your recommendations for their needs and space.

1. What are the most energy-efficient appliances?

2. What appliances would you recommend, since they have limited space?

3. Is there anything else specifically you can recommend for sustainability?

TYPES OF APPLIANCES

Appliances are a very important part of the kitchen. They are the primary components to working in the kitchen. Although the refrigerator, cooking surface, and oven are the primary appliances needed, there are many more that may be included; various types of specialty refrigeration, dishwashers, microwaves, and built-in coffee systems, just to name a few. Even the primary appliances have many options to choose from.

Bathrooms are starting to see the use of appliances more frequently. As technology advances and bathroom spaces become larger, more appliances are being incorporated into this space as well. By the end of this chapter, you will have a thorough understanding of the diverse appliances that are available.

DESIGNER'S DIALOGUE 6.1

"Clients need to get appliance recommendations from the designer based on what their needs are. Appliance stores can help, but ultimately they are salespeople. Many times the client will go ahead of time to select things and they won't be usable. People don't know about things such as induction cooktops or convection ovens. A client once asked me for a gas oven and they aren't even available anymore except with a range. Nobody makes a stand-alone gas oven. The client can also end up buying appliances just because there's a rebate for a package, when they can get better products selected individually."
—Lisa McManus, ASID, Kitchen and Bath Designer

REFRIGERATORS

The refrigerator is a vital component of the kitchen. When selecting a refrigerator it is important to consider the quantity and quality of the storage. Although a deeper refrigerator will have more storage, it will be harder to see what is being stored. Most will have special compartments for vegetables, fruits, butter, and meat with specific temperatures and humidity levels. The ideal temperature ranges from 36 to 40 degrees Fahrenheit.

As with the other appliances that are discussed in this chapter, there are several styles to choose from. The styles that are the most functional and aesthetically pleasing always end up being the most costly of the choices. Of the styles mentioned below, most are available with ice and water either outside or inside the refrigerator.

Freestanding versus Built-in and Counter Depth

Refrigerators are available in one of three main of styles: freestanding, counter depth, or built-in. Freestanding refrigerators are typically deeper than the standard 24-inch-deep cabinets. They may be 28 inches, or even more than 30 inches deep. Although this is the least expensive type of refrigerator up front, the cost of wasted food due to the large depth can add up. These refrigerators also need more thought when installing to look built-in. A refrigerator with a standard condenser may build up heat when closed in.

Counter-depth refrigerators are made to be the same depth as a standard 24-inch deep cabinet. These too are technically freestanding. Although these refrigerators will have less storage due to the smaller depth, they always cost more because of the design appeal. In addition to the aesthetic benefit, this type is also more functional (Figure 6.1). Foods are not lost in the back and forgotten, likely resulting in less food being wasted.

Built-in refrigerators are counter depth, but also require custom panels. These refrigerators resemble cabinetry with custom panels applied (Figure 6.2). A built-in refrigerator is one of the more expensive refrigerator options available. They are available in 27-, 36-, 42-, and 48-inch widths. Most will be 84 inches high. The compressor is usually separate and above the storage. Built-in refrigerators also typically are better at maintaining consistent temperature and humidity, which keeps food fresh longer. One company has separate compressors for the freezer and refrigerator. Built-in refrigerators also require a little more maintenance; the vent should be vacuumed once a month. Built-in refrigerators require a tune-up once a year.

Figure 6.1 This image shows the difference between free-standing and counter-depth refrigerators. *Courtesy of Novak and Parker by Brad Wilkening.*

Figure 6.2 A built-in refrigerator typically requires custom panels. This refrigerator is a side-by-side style. *Courtesy of Novak and Parker by Brad Wilkening.*

Top Freezer

Top-freezer refrigerators typically are the least expensive option. This style has been around the longest, but now other styles are available, which have become more popular. This style simply has a freezer door at the top and a refrigerator door at the bottom.

Side-by-Side

Side-by-side refrigerators were very popular for a time, but have been losing popularity. This style of refrigeration has one tall refrigerator door and one tall freezer door. The problem with this style is that the two doors end up being rather narrow. This limits the size of items that may be stored in this refrigerator.

Bottom Freezer

Refrigerators that have bottom freezers have become popular in recent years. They offer a width that is useful for storing large items, such as party trays. They also put the area of storage that is used the most at a preferable height. The freezer, which typically is not used as frequently, is placed lower, as a drawer. These refrigerators are available with a single door or double doors at the top (Figure 6.3). Double-door versions are frequently referred to as "French-door refrigerators." When the unit has a single door it can be hinged right or left.

Column

A newer style of refrigeration is column storage (Figure 6.4). These were introduced and expanded the options for refrigerator and freezer layout. Since a whole column is refrigerator or freezer, a side-by-side setup can be used (Figure 6.5). These columns also allow for the option of mixing the types of appliances. For example, a kitchen can have a refrigerator column and freezer drawers located somewhere else.

Figure 6.3 A bottom freezer refrigerator is available in a few different versions. They are also available with one door and one freezer drawer. *Courtesy of Novak and Parker by Brad Wilkening.*

DESIGNER'S DIALOGUE 6.2

"Most people don't like side-by-side refrigerators these days. They seem to like columns and French door refrigerators."
—*Gladys Schanstra, CKD, CBD, Allied ASID*

Figure 6.4 This paneled refrigerator column is hidden with a custom panel that looks like a door. *Courtesy of Abt Electronics by Brad Wilkening.*

Figure 6.5 The interior of the concealed refrigerator column. *Courtesy of Abt Electronics by Brad Wilkening.*

Undercounter Refrigeration/Freezer

Undercounter refrigeration has become a luxury afford-able to more people and is a great way to gain some additional storage. There are two different types of undercounter refrigeration: those with a door and those with drawers.

Door. Undercounter refrigerators with doors also may be called *beverage centers*. Beverage centers are great for storing beverages and snacks. These units are excellent for flexibility in additional storage location. They are typically 24 inches wide. Some beverage centers will offer a small amount of wine storage. They may have both refrigeration and freezer control and some may have an ice maker.

Drawers. Another option for refrigerators and freezers is drawers, which allow more storage and flexibility opportunities for a kitchen. If a standard refrigerator is not enough storage, one or two refrigerator or freezer

Figure 6.6 Undercounter refrigeration is a great opportunity for point of use storage. *Courtesy of Abt Electronics by Brad Wilkening.*

DESIGNER'S DIALOGUE 6.3

"Don't forget to account for the handle that sticks out from the refrigerator if the fridge is at the end of the run against a wall. If the door doesn't open fully the roll-outs won't be able to roll out."
—*Lisa Godsey, ASID, LEED AP, IDEC, IESNA, Interior Designer, Adjunct Instructor*

drawers can be added. Like with the other refrigerator styles, these are available in stainless steel or to accept custom panels (Figure 6.6).

Wine Storage. Undercounter wine refrigerators have also become very popular. These units are typically 24 inches wide, although there are also models at 15 inches wide. Many are available with different temperature zones to allow for storing different types of wine; white wines can be stored in one zone and red wines in another. Although undercounter versions of these refrigerators are most popular, there also are tall column wine refrigerators available as well.

OVENS

There are several different types of ovens to choose from for a kitchen (Figure 6.7). It is important to keep the client's budget in mind when helping to select appliances, because there is always a wide range of pricing available for various items. Most ovens will open down, but there are a few that open to the side. The disadvantage of the oven that opens to the side is there not being a close place to set down what is being cooked if something needs to be added while it is cooking. Another thing to consider with ovens is the racks. Higher-end ovens will have racks that slide out completely while remaining stable.

Self-cleaning capabilities also are an important consideration for ovens. There are two basic systems for self-cleaning: pyrolytic and catalytic. In pyrolytic cleaning, the oven has a specific cleaning cycle during which the oven heats up to between 850 and 950 degrees. The door locks in this state. The heat remains high for 2 to 4 hours, after which the oven cools, which takes another 2 hours. The entire cleaning therefore lasts about 6 hours. The grease and dirt in the oven turn to ash, which can then be easily wiped up. For catalytic cleaning, the oven has a porcelain interior that allows grease and oils to burn off during regular baking use. Oven racks and windows will need to be cleaned regularly. Chemicals should not be used in ovens with this system of cleaning.

Gas

Gas ovens are available but are now harder to find than electric or convection ovens. These are simply ovens that

Figure 6.7 Ovens that open to the side are available, but may not be the safest option. *Courtesy of Abt Electronics by Brad Wilkening.*

have gas as the primary heat source. Because gas needs oxygen for combustion, these ovens are not sealed as tightly as electric ovens.

Electric

Electric ovens have tighter construction than gas ovens. Electric ovens typically have two heating sources: one at the top for broiling and one at the bottom for baking. In standard electric ovens, heat rises, pushing cold air down. This can cause hot and cold spots within the oven. These spots lead to uneven cooking. Items placed on the bottom shelf will cook faster. If multiple shelves are used for baking, the items will have to be rearranged halfway through so the baking will be even.

Convection

Convection ovens are the best ovens to work with. There are two basic types of convection oven: fan-assisted and true convection. For the fan-assisted convection oven, a fan is added to the back of a standard oven (Figure 6.8). Most gas ovens that have a fan will be fan-assisted and not true convection. In fan-assisted ovens, items on two racks will cook evenly. If a third rack is used, the middle rack will not heat as evenly as the other two racks. A true convection oven has a third heating element wrapped around the fan. This causes the heat to flow evenly over all the racks. Three or even four racks can be used and the items being cooked will not need to be repositioned. Another feature of true convection ovens becomes apparent when separate foods are being cooked simultaneously: The aromas and flavors will not mingle. The element that is wrapped around the fan burns the oils, which cause aromas and flavors, and therefore separate dishes being cooked simultaneously keep their flavors intact. Convection ovens also

Figure 6.8 Fan-assisted convection ovens have a fan at the back, which results in even cooking. *Courtesy of Novak and Parker by Brad Wilkening.*

cook faster than conventional ovens. The cook times are 25 percent shorter. Alternatively, the same cook time may be used, but the temperature should be lowered by 25 degrees in the convection oven. On occasion, convection cooking will dry some foods, but liquids may be added to prevent this. Most home convection ovens can be switched between convection and standard.

Steam

Steam ovens are another option. When cooking with a steam oven, foods remain moist and do not require as many oils or sauces. These ovens are usually not plumbed, but have a reservoir to fill. The water is heated and then moves into the cavity. This method of cooking is faster than stovetop steam cooking. This is a benefit because it will leave the food and its nutrients more intact than with stovetop steaming. Steam ovens also are convenient for reheating, they will cook as quickly as a microwave but more evenly and with better results. In addition, as more items are added to cook in a microwave, the time for cooking needs to be increased. This is not the case for a steam oven.

Combination Steam and Convection

The combination steam and convection oven is yet another option in ovens. These ovens, unlike the standard steam oven, need to be plumbed. As the name indicates, they are a combination of the above-described steam and convection ovens.

COOKING SURFACES

Cooking surfaces are simply appliances with burners for cooking. There are several different types of cooking surface available. Although it may be argued that one is better than the other, it is really about cooking preference. Many people favor cooking with gas, but electric or induction cooking is just as good. The important things to consider when selecting a cooking surface are the number of burners required, the range and power of the heat, and the ease of maintenance.

Range

A range is a single unit with both a cooking surface at the top and an oven below. Ranges typically will have the same type of heat source for both the top and the oven. The exception to this is a dual-fuel range.

Gas Ranges and Cooktops

Gas cooktops are generally the favored type of cooktop. Professional chefs use gas. The heat produced by gas burners is measured in British thermal units (BTUs). One BTU is the heat required to raise the temperature of 1 pound of water by 1 degree Fahrenheit. The burners of residential cooking surfaces range between 6,000 and 9,000 BTUs, and there is usually one burner that produces 12,000 to 15,000 BTUs. Gas cooking surfaces are offered in standard sizes between 12 and 60 inches. Gas ranges are generally 30, 36, 48, or 60 inches. When helping clients select a gas cooktop, or range, it is good to know their personal style; for example, how large and varied their pans are, and whether they entertain large groups on a regular basis. Keep in mind, too, that sealed gas burners are easier to clean because only one surface needs to be cleaned, instead of both the top and the catch pan. Because this is a benefit, gas ranges and cooktops with sealed burners will be more expensive.

Electric Ranges and Cooktops

Electric cooktops are the second most favored type of cooktop in the United States. The power of these cooktops is measured in watts. To compare the power of electric and gas cooktops, 1,000 watts are roughly equal to 3,500 BTUs per hour for a gas cooktop. The benefits to electric cooking surfaces are that they are cleaner and emit no gas fumes. When selecting an electric cooking surface it is often best to choose one with more elements; because heating and cooling times can be slower than with gas, having more elements helps for flexibility in cooking. When using an electric cooking surface, the best way to match the quick temperature changes of a gas cooking surface is to have one element going at high heat and another at low heat—moving a pot or skillet from one to the other will change the temperature more quickly, more like on a gas cooktop. Electric cooktops can be made with coils or with a ceramic glass top. Higher-end electric cooktops are composed of ceramic. The ceramic cooking surface can be damaged by intense heat and therefore the heat may be inconsistent. Electrical ranges are simply ranges with both an electric cooking surface and an electric oven.

Dual-Fuel Range

Dual-fuel ranges are ranges that have gas burners and an electric oven or ovens. This type of range is generally more expensive than a standard range. It is a popular option because most people like gas burners and electric ovens. The electric oven in a dual-fuel range is usually convection, which adds to the appeal of this option. Some dual-fuel ranges, and some gas ranges, offer an infrared broiler. The dual-fuel broiler has high consistent heat and will be the best for even cooking by this method.

Freestanding versus Slide-in versus Drop-in Ranges

In addition to the various choices in heat sources, ranges also are available in different styles. A freestanding range is installed just as its name implies, freestanding (Figure 6.9). These ranges typically have a splash on the back with controls or a timer and clock. Slide-in ranges will usually not have a splash in the back, and the controls will be placed on the front (Figure 6.10). When the controls are on the front, typically there will be a feature for child safety. This unit slides in and very slightly overhangs the top of the countertop, eliminating gaps between the range and countertop. This type of range is usually more expensive than the freestanding range. The benefit of the slide-in is that the lack of a splash allows for less interference in a tile design that may be behind the range. Eliminating the gap between the counter and range also makes for easier cleaning in the kitchen. Drop-in ranges do not sit on the floor, but on a platform.

Figure 6.9 Freestanding ranges will typically have a splash with controls or a clock. *Courtesy of Novak and Parker by Brad Wilkening.*

Figure 6.10 A slide-in range slides into place and sits very slightly on the countertop, leaving no gap. *Courtesy of Novak and Parker by Brad Wilkening.*

Rangetop

A rangetop is available with gas burners only, because the idea of the rangetop is to look like a professional appliance. These units fit on top of a cabinet (Figure 6.11). The cabinet is made at a lower height than standard to accommodate this appliance. The controls are always on the front. They are generally 24 to 27 inches deep and allow bigger pots to be used when cooking. They also typically have higher BTUs because they are intended to work similarly to a professional appliance.

Cooktop

The cooking surface of a cooktop may be gas or electric. The cooktop drops into a cabinet through a hole in the countertop. The gas and electric burners are the same as described previously, but there is an additional choice, the induction cooktop.

> **DESIGNER'S DIALOGUE 6.4**
>
> "I like to use a 36-inch cooktop above a 30-inch oven because then there is space to install spice pull-outs."
> —*Gladys Schanstra, CKD, CBD, Allied ASID*

Induction

Induction cooking has not gained popularity in the United States; it is used more often in Europe. This type of cooking is the most environmentally friendly of all the options available. It uses the least amount of energy. It works using electric current generated from a magnetic field. It requires pots and pans made of ferrous metal (if a magnet sticks, it is usable). This cooking surface has no direct heat source (Figure 6.12); the metal molecules of the pan vibrate in response to the magnetically induced electric current, which generates heat. The surface stays cool, but the pot gets hot. Induction cooking is great for low-heat cooking but takes time to get very hot and more time to drop the temperature.

> **DESIGNER'S DIALOGUE 6.5**
>
> "I think an induction cooktop is a good choice, but people are still scared of it. Some people still like to see the flame."
> —*Gladys Schanstra, CKD, CBD, Allied ASID*

SPECIALTY COOKING

In addition to standard cooking surfaces, there also are a few options for specialty cooking. These options have become more affordable, but still are seen as a luxury. Some of these options may be incorporated within a range or rangetop in place of two burners.

Fryers

One specialty item that is available is a fryer (Figure 6.13). These have high BTUs, which are important for this type of cooking. When selecting a fryer, it is very important that it be easy to drain the fat and that the interior be made of stainless steel. Be sure to thoroughly read the product's specifications regarding a fryer's installation and use. The specifications will likely describe in detail where the fryer can and cannot be located.

Steamers

Steamers also are available for counter cooking and work differently than steam oven cooking (Figure 6.14). Steamers are typically used for vegetables and for poaching fish or chicken.

Wok Burners

Wok burners also are available. These typically generate about 30,000 BTUs and are expensive. They are available in 15-inch units. This type of burner is recommended only for households that cook with woks on a regular basis.

Figure 6.11 Rangetops sit on top of a lower cabinet. *Courtesy of Novak and Parker by Brad Wilkening.*

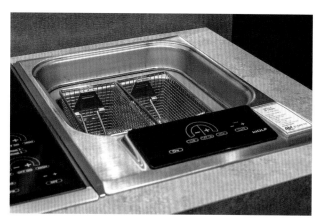

Figure 6.13 A counter-installed fryer is available for specialty cooking. *Courtesy of Novak and Parker by Brad Wilkening.*

Figure 6.12 Induction cooktops are a more sustainable option for a cooking surface. *Courtesy of Novak and Parker by Brad Wilkening.*

Figure 6.14 Steamers are another appliance available for specialty cooking. Steam cooking helps cooked foods retain their nutrients. (Steamer, left. Burners, right.) *Courtesy of Novak and Parker by Brad Wilkening.*

Grills

Grills are available as part of a range or rangetop. They are available as gas or electric and take up the space of two burners. There is a grill over the burner with simulated charcoal briquettes or stainless steel diffusers in between and a collection pan below. They also can be installed separately in a 15-inch unit. Grills should have extra ventilation. It is also best if they have a removable collection pan for easy cleaning. Again, it is best to thoroughly read the product's specifications regarding installation and use when planning to use a grill.

Griddles

Griddles are great for cooking foods that are normally cooked in a frying pan. They too require the space of two burners if included with a range or rangetop. The disadvantages of griddles are that the temperature cannot be changed quickly and they require a bit more maintenance. They need to be oiled to prevent rust.

VENTILATION

Ventilation is required in every kitchen; it is not optional. Without ventilation, grease will end up soaking into items all over the home. How efficiently the ventilation works is measured as cubic feet of air moved per minute (CFM). At minimum, the ventilation unit should be at least the same width as the cooking surface. It is more desirable that the ventilation be wider, as this will capture more of the grease and smoke. Several types of ventilation can be used in the kitchen.

Hoods/Updrafts

Hoods are the most common type of ventilation for a kitchen. A hood works by taking the air in with a blower; the air then passes through a filter and out via a duct to the exterior of the home. These hoods are typically placed 30 inches above the cooking surface, but the manufacturer's specifications should always be referenced to be certain. The specifications also will typically give a range of space where the ventilation can be installed. It is important to consider the height of the cook when locating the hood. A hood installed 30 inches above the cooking surface may be too low for some clients. Hoods of many shapes and sizes are available to match the style of any kitchen.

Chimney Hoods

Chimney hoods are hoods shaped like a chimney (Figure 6.15). They are often made of metal, but can also be wood. A metal chimney hood generally will include a blower as well. For a wood chimney hood, the **blower** may need to be purchased separately and installed on site. Some cabinet companies will offer the option to order wood hoods with the blower installed at their cabinet shop.

Professional Hoods

Professional hoods are made for residential use but resemble those used in a commercial kitchen (Figure 6.16). They are stainless steel and have a lower profile, usually allowing for cabinets above.

Figure 6.15 Chimney-style hoods are available in various styles and finishes. *Courtesy of Novak and Parker by Brad Wilkening.*

Figure 6.16 A professional hood mimics a commercial-style hood. *Courtesy of Novak and Parker by Brad Wilkening.*

Mantle Hoods

Mantle hoods are generally a larger style of hood (Figure 6.17). These are aesthetically impressive, intended to make a design statement. In addition to their aesthetic focus, mantle hoods with their concealed blowers are superbly functional.

Figure 6.17 Mantle hoods commonly create a focal point. *Courtesy of Novak and Parker by Brad Wilkening.*

Blowers

When using a wood or custom hood, the blower will generally need to be purchased separately. The two main choices for hood blower, in-hood or remote, will be either in-line or external. In-hood blowers are simply located inside the hood. For in-line blowers, the hood is the part located directly above the cooking surface, and the blower is located inside the duct. An external blower is a motor located outside of the home. The advantage of the in-line and external blowers is that their size is not determined by the hood size. A remote blower also will not be as noisy as other blowers.

Downdrafts

Downdrafts are a type of ventilation that either pops up behind the cooking surface or lies centered between the burners to provide ventilation (Figure 6.18). Because they need to be recessed below a cabinet, they only work when a cooktop is being used. If a rangetop or range is used, there is nowhere for the downdraft to be located. It is also important when specifying a downdraft to be sure it works with the cooking surface that is being specified. This type of ventilation will pull the smoke down and out through the floor. Downdrafts can be especially useful when the cooktop is on an island and a large ceiling-mounted hood is not wanted.

Recirculating

Recirculating ventilation is the least ideal of all the options. Because there must be some type of ventilation, it is still better than no ventilation. This type gathers in the air, which passes through a filter (sometimes called a charcoal filter), and then pushes the air back into the room. The charcoal filters need to be replaced approximately every 3 to 6 months. The manufacturer's recommendations should be followed concerning the frequency for replacement and cleaning of this filter. Although recirculating ventilation is not ideal, sometimes it is required in high-rise buildings or other situations where the hood cannot be vented outside directly.

Figure 6.18 Downdrafts can be used only with certain cooktops, so it is important to check the specifications for both appliances. *Courtesy of Abt Electronics by Brad Wilkening.*

MICROWAVES

Microwaves have become a staple in most kitchens. It is very important to consider the location of the microwave when designing a kitchen. It is not ideal to end up with a microwave sitting on a countertop taking up valuable work space. There are many ways to plan for a microwave in a kitchen design.

Microwaves cook food, from the outside in, by agitating the molecules in the food. This creates friction, which in turn creates heat. When selecting a microwave, the higher wattage it has the better. Although some companies make microwaves that will fit in a 12-inch-deep cabinet, there are still many that are 16 inches deep or deeper. Typically, smaller microwaves will cook faster and better. Let us look at the various styles of microwaves.

Built-in Microwave

Because microwaves have become so common, there are many ways to build one into the layout of the kitchen. One way is by using a built-in microwave. These microwaves can be built into a base, wall, or tall cabinet. Built-ins require the use of a trim kit, which can be purchased separately. These trim kits hide the shelf where the microwave sits, giving a very clean and seamless look (Figure 6.19). Some microwave models are offered with a hanging kit, so that they can be hung from a wall cabinet. A light rail molding, as discussed in Chapter 5, can be added to the bottom, making the microwave appear built into the cabinet.

Figure 6.19 Built-in microwaves require a trim kit. *Courtesy of Pamela Polvere Designs and Dennis Jourdan Photography Inc.*

Figure 6.20 A microwave/hood combination acts as two appliances in one and is a good option for smaller kitchens. *Courtesy of Novak and Parker by Brad Wilkening.*

Microwave/Hood

Another option for the microwave is to have a combination microwave and hood in one (Figure 6.20). This is a fitting option for smaller kitchens with limited space because this appliance is really two items in one.

Microwave/hoods can be vented outside or be recirculating. As mentioned previously, it is better when vented outside, but sometimes this is not possible.

Microwave Drawer

A newer technology for microwaves is the microwave drawer option. This is a microwave where a button is pressed and it slides open for use (Figure 6.21). Because of the top access for this microwave, it is best installed at a lower height. In general, this style of microwave is at the ideal height for use. Because it is accessed from the top, a microwave drawer does not require the user to bend down, as would a standard microwave installed in a base cabinet.

Convection Microwave

Convection microwaves are newer and are also gaining popularity. These microwaves will not change the texture of the food as much as a standard microwave. The disadvantage is that they usually take longer to cook the food. This appliance works well for baked goods, but is not as good for cooking meats.

WARMING DRAWERS

Warming drawers do exactly that—keep food warm. These drawers are typically available in 27- and 30-inch widths, which ideally line up underneath a standard oven width (Figure 6.22). They are available in stainless steel, other metallic finishes, or accept a custom panel. Although they are intended to keep food warm, it is nonetheless best to cover the food in a warming drawer so it will retain its moisture. They are convenient for the baker who needs a warm, out-of-the-way place to let dough rise, or simply to warm plates. Warming drawers are a luxury as they require additional money and space in the kitchen.

DISHWASHERS

The dishwasher is another appliance that is seen in most kitchens. The advantage of dishwashers, as discussed

Figure 6.21 Microwave drawers are a newer technology, which make sense for undercabinet installation. *Courtesy of Novak and Parker by Brad Wilkening.*

justable racks, versus the immovable racks in less expensive models. The most energy-efficient dishwashers use condensation drying. These dishwashers condense the heated water on their stainless steel interiors and drain without wasting energy.

in Chapter 3, is that they are more environmentally friendly than hand-washing dishes. Obviously, running a properly loaded dishwasher will most effectively use water for cleaning dishes. Dishwashers are most often seen in 24-inch widths, but there also are 18- and 36-inch widths available, just not as readily. Like other appliances mentioned, they too are available in a stainless steel or metal finishes; otherwise there are custom panel options as well.

The best dishwashers will heat the water for sanitation no matter what the incoming water temperature is. Higher-end models also have inline heaters instead of exposed elements at the base, preventing nearby plastic from melting. Most dishwashers do not require prerinsing and, in truth, this habit can be harmful to dishes; if food is not on the dishes placed in a dishwasher, they may become etched by strong detergents. Better dishwashers will have stainless steel interiors. Despite the fact that most dishwashers are the same 24-inch width, their capacities can vary. The better quality dishwasher will have more space inside for loading. Higher-end dishwashers also will have ad-

Figure 6.22 A common way to install a warming drawer is in combination with a microwave and oven. *Courtesy of Novak and Parker by Brad Wilkening.*

Dishwasher Drawers

A newer trend has been the use of dishwasher drawers (Figure 6.23). The advantage of this style of dishwasher is the flexibility it offers. These units allow one drawer to run at a time. This is a great option for a home with only one or two people. A single dishwasher drawer can be installed in addition to a dishwasher, allowing for additional dish cleaning in a larger, more frequently used kitchen.

Figure 6.24 Air switches allow a garbage disposal to be turned on by a button instead of a switch. *Courtesy of Allied Plumbing by Brad Wilkening.*

GARBAGE DISPOSALS

Garbage disposals remain popular in the kitchen. This appliance, installed under a sink, finely shreds scraps of food. It is argued that using a garbage disposal is not environmentally friendly for two reasons. First, it requires energy to operate, which is not ideal. Second, this waste ends up at the wastewater treatment plant. This increases the possibility of clogs at these plants, and it is wasteful of water and energy to remove these clogs. Garbage disposals can be operated by a switch located on a wall or by an air switch located on the sink (Figure 6.24). Newer garbage disposals are being made to operate more quietly, so as not to be a disturbance in the kitchen. Let's look at the two main types of garbage disposals available.

Continuous Feed

The continuous feed garbage disposal operates as it is named, working continuously while scraps are being fed into it. This type is considered dangerous because it operates without a cover, allowing the opportunity for a person's hand to get caught.

Figure 6.23 Dishwasher drawers allow flexibility because one drawer can be run at a time. *Courtesy of Abt Electronics by Brad Wilkening.*

Batch Feed

A batch-feed garbage disposal starts working only when its stopper, or lid, is placed inside the disposal opening and turned. The presence of a lid makes this a safer garbage disposal to use. It can be a little trickier to use than the continuous feed type, but homeowners might appreciate its safety if they have small children in the house.

TRASH COMPACTORS

Trash compactors have become less popular over time, and are not considered a very "green" choice for the kitchen. It is argued that trash that has been compacted does not break down as quickly, due to less air circulation, which slows decomposition. Because many people have started recycling and require sorting to do so, a trash compactor does not seem like a beneficial use of space. These units are typically 18 or 12 inches wide. The disadvantages of having a trash compactor are the potential for odors and the fact that the garbage, once removed, is usually heavier to carry. When selecting a trash compactor it is important to consider the compacting pressure, safety, level of noise, and cleaning requirements.

WATER FILTRATION SYSTEMS

Water filtration systems have become popular along with the sustainable movement. A water filtration system in the home promotes the drinking of tap water instead of buying bottled water.

HOT WATER DISPENSER

In addition to water filtration systems, there also are hot water dispensers. These units instantly dispense hot water. This is a great appliance for those who frequently drink hot beverages.

COLD WATER DISPENSER

The opposite of the hot water dispenser is the cold water dispenser. These fixtures are great for those who enjoy drinking chilled water. There are some fixtures available that will have both hot and cold water options (Figure 6.25).

Figure 6.25 Hot and cold water dispensers allow for heated or chilled water on demand. *Courtesy of Allied Plumbing by Brad Wilkening.*

BUILT-IN COFFEE SYSTEMS

Built-in coffee systems are becoming more popular (Figure 6.26). There are a few different types of these systems. Some are plumbed directly to a plumbing line whereas others require that a reserve of water be filled.

ICEMAKERS

Icemakers are an appliance option for clients who have a significant need for ice. If the homeowner has a lot of parties, this could be a nice option to offer. Although ice may seem like a simple thing, different manufacturers make machines that produce different styles of cubes. It is best to be aware of this, so as to educate the client about his or her choices. The client may have a preference for a specific type of ice cube.

Figure 6.26 Built-in coffee systems are a nice luxury for the serious coffee drinker. *Courtesy of Novak and Parker by Brad Wilkening.*

APPLIANCES FOR THE BATH

As technology continues to advance, more appliances are found in the bathroom. These items contribute to making the bath feel more like a retreat, which is a popular goal. Among the features available are televisions, mirror defoggers, towel warmers, heated flooring, and sound systems.

TELEVISIONS

With the increase in plasma and flat-screen televisions, clients are finding more locations for these slim and sleek items. A television could easily be hung on the wall in a bath, so the news could be watched in the morning as the users are getting ready for the day. There also are mirrors with televisions available. These high-tech mirrors are still on the expensive side, but are a delightful feature if the budget allows.

MIRROR DEFOGGERS

In addition to mirrors with televisions, there are also mirrors with an antifog feature. These mirrors have a heating element, so that when the bathroom gets steamy the mirror does not. This feature is available at a reasonable price and can be incorporated easily.

TOWEL WARMERS

Towel warmers are frequently used in bathrooms. It is a wonderful treat to have a warm towel waiting at the end of a shower or bath. Two types of towel warmers are available: electric and hydronic. Electric towel warmers are powered simply by electricity whereas hydronic towel warmers use hot water for heating. The electric versions are used more often because of the ease of installation compared with the hydronic version. Both types of towel warmer are available in many different sizes, finishes, and styles.

HEATED FLOORING

Heated flooring can be used in a bathroom or a kitchen, but is found more frequently in the bathroom. This is also a beneficial feature to incorporate when possible. Like towel warmers, these too can be electric or hydronic. And again, as with towel warmers, the electric versions are generally easier to install. Many heated floor manufacturers offer features, such as timers. Timers are convenient because they allow homeowners to set when the heat turns on and off. If the homeowners always wake up and get ready for the day at 7:00 A.M. they could set the flooring to heat at 6:30 A.M. every morning, so that they are greeted with a warm floor. Heated floors also can help reduce heating costs, because they are efficiently heating the space.

SOUND SYSTEMS

Sound systems are becoming more popular as whole-house technology systems are gaining popularity. It is very easy to incorporate speakers and other sound system pieces into a bath. These can even include a dock for the homeowner's iPod to play his or her music of choice. Speakers can be installed in the ceiling, walls, or even the tub, as is discussed further in Chapter 7 (Kitchen and Bath Design: Plumbing). The other components can be installed in a cabinet, closet, wall, or any other creative location conceptualized by the designer.

When sound systems are included, it is often best for the client to hire a specific home-technology specialist. These specialists can design the whole system, sell all the parts needed, and possibly provide the installation. This is really the best way to proceed when choosing a sound system, because the specialist will know what is most up to date and have a better understanding of the acoustics for the space. More frequently than not, sound systems are not the kitchen and bath designer's specialty.

INFORMATION FOR THE DESIGNER

As the designer, the dimensions of the various appliances are very important. They are important when planning the space to determine what size and how many appliances will fit logically within the space. After the plan and appliances are finalized, the specific appliance dimensions become more important to the designer. When semicustom or custom cabinets are ordered, these dimensions must be known to place the order correctly. The designer must specify to the cabinetry company the exact size of cut-outs needed for ovens, microwaves, or any other appliance being installed within a cabinet (Figure 6.27). Stock cabinets will require that openings be cut on site by the installer.

DESIGNER'S DIALOGUE 6.6

"Appliance companies don't always give good specs for panels. If you're not sure, ask somebody. Some need a backer while some just need a panel; it's best to ask someone."

—*Therese Kenney, Kitchen and Bath Designer*

INFORMATION FOR THE CONTRACTOR

The information that the contractor needs is similar to what the designer needs. The contractor, too, will need to know the general sizes of the appliances (Figure 6.28). In addition, he or she will need to know what type of power is required and where the power and/or water supply should be located, depending on the appliance.

TABLE 6.1 ANNUAL ELECTRICITY CONSUMPTION

Appliance	Annual Percentage*
Refrigerators	13.7%
Freezers	3.5%
Water heaters	9.1%
Dishwashers	2.5%
Electric range tops	2.8%
Electric ovens	1.8%
Microwave ovens	1.7%

*Represents annual electricity consumption percentages of a typical household by appliance.
Source: http://www.eia.gov/emeu/recs/recs2001/enduse2001/enduse2001.html

SUSTAINABLE CONSIDERATIONS

As discussed in Chapter 3, the most helpful thing to keep in mind when specifying sustainable appliances is to look for Energy Star–rated appliances (Table 6.1 and Box 6.1). These appliances offer the best options for conserving energy and water use. Clients are selecting these appliances more and more often, as people become more concerned about these issues. Read further about sustainable design in Chapter 3 for more ways to accomplish a "green" project.

TRADE TALK 6.1

"As long as the designer pulls the specifications from the manufacturers, there will be no problem with the installation of the appliances."
—*John Gruszka, Jr., President, Fair Oaks Contractors*

OVERALL DIMENSIONS

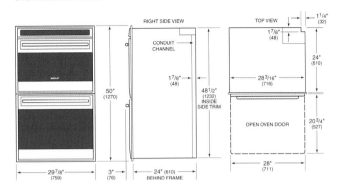

L Series Built-In Double Ovens

Unit dimensions may vary by ± 1/8".

SPECIFICATIONS

Overall Width	29 7/8"
Overall Height	50"
Overall Depth	24"
Oven Door Clearance	20 3/4"
Overall Oven Interior Capacity (per oven)	4.5 cu ft
Oven Interior Dimensions (per oven)	25" W x 16 1/2" H x 19" D
Minimum Cabinet Width	30"
Minimum Cabinet Depth	24"
Minimum Base Support	400 lbs
Opening Width	28 1/2"
Opening Height	49 5/8"
Electrical Requirements	240/208 V AC 60 Hz, 50 amp circuit
Conduit	5' flexible 4-wire
Electrical Rating	8.9 kW at 240 V 6.7 kW at 208 V
Total Amps	37
Shipping Weight	466 lbs

INSTALLATION SPECIFICATIONS

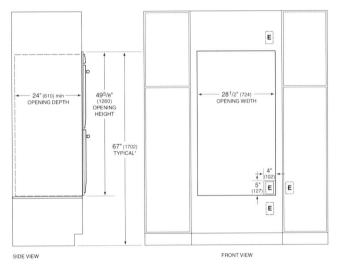

SIDE VIEW   FRONT VIEW

Dimension must accommodate height of oven trim.
NOTE: Location of electrical supply within opening may require additional cabinet depth. Dashed line represents profile of unit.

IMPORTANT NOTE: *Unless you are using cabinets deeper than 24", it is recommended that the electrical supply be placed in an adjacent cabinet within reach of the conduit. Choose the location shown in the illustration that best suits your installation.*

INSTALLATION NOTES

Complete installation specifications can be found on our website, wolfappliance.com.

Dimensions in parentheses are in millimeters unless otherwise specified.

Figure 6.27 These double-oven specifications are a good example of the information needed by designers and contractors. *Specifications courtesy of Sub-Zero, Inc., and Wolf Appliance, Inc.*

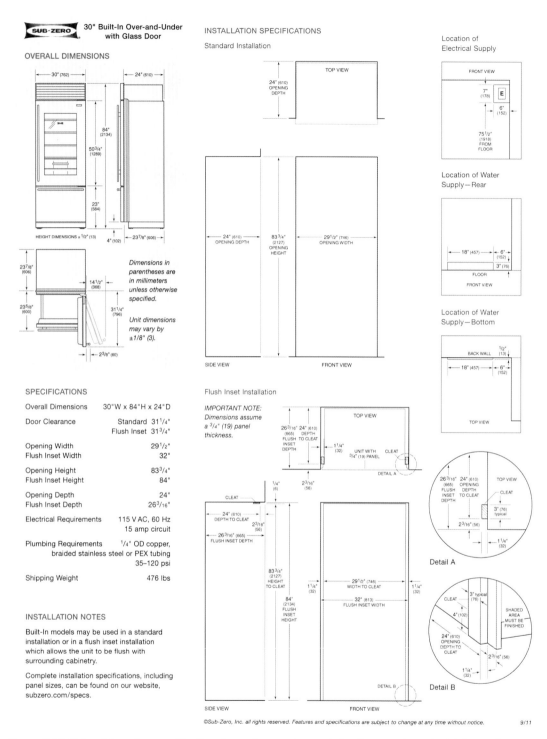

Figure 6.28 This refrigerator specification shows the requirements for the opening, electricity, and water. It also points out the needed location for the electricity and water. *Specifications courtesy of Sub-Zero, Inc., and Wolf Appliance, Inc.*

SUMMARY

The appliances are a key part of any kitchen project and an added bonus to bath projects. They greatly affect the functionality of the kitchen and add modern technology to the bath. Many types of appliances are available, and therefore it is important that the designer stay informed about the newest technologies and the most recent trends. Manufacturers are very willing to offer assistance in educating designers about their available products. They offer classes or will send sales representatives to visit designers to keep them up to date. It is important for the designer to take advantage of this so as to be able to assist clients with making the best decision for their project.

CHAPTER 6 EXERCISES

I: Select the appliances you would recommend for the Benners' kitchen, mentioned in the Design Scenario at the beginning of this chapter. Explain why you chose them. Pull up the specifications on each appliance and highlight or circle the information that will be needed by both you, as the designer, and the contractor. Be sure, if you are printing this information, to print only the pages with the needed information. Do not retype specification information, as this allows for error.

II: Research an appliance manufacturer. Select one appliance manufacturer and create a report summarizing its history and products. Share your findings with the class.

CHAPTER 6 DISCUSSION QUESTIONS

1. What type of cooking surface is the most energy efficient and uses electric current generated by a magnetic field?

2. What style of refrigerator has become the most popular recently and why?
3. How much shorter is the cook time for convection ovens?
4. What is the ideal width for a cooking surface's ventilation?
5. What types of wines can be stored in a wine refrigerator?

REFERENCE

Silvers, Donald E., and Moorea Hoffman. *Kitchen Appliances 101: What Works, What Doesn't and Why*. Tarzana, CA: NMI Publishers, 2005.

ADDITIONAL RESOURCES

Energy Star. http://www.energystar.gov (home page). This website has additional information about the Energy Star program and products.

BOX 6.1 ENERGY STAR–RATED APPLIANCES

Energy Star is a joint program of the U.S. Environmental Protection Agency and the U.S. Department of Energy. The voluntary Energy Star labeling was introduced in 1992. It started with labeling computers and monitors but gradually expanded to include appliances. Products earn Energy Star labeling by meeting specific energy efficiency requirements set by Energy Star. Additional information about the program and specific Energy Star products can be found on their website at: http://www.energystar.gov.

CHAPTER 6: APPLIANCES CHECKLIST

___Does the client's preferences, budget, and kitchen space allow for a separate cooking surface and oven or ovens?

___Does the client prefer cooking on a gas, electric, or induction cooking surface?

___Is a convection oven within the client's budget?

___What style of refrigerator makes the most sense for the client?

___Review Energy Star's options for efficient appliances.

___What specific appliance requests did the client make?

___Should heated flooring be incorporated?

___Does the client require a television or stereo system in the bath?

___Would the client(s) like a towel warmer? Should it be electric or hydronic?

___Locate the information you need from the specifications for your cabinet order.

___Locate the information from the specifications that the contractor is going to need for the electrician.

KEY TERMS

BTU: British thermal unit, the heat required to raise the temperature of one pound of water by 1 degree Fahrenheit.

Blower: A hood blower pulls in the grease and smoke–laden air that needs to be removed while cooking. A blower may be incorporated into the hood or bought separately to install into a decorative hood.

CHAPTER 7 KITCHEN AND BATH DESIGN: PLUMBING

OBJECTIVES

After reading this chapter, you will:

- Understand the basics of how plumbing works in a home.

- Recognize that most homeowners no longer want a utilitarian bathroom but a luxurious retreat, and be able to achieve that for them.

- Be familiar with items that contribute to making the kitchen as functional as possible for the cook.

- Identify the various plumbing fixture options available for the kitchen and bath and their characteristics so as to make the most informed suggestions for the client(s).

DESIGN SCENARIO

Your client, the Kings, have decided to redesign their master bathroom. They both prepare for work at the same time in the morning, so two sinks and a toilet in its own room would be preferred. Having traveled to hotels with exquisite spas, the Kings would like some spa aspects incorporated into their bathroom. Mrs. King enjoys relaxing with long baths, and Mr. King wants a steam shower. They have hired you to lay out the most functional space possible and help make the best selections for materials, fixtures, and fittings.

1. What type of tub should you specify if Mrs. King likes to use bath oils for her baths?

2. What is the ideal size for Mr. King's steam shower?

3. What other features can you incorporate to give the Kings their dream spa bath?

Plumbing is an important area for consideration for the kitchen or bath project. In this chapter, we discuss a general overview of the house plumbing system. We then look closer at the specific considerations for the kitchen or bath project's plumbing fixtures. Plumbing in the bathroom is a large part of the aesthetic and functionality of the bathroom design. These selections make a significant statement about the bathroom that is being designed. Is it a decorative powder room with minimal storage and a vessel bowl sink, or a master bath with all the lavish options available? We discuss the various plumbing options available to specify in the bath, from lavatory sinks and faucets, to toilets, tubs, and shower systems. Although the plumbing plays a smaller role in the kitchen, it is still significant. The main sink area is one of the primary parts of the work triangle. We examine the selections available for this area as well.

WATER SUPPLY

Plumbing is another essential component of the kitchen or bath design. Before we discuss the specific types of fixtures available for the kitchen or bath, it is important to understand how plumbing works in a home. Water is brought into the home either from a municipal supply system or, in the case of most rural homes, from a well. Cold water enters the house through ¾- or 1-inch diameter pipe. Water will first pass through a **water softener** if there is one, and then through the water heater. **Branch lines** run to the plumbing fixtures throughout the house. Plumbing fixtures have a stack that goes down to the sewage line and up for venting (Table 7.1).

WATER HEATING

The water heater is an important consideration when determining plumbing fixtures. The kitchen faucet should not have a drastic effect on the capacity of the water heater; the bathroom fixtures will be more important to look at closely. Most homes use conventional water heaters with a tank. The tank is insulated and stores hot water ready to use. These tanks may hold anywhere from 30 to 82 gallons of water. What size is appropriate depends on how much water is used at the time of maximum usage. If more hot water is needed either a new, larger conventional tank may be installed in place of the existing one, or an additional water heater that is tankless may be added. Tankless water heaters are sometimes referred to as *on-demand* or *instantaneous*. They heat water only when it is being used. They are a good option when replacing an old water heater or when the fixtures being used are far from the central heater.

DRAIN, WASTE, AND VENTING

The drain, waste, and venting system removes used water and waste from the house. Small-diameter drain pipes from the fixtures feed into the branch lines and then to the **soil stack,** which is generally 4 inches in diameter, and then to the house drain, which leads to the municipal sewer system or septic tank. The waste pipes slope, using gravity to move the flow, not pressure. The larger piping of the soil stack is necessary to allow for both solids and liquids. Venting is required to prevent sewer gas from entering the home. Code makes it mandatory that each fixture be vented. The soil stack of the house will typically extend up to vent through the roof. Once the waste reaches the septic tank it is held while bacteria and organisms partially digest the waste. Undigested solids end up at the bottom as sludge, while water runs out the top to the drain. It is important to consider the size of the septic tank if a food disposal is being added. Disposals will increase the load to the septic tank, and therefore it needs to be appropriately sized to handle the extra load.

TABLE 7.1 TYPICAL HOUSEHOLD WATER CONSUMPTION	
Appliance or Task	Gallons Used per Day
Bathroom	
Toilet (four flushes per day at approximately 1.6 gallons per flush)	6
Showerhead (10 minutes per day at 3–8 gallons per minute)	30–80
Showerhead with aerator (10 minutes per day at 2.5 gallons per minute)	25
Bathtub	
• Once per day	30–45
• Filled one-quarter to one-third full	9–12
Shaving (once per day)	5–10
Brushing teeth (twice per day at 2–5 gallons)	4–10
Kitchen	
Dishwasher (one cycle per day)	4–8 gallons per cycle
Washing produce	5–10

BATHROOM PLUMBING

LAVATORY FAUCETS

Lavatory faucets bring the water to the lavatory, or bathroom sink. They are available in many different styles and finishes. It is best to try to use manufacturers known for having good-quality products. If a faucet is not plated well, the user may inadvertently scratch or chip away the finish. Bathroom faucets are available with aerators to help conserve the amount of water used. There are various aesthetic faucet styles to select from, and there are also a few different installation styles to decide between for the lavatory faucet. Faucets may have an 8-inch spread, a 4-inch spread, or a single-hole installation when deck mounted. Alternatively, the faucets also can be wall mounted.

Eight-Inch Spread or Widespread

Faucets with an 8-inch spread, or widespread faucets, are among the most popular for baths today. They allow generous space to control the handle of the faucet. They are referred to as 8-inch spread faucets because there is 8 inches from the center of one handle to the center of the other.

DESIGNER'S DIALOGUE 7.1

"Curving the lavatory faucet spread-set around an oval bowl gives more space for turning the levers in a tight countertop situation; that has been a problem solver for me."
—*Lisa Godsey, ASID, LEED AP, IDEC, IESNA, Interior Designer, Adjunct Instructor*

Four-Inch Spread or Centerset

There are also faucets with a 4-inch spread. As for the 8-inch spread, the measurement is taken from the center of one handle to the center of the other handle. This style is typically less expensive than the 8-inch spread. The handles are closer to the spout, making for overall tighter faucet control.

Single Hole

Single-hole faucets are simply faucets that install into one hole and have a single control. Faucets with a single lever control are ideal for users with arthritis, because they require less grasping.

Wall Mount

Wall-mount faucets have become more popular, along with vessel bowl sinks. Like it sounds, they are faucets that are mounted to the wall. Although many have a contemporary style, there are options that have a traditional aesthetic as well.

SINKS

Bathroom sinks are available in many shapes, sizes, and materials. The drain often is sold separately, so it is important to confirm whether it is included or not. It is also important to consider the size of the sink in relation to the faucet and backsplash. All too frequently it is assumed that everything will fit just fine, only to find that there is not enough space for the faucet to be installed.

China

China sinks are similar to glazed tiles. There are many china lavatory sinks available to choose from. They have a painted layer and are susceptible to chipping. They are still considered very durable and can be cleaned with abrasive cleaners.

Figure 7.1 Glass is a newer material being used for lavatory undermount sinks. *Photograph courtesy of Kohler Co.*

Glass

Glass is being used for bath sinks more often, matching the trend toward using vessel bowl sinks. Glass is hard and durable but can still chip. It resists chemicals but can also require more maintenance, especially if a clear glass is used. Although in the past glass sinks have been used only as vessel bowls, more recently undermount and **integrated sink bowl** options have become available (Figure 7.1).

Pedestal

Pedestal sinks are a traditional style, although lately more contemporary versions have become available. This is a sink that essentially has its own pedestal incorporated, making it one free-standing piece. When using a pedestal sink it is important to consider the amount of counter space that will be available to the user. Some pedestals are larger and have more landing space in general. If a smaller pedestal is used, will there be enough landing space? In the case of a powder room, it may not be an issue at all. In a master bath, where in the morning the user prepares for the day, there may not be enough space for toothpaste, a toothbrush, mouthwash, face wash, and other essentials. Perhaps a small shelf could be installed near the sink or an alcove, soap dish, or other accessory for extra landing space (Figure 7.2).

Undermount

Undermount sinks are mounted to the underside of the countertop. This style has been very popular recently, as it has a sleek look and is easy to clean. Sometimes the dimensions given in a sink's description consist only of the bowl size, not the overall dimensions. It is important to look at the specifications to verify the sink's overall dimensions to be sure it will fit in the cabinet.

Integrated

The term *integrated sink* describes a sink bowl made from the same material as the surrounding countertop, thus allowing a seamless integration between the two.

This is another sink style that is easy to clean because of the lack of edges where dirt can collect. In kitchens, integrated sinks are typically seen only with **solid surfacing** material. In baths, integrated sinks are available in many materials such as solid surface, glass, or china.

Self-Rimming

Self-rimming sinks also may be referred to as *overmount*. This style of sink drops into a cutout in the countertop. Many self-rimming sinks have predrilled holes for faucets. It is important to know how many holes the sink has, as this will dictate what type of faucet can be used with it.

Figure 7.2 This pedestal sink has a generous landing area, which is nice. *Courtesy of Pamela Polvere Designs and Dennis Jourdan Photography Inc.*

Figure 7.3 Vessel sinks are often best used in powder rooms, but depending on the style can also work in a master bathroom. *Courtesy of Drury Design Kitchen & Bath Studio.*

Vessel

Vessel bowl sinks have become popular in recent years. The designer must be especially careful when specifying this type of sink. If a proper faucet is not used or an incorrect height for the faucet is specified, the vessel may have problems with splashing water. Vessel bowl sinks are available in various heights, sizes, and materials, and the type of faucet is specific to the vessel selected (Figure 7.3). Another important consideration for vessel sinks is the height of the countertop. If the sink is a tall vessel, the countertop must be lowered to adjust for this. It is also not typically recommended that vessel bowls be used in a master bath. Although lower-height vessel bowls are available, many are tall and make some tasks challenging, such as washing the face or brushing teeth. They also may restrict the amount of accessible counter space. Because the vessel bowl sink is such a statement piece, it would be ideal for use in a powder room.

TOILETS

Besides the sink, another very important fixture in the bath is the toilet. Toilets may occasionally be referred to as "water closets." This term originated from Europeans putting the toilet in its own room (a water closet), with a door, inside a bath.

Before considering the type of toilet that will be used in a bath it is important to consider the location. When working on a remodeling project it is vital to consider the existing location of the toilet. Waste stacks are not easy to move because the waste is removed by gravity. A slope is required with a vertical waste pipe. Even if it is possible to move the toilet location, it will be quite costly; this is something the designer should consider regarding the client's budget.

One Piece versus Two Pieces

Toilets may be constructed as one piece or two pieces. A two-piece toilet is more traditional, and is also less expensive than one-piece versions (Figure 7.4). The

Wall Mount

Wall-mount or wall-hung sinks are another option for sink installation. These sinks are useful for bathrooms that need to be universally designed. They allow for open space below, which is necessary for wheelchair users. If using a wall-mount sink, it is important to consider the plumbing pipes. Pipes should be protected so that anyone using the sink will not burn themselves from touching a hot pipe. It is also important to be aware that this style of sink will require additional support in the wall. When determining how much support is needed, the sink's weight is not the only consideration; the user may place additional weight in the sink, such as when bathing a baby. Such possibilities should be discussed before the sink is installed.

two-piece toilet is less expensive for production reasons. If something is wrong with one of the two parts, only that half has to be replaced. If something is wrong with a one-piece toilet, the whole toilet will be defective. The one-piece style has become the preferred style because it is often sleeker looking and easier to clean (Figure 7.5). Either type of toilet typically requires that the seat be purchased separately. There are seats available today that close softy, called "soft close." There are also toilets that will not flush unless the seat is down.

Elongated

Toilets that have an elongated seat are called just that: elongated. They are considered to be more comfortable than round-bowled toilets. They are also about 3 inches longer than round toilets, so this should be considered when deciding what will best fit in the space.

Round

Round toilets simply have a round seat. They are not as deep as the elongated toilets and therefore may be a good option in baths with limited space.

ADA Height

"ADA height" is a term sometimes used for toilets that have a higher toilet seat. Toilet seats are typically 14 or 15 inches high, but ADA height toilets have a higher seat, at about 18 inches high. An ADA height toilet is more comfortable because the user does not have to bend the knees quite so much to sit on it. As the name implies, this style of toilet is recommended for universal design.

Flushing Systems

In addition to the number of pieces or the shape of the toilet seat, there are also several different flushing systems that may be used. Toilets are required to use no more water than 1.6 gallons per flush **(GPF)** according to code. Newer toilets have been designed to be more efficient, so that a single flush at 1.6 GPF will remove everything (in the past, consumers had to flush twice

Figure 7.4 Two-piece toilets are less expensive than one-piece toilets. *Photograph courtesy of Kohler Co.*

Figure 7.5 One-piece toilets are sleeker and easier to clean. *Photograph courtesy of Kohler Co.*

or more, which went against the idea of conserving water). The various flushing systems are gravity, wash-down, vacuum assist, pressure-assist, electrohydraulic, flushometer, and dual-flush.

Gravity

Gravity toilets are the most common type. Water in the tank is released into the bowl. Gravity pushes the water and waste out of the bowl. Newer designs have taller and narrower tanks with steeper bowls and smaller water surface areas, making for an improved flush.

Wash-Down

Wash-down toilets are less likely to clog than the others. They have large trapways and a small surface area of water in the bowl. They sometimes do not clean the bowl surface as well.

Vacuum-Assist

The vacuum-assist toilet has a vacuum tank, within the toilet tank, that is connected to the trapway. When this type of toilet is flushed, a vacuum is created that pulls water into the bowl for a more efficient flush.

Pressure-Assist

Pressure-assist toilets have a louder and more powerful flush. Because of this extra power they really do empty the bowl with only one flush. It works by compressing air and water in the tank; the compressed water then shoots out under the rim by means of a siphon jet and flushes the toilet.

Electrohydraulic

Electrohydraulic toilets use electric motors, pumps, and controllers when flushing. These parts control the flush and the amount of discharge from the tank into the bowl.

Flushometer

A flushometer is used with a toilet that does not have a tank. These used to be found only in commercial applications, but they are now being used more often in residences for a contemporary style. The flushometer is available as a floor outlet or as an in-wall outlet.

Dual-Flush

The dual-flush toilet is a newer technology. This is a good option when trying to design a bath that is sustainable. This toilet has two separate buttons for flushing. One button uses a smaller amount of water, such as 0.9 GPF, whereas the other uses more water, such as 1.6 GPF (Figure 7.6).

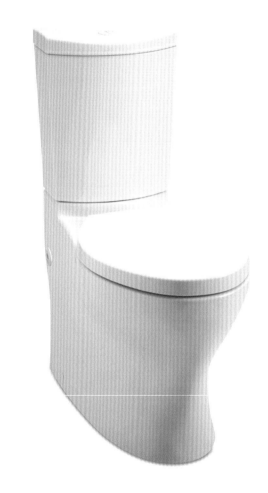

Figure 7.6 Dual-flush toilets are a nice sustainable option.
Photograph courtesy of Kohler Co.

Rough-ins: 10, 12, and 14 Inch

The toilet "rough-in" is the measurement from the toilet bolt, which is the toilet outlet, to the back wall. Although the plumber may be able to use an offset flange to change the rough-in of the toilet, it is best to try to specify a toilet that will work with the existing rough-in dimension. Twelve inches is the most common toilet rough-in available because this is what is used for new construction. The 10- or 14-inch rough-ins may be found in older homes. Fewer toilet options are available with these.

Other Toilet Considerations

A few other things should be considered when selecting a toilet. The lever or button that controls the toilet flush is called the *actuator*. This actuator can be ordered in various finishes so that it can match the finish of other fixtures in the bath.

Bidets

A bidet is a fixture that is very popular in Europe, but has not been as popular in the United States. It looks similar to a toilet, but is for cleaning rather than waste. The user sits on the bidet, facing the wall, and is cleaned with a spray of warm water. Bidets need both a hot and cold water supply along with a drain. They may have a standard tap, vertical spray, or horizontal spray. The fittings may be deck mounted or wall mounted, depending on the fixture (Figure 7.7). A vacuum breaker must be installed behind the bidet to avoid back flow, or suction causing contaminated water to enter from the city's water supply. If the bidet has a deck-mounted faucet it will not need a vacuum breaker. It is also important to realize that not all parts from other manufacturers will work with all bidets. It would be simplest to purchase all the parts from the same manufacturer. If having a separate bidet is not possible, bidet seats for toilets are also available.

Figure 7.7 Bidets are more popular in Europe than in the United States. *Photograph courtesy of Kohler Co.*

Bidet Seats

An alternative to the standard bidet that has become available recently is the bidet seat. Manufacturers are making these seats to work with toilets. There is a control panel to operate it on the toilet. These seats also have an air dryer and can be heated. This seat requires power, which is important to note for the electrician. A benefit to using a bidet seat instead of a separate bidet is that the homeowner can have essentially two plumbing fixtures in one (Figure 7.8).

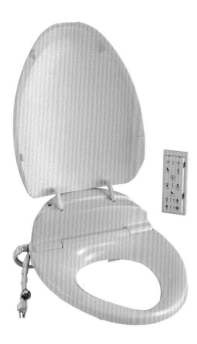

Figure 7.8 Bidet seats are a nice way to get the bidet features without the need for a separate fixture. *Photograph courtesy of Kohler Co.*

Figure 7.9 Urinals are primarily seen commercially, but they are available residentially. *Photograph courtesy of Kohler Co.*

Urinals

Although urinals are typically seen in commercial applications, they are also available for residences. They may be wall hung or floor mounted. They typically use the flushometer system for flushing. Waterless urinals are also available, which do not flush. These have a special configuration and a replaceable cartridge to conceal odors. Urinals are typically made of vitreous china (Figure 7.9).

TUBS

Although some homeowners decide to forgo a tub in the bath to allow for a larger custom shower, there still remain many who would not give it up for anything. It is recommended that there be at least one tub in the home, even if there is not one in every bath. This is recommended to enhance the resale value of the home. When specifying a tub, it is important to consider the weight of the tub with the water and people in it. Will the floor be able to support the weight? If not, the floor will need to be reinforced to support it. Tubs also require a waste and overflow system that needs be purchased separately. It is important to be sure to order this. There are several different installation styles of tubs to select from.

Freestanding

Freestanding tubs were considered traditional for a long time, but now there are also many contemporary versions available. Claw-foot tubs are used for Victorian style bathrooms. Although older bathrooms can be found with freestanding tubs that also have shower systems, this is not ideal. Usually freestanding tubs do not have enough standing space to allow for comfortable and safe showering (Figure 7.10). Although freestanding tubs make a beautiful statement piece, they require special attention when being used. It is important to be sure the height of the tub filler works with the tub. It also is important to consider how it will be plumbed, especially when using a floor-mounted filler. It is best to check with local codes about any restrictions as well. Some cities will not allow the tub filler to extend past a certain depth into the tub so as to avoid backflow from the city water. Because freestanding tubs vary in style between manufacturers it is usually best to order the waste and overflow system for the tub from the tub manufacturer. If not ordering the waste and overflow from the same manufacturer, it is very important to look at the specifications closely to be sure they are compatible.

Figure 7.10 Freestanding tubs can be tricky to install but make a beautiful statement. *Courtesy of Drury Design Kitchen & Bath Studio.*

Alcove

Alcove tubs are intended to fit into an alcove of three walls. These tubs have three unfinished sides and one finished side (Figure 7.11). When ordering, it must be specified whether the drain will be to the right or left (facing the tub). These tubs are typically 30 to 34 inches wide, 14 to 20 inches deep, and 60 to 72 inches long (Figure 7.12).

Corner

Corner tubs are made to fit into a corner. The two sides that will butt against the walls will not be finished, but the exposed sides will be finished. Corner tubs are typically larger and therefore may not work in smaller bathrooms.

Figure 7.11 It is necessary to specify whether an alcove tub drains right or left. *Courtesy of Drury Design Kitchen & Bath Studio.*

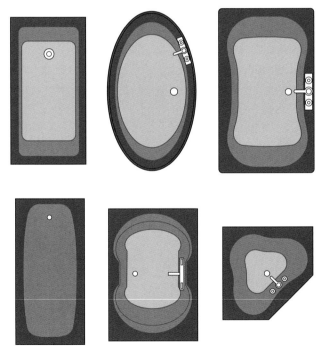

Figure 7.12 Tubs are available in many different configurations.

Drop-In

Drop-in tubs are intended to drop into a platform. This platform may be larger than the tub, allowing for surface around the tub, or simply a platform directly under the tub. These tubs are unfinished on all sides. If the tub also is used as a shower and installed on a platform with a larger ledge, it is possible that water will collect in the corners. The nice thing about drop-in tubs is the opportunity for customizing the design. These tubs can be installed into an alcove, leaving one side exposed to create a customized front. Exposed unfinished tub fronts may be tiled or have a custom wood-panel front or stone slab front, just to name a few options.

Undermount

Undermount tubs are unfinished on all sides. Some tubs will have the option to drop-in or undermount for the installation. Although undermount installation provides a cleaner look, it can cause issues later. When a tub is undermounted, the entire deck surface above it must be removed if the tub needs to be repaired or replaced. This makes the repair or replacement of the tub more costly than if it had been installed as a drop-in. Undermount tubs also may be less comfortable for the user trying to rest his or her head on the tub ledge (Figure 7.13).

Figure 7.13 Undermount is one method that can be used to install a drop-in tub. *Courtesy of Drury Design Kitchen & Bath Studio.*

Tub Materials

Not only are there several installation styles to choose from, but there are also several materials commonly used for tubs. Let's look at the most common materials being used to make bathtubs.

Cast Iron. Cast iron is a heavy and tough material that has been used for bathtubs and kitchen sinks for more than a century. Cast iron is cool to the touch and will cool bath water faster than a plastic material. The weight is an important consideration if a cast iron tub is being used on a second floor. It will require multiple men to carry and clearances may be an issue when traveling upstairs. Cast iron is more expensive, but it will last for decades. Cast iron tubs are available in a range of glossy enamel colors. It is a very durable material and can be cleaned with abrasive cleaners. They may chip under forceful impact.

Acrylic. Acrylic is a lightweight material that is popular for tubs. Acrylic tubs are also less expensive and are warm to the touch. Abrasive cleaners should not be used on acrylic tubs, and some chemicals will damage them. Acrylic is also available in many colors, like cast iron. Acrylic's color is found throughout the material. It can be scratched, but it is repairable.

Gel Coat. Gel-coat tubs are made of fiberglass and finished with a gel coat, a polyester resin that comes in many colors. These tubs may be referred to as gel coat or fiberglass, and are not as durable as acrylic.

Standard Sizes. Although it is possible to order custom-sized tubs, there are a variety of standard sizes available. The most common tub widths are 30 and 32 inches; there are certainly many others. Some very common options for tub length are 66 and 72 inches. It is helpful to have a basic idea of general tub sizes when space planning a bathroom and deciding what will work for the space.

Spa Experience

Bathrooms are no longer simply a utilitarian space where people groom. It has become a luxurious space where the goal is to relax and indulge. Many homeowners take a vacation and visit a nice spa, and then decide they want that for their own homes. There are now many products available for the residential project to accomplish this goal.

Air Tub

Air tubs are one type of tub used for spa-like relaxation. One benefit of air tubs is that bath oils may be used: Because air, not water, is pushed through the pipes, oil will not end up inside the pipes. Air tubs are quieter than whirlpool tubs. The motor can also be located remotely, for even greater quiet. Some air tubs will blow air through the pipes after the tub is drained to remove excess water. Although air tubs are a nice option, they have a more gentle feel compared with a whirlpool tub, which has jets that push water instead of air (Figure 7.14).

Blowers. Air tubs require a blower, which provides the power to create the air bubbles in the tub. The benefit of an air tub is that, oftentimes, the blower can be located away from the tub, helping reduce the amount of noise when the tub is in use. Because things can go wrong with the blower, it needs to be accessible for repairs. If the blower is not accessible, it could mean the whole tub will need to be removed if something goes wrong with the blower (Figure 7.15).

Whirlpool

Whirlpool tubs are another popular style of tub conveying the spa experience. Whirlpool tubs push the bath water through pipes and out of jets to massage the user. Jets are usually located at the feet or back area. Because water from the tub is what is pushed through the pipes, it is not recommended that bath oils be used in a whirlpool tub. Once the whirlpool is turned off, remaining water sits in the pipes. If this water has oils in it, it will attract more dirt and bacterial growth.

Figure 7.14 This freestanding tub is an air tub with a floor-mounted filler. *Courtesy of Pamela Polvere Designs and Cindy Trim Photography.*

Figure 7.15 This air tub has its blower located away from the tub, in a cabinet, to lessen the noise. It also has a cleaning system and speakers installed in it. *Courtesy of Pamela Polvere Designs.*

Pumps. Just as air tubs have blowers, whirlpool tubs have a pump that provides the power to push the water through the jet system. And like air tub blowers, whirlpool pumps need to be accessible for repairs.

Cleaning Systems

A newer feature that some tub manufacturers are offering is a cleaning system for the whirlpool tub. Mold and bacteria are a concern with whirlpool tubs because the water may just sit in the pipes when the whirlpool is not on. Cleaning systems flush out the pipes; some use a special cleaning solution. If the whirlpool tub does not have a specific cleaning system, it is recommended that it be cleaned by first filling the tub with warm water to just above the jets. Nonfoaming dishwasher detergent should then be added with bleach, and the whirlpool run for 5 to 10 minutes. Afterward, simply turn off the whirlpool and drain the water.

Soaking Tub

Soaking tubs with Asian-inspired designs have been popular. These tubs are deeper than standard tubs because the intent is that the user soak in it (Figure 7.16). As mentioned previously, it is important to confirm that the weight of the tub, when filled, will be adequately supported and that the tub fillers specified will work correctly. The safety of the person or persons who will be using the tub also needs to be considered. Should a grab bar be installed to make entering and exiting easier?

Figure 7.16 Soaking tubs are deeper than standard tubs. *Courtesy of Drury Design Kitchen & Bath Studio.*

Chromatherapy

Chromatherapy is a newer spa experience available for the residential consumer to purchase. It is the use of colored lights in the bathtub and/or shower. Different colors have different effects on how a person feels. Warm colors stimulate while cool colors calm the senses. Some homeowners like the idea of incorporating chromatherapy to enhance their bathroom spa experience.

In-Line Heaters

An in-line heater is something that can be added to a whirlpool or air tub to enhance the bathing experience by allowing the user to bathe longer. In-line heaters maintain the temperature of the bathtub. It does not raise the temperature, but keeps the temperature from dropping. Like the pump, this too needs to be accessible in case it needs repairing.

Tub Fittings

Tub faucet options are similar to lavatory faucet options. They are available in different spreads and may be deck, floor, or wall mounted. The simplest fitting configurations are when a tub is being used only as a tub. If the tub is designed as a tub and shower combination, more fittings are required. Let's look at showers now, as these controls will be used if combined with a tub.

SHOWERS

Showers have become the preferred method for bathing in the United States. Many homeowners decide to have a bathroom with only a large shower and completely forgo a bathtub at all.

Standard Components

The standard components of the shower include the shower pan, drain, various fittings, and the glass enclosure. Three main systems may be used to control the shower fittings: pressure balance valve, thermostatic, or electronic. These systems control the various showerheads, rainheads, body sprays, and handheld showers

available. Showers can also have a steam generator if a steam shower is desired.

Shower Pan

The shower pan is the base of the shower. It can be a prefabricated base or it can be fabricated by the installer to allow for a tile or concrete base. Tile or concrete shower bases are custom and therefore more expensive, whereas prefabricated shower bases are easier to install and less expensive.

Prefabricated Shower Base

Prefabricated shower bases are the most economical route for a shower (Figure 7.17). Acrylic is the material most commonly used for these shower bases. There are shower bases available that even extend up the wall, so that no wall tile is needed. Another available option includes the water fixtures. Terrazzo and gel coat are also commonly used materials for these shower bases.

Custom Shower Base

Custom shower bases are very popular in high-end baths. This type of shower base allows flexibility in the size of the shower. Because the installer will have to pitch the floor to the drain, the shower can be made virtually any size or shape. These bases may be covered with tile or can be made of concrete poured on site.

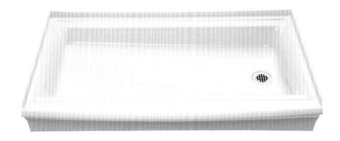

Figure 7.17 Acrylic shower bases are economical for a shower. *Photograph courtesy of Kohler Co.*

When creating a custom shower base with tile it is important to consider the size of the tile. Because shower floors are slippery, it is better to use smaller tiles. When smaller tiles are used there are more grout lines, which adds texture. Even if the floor is covered with polished tile, so long as they are small, the floor will not be too slippery. Ideally, shower floor tile should not be any larger than 2 by 2 inches in size. Smaller tiles are also a better choice because the floor will be pitched to the drain. It is easier to pitch a floor with smaller tiles than with larger tiles.

Zero Threshold Showers for ADA

Standard shower bases and even many custom tile shower bases will have a curb where the shower door sits. The thresholds are generally about 3 inches high and 4 inches deep, although that can vary. Zero threshold showers are a good alternative for showers that need to be designed for compliance with the Americans with Disabilities Act (ADA). A wheelchair would be very difficult to roll into a shower that has a 3-inch high curb at the entrance. **Trench drains,** which are a long narrow trough along the shower opening, prevent water from flowing into the bathroom. The use of trench drains has become popular not only for ADA-designed bathrooms, but contemporary styled bathrooms as well.

SHOWERHEADS

Showerheads are used for washing one's hair. This is obviously a very important part of the shower. As mentioned in the discussion of sustainable design in Chapter 3, showerheads equipped with aerators, which use less water, are available. Showerheads with aerators still have good pressure, due to the addition of air to the water flow. With the trend toward spa showers, these fixtures also are being made with more features. Several companies make showerheads with various water spray patterns. The user can get in the shower to bathe, but then switch the showerhead water flow to a massage setting for relaxation.

Showerheads have a flow restriction, based on federal law. They are limited to 2.5 gallons per minute for 80 pounds per square inch of pressure. Flow restrictors are included in the showerhead to comply with this law.

When placing the showerhead it is important to keep in mind that the spray should reach toward the body, not the face and hair. The user should be able to step out of the water to allow for lathering when shampooing the hair. Showerheads are typically located between 72 and 78 inches above the finished floor, depending on the heights of the users.

RAINHEADS

Rainheads are similar to showerheads, but produce more water flow and are larger. They are often mounted at the ceiling, but wall-mount versions are also available. It is important to remember with rainheads that a standard showerhead should also be installed; most rainheads provide so much water flow that it may be difficult, when washing hair, to get out of the way of the water to lather in shampoo. Rainheads are intended for use as part of a steam shower experience rather than for functional grooming.

BODY SPRAYS

Body sprays are small jets that can be installed in showers at whatever height is ideal for the user. Like showerheads, body sprays are now being made with various water spray patterns to maximize the spa showering experience. Body sprays should be located according to the user's preference. Typically, body sprays are placed so they can be aimed at the calves of the legs, or at the back, for relaxation.

HANDHELD SHOWERS

A handheld shower is a nice accessory to add to the shower. It gives the user flexibility in bathing. They are great to have when there are people of different heights using the same shower. Handheld showers can be attached to a slide-bar or hung from a hook. If the shower has seating, the handheld shower can be used while sitting. It's also helpful to specify a handheld shower because it makes cleaning the shower easier. Some clients like having a handheld shower if they have pets and want to bathe their pets in the shower. If the handheld shower is to be used as the main showerhead it should be located higher, like a showerhead. If it is being used in addition to a showerhead, it should be located lower, between waist and shoulder height.

CONTROLS

There are three systems that can be selected to control the parts of the shower. A pressure balance valve system is simplest and least expensive; a thermostatic system will typically require more pieces, making it more complex and expensive; and an electronic system is the most modern and expensive. All of these systems use valves and fixture trim pieces. The water enters the system through the valves, which are located inside the wall. The trim is the decorative part that is exposed and used to control the water.

Pressure Balance Valve System

Pressure balance valve systems are the simplest of the three options. The purpose of this system is to compensate for changes in water pressure or temperature. This system prevents water flow or temperature change when, for example, a toilet is flushed or a lavatory faucet is running (Figure 7.18). The valve has either a diaphragm or piston mechanism to balance the hot and cold water. The water temperature remains consistent

Figure 7.18 A pressure balance shower system is simpler and generally less expensive than a thermostatic system. *Courtesy of Pamela Polvere Designs and Cindy Trim Photography.*

within 2 to 3 degrees Fahrenheit. This is accomplished by the valve reducing the flow of either the hot or cold water so it will remain consistent.

Thermostatic System

Thermostatic systems are typically more expensive than pressure balance valve systems because they require more pieces, and more labor to install these pieces. This system is capable of supplying more fixtures at once than a pressure balance valve system. It typically has ¾-inch inlets to allow for this, but if water is needed for more than four or five fixtures a system with a 1-inch inlet may be wise to consider. Thermostatic systems have a thermostat control that adjusts the temperature of the water and a volume control that changes the flow. When using this system, there is one thermostat control and multiple volume controls, one for each fixture. The advantage of having a thermostat control is that, once the ideal temperature is found by the user, it can remain at that spot (Figure 7.19). The water is then turned on by the volume controls. Whereas each fixture will need a volume control, body sprays can be combined onto one control. Having multiple volume controls is nice because it allows flexibility in what can be on at the same time. One item, multiple items, or everything can be turned on at the same time.

Diverters

Diverters may be used in either pressure balance valve or thermostatic systems, although they are more typically found with a pressure balance valve system. Diverters simply divert where the water is going. In a pressure balance valve system, the diverter typically allows only one item to be on at a time. Diverters are now available that can allow two items to be on at the same time, but that is the maximum. Diverters can also be used with thermostatic systems, but in this case separate volume controls are typically used instead to allow for more flexibility. When a combination shower and tub is used, the diverter is commonly found on the tub spout.

Electronic System

More recently, electronic systems have become available to control all the pieces in the shower. These systems have a digital display where the user can select what should be on and at what temperature. Not only do these systems control the water, but they can control lighting and music in the shower as well. They can even be programmed to save preferences (Figure 7.20).

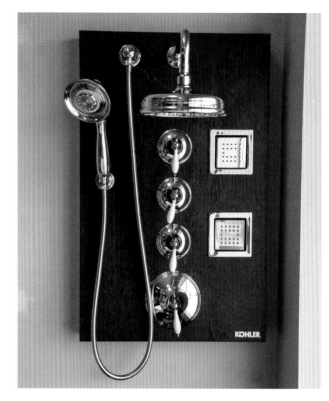

Figure 7.19 Thermostatic shower systems allow the user to leave the temperature set where he or she likes it. The bottom control pictured adjusts the temperature while the three above it control the volumes. *Courtesy of Allied Plumbing by Brad Wilkening.*

Figure 7.20 Electronic systems are a newer technology being used for showers. *Photograph courtesy of Kohler Co.*

SHOWER SPA EXPERIENCE

As mentioned previously, bathrooms are no longer simply a utilitarian space. The spa experience can be incorporated in many aspects of the bathroom. In addition to the tub, the shower can also be designed to replicate a spa shower. It too can have chromatherapy but can also be made to function as a steam shower.

Chromatherapy

Chromatherapy is also available for shower applications. When used in a shower it is typically part of the showerhead or rainhead. As mentioned previously, this is a newer spa experience that people enjoy. The colors can be relaxing or invigorating. Many people enjoy this feature.

Steam Showers

As the spa experience has become popular for people to incorporate into their homes, so have steam showers (Figure 7.21). It is best to include a rainhead in the steam shower because the typical user turns on a cool rainhead after spending time in the steam. When designing a steam shower, it is also important to include a standard showerhead in addition to the rainhead. Most rainheads will have too much water flow for the user to wash their hair. The person needs to be able to get out of the water to lather the shampoo.

To maximize the steam shower experience it is also ideal to include a place to sit. Although built-in benches are best when space allows, fold-down benches are available. Teak fold-down benches are popular for steam showers, or any shower really, where space is limited. If using a fold-down bench, it is important that the contractor be prepared to provide additional support in the wall to hold the bench and the person sitting on it. If the bench is being built, it is best for it to be at least 15 inches deep and between 16 and 19 inches high. It is also important to be sure the bench is not located directly by the steam nozzle so the user does not get burned.

Steam showers get their steam via a steam generator. Different-sized steam generators can be used. To determine what size generator is best to use, the volume, in cubic feet of the shower interior needs to be determined. Once this is figured, the appropriate generator may be selected. Steam showers also need to be entirely enclosed so the steam does not escape. To accomplish this, the shower may have full-height walls or full-height glass. Sometimes, when full-height glass

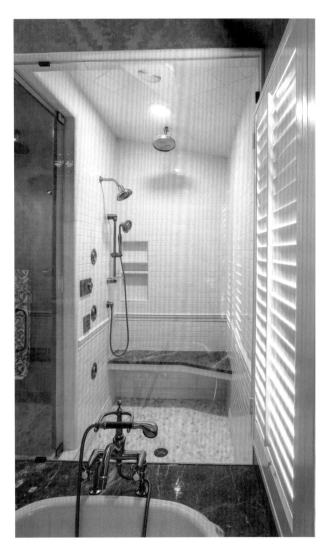

Figure 7.21 Steam showers should have full height glass, a place to sit, and a rainhead. *Courtesy of Drury Design Kitchen & Bath Studio.*

is used, a transom window is incorporated. A transom window may be opened to allow some of the steam out, but not all of it at once.

It's important to be sure that all the surfaces in the steam shower are moisture resistant. This means no exposed drywall in a steam shower. The moisture stays in the shower for a long time, so it is essential to use materials that will hold up.

SHOWER ENCLOSURES

The final part of the shower is the shower enclosure. This refers to the glass used to enclose the shower. Shower enclosures can have sliding doors, swing doors, or even be simply a screen. Shower enclosures can be prefabricated or custom. Obviously, the prefabricated enclosures are more limited in options, but also less expensive. Prefabricated enclosures are made to work with either a tub and shower combination or a shower alone. More styles have appeared lately with smaller tracks for a cleaner, more seamless look. Shower screens do not run the whole length of the shower. They sometimes have both a fixed panel and a smaller glass panel that can swing in or out of the shower (Figure 7.22).

Shower doors are always made to be able to swing out at minimum, although many will swing both in and out. It is crucial that they be able to swing out in the event that someone falls in the shower. If the door only swings in, it would not be possible to move the fallen person out of the shower.

Custom shower enclosures are desirable because they can be made for almost any shower shape or size. The glass is measured once the shower tile and curb are installed. This type allows for a choice between a decorative handle for the door or a towel bar. The exact height of the glass can also be specified, which can be useful. Many glass fabricators will also offer an option of applying a coating to the glass that helps wick the water off the glass better to avoid water spots appearing quickly. The glass fabricator also prefers when the door can be hinged on a full-height wall versus a half wall of glass, as this will lessen the chance of problems later.

Figure 7.22 Shower screens are an alternative option for the shower enclosure. *Courtesy of Pamela Polvere Designs and McShane Fleming Studios, Chicago.*

KITCHEN PLUMBING

SINKS

Now let's take a closer look at the fixtures used in a kitchen. There are various things to consider when selecting a sink. First, will the kitchen have only one main sink, or will there also be a second sink? What should the shape be for the main sink? Homeowners have the choice of one large bowl, double bowls, triple bowls, a bowl and a half, or a specialty shaped bowl. What sink installation style does the client prefer? They can have undermount, self-rimming, apron, or integrated. Finally, what material would the client like the sink to be made of? They can have it in stainless steel, fireclay, cast iron, solid surface, stone, copper, or other metals.

MAIN SINK

The main sink is very important for the kitchen. It makes up one of the corners of the work triangle. It is likely the area traveled to most during the cooking process. Items taken from the refrigerator are brought to the sink to be cleaned and then to the cooking surface. Once the food is prepared, the dirty dishes go in the sink. There are several different styles of sink to choose from. Although some are more practical than others, for the most part the decision can be based on the preference of the homeowner. What material to use, and how many bowls are preferred, are important to discuss with the client in addition to everything else.

Second or Auxiliary Sink

Incorporating a second sink whenever possible is an ideal goal. The sink is a high-task area in the kitchen. Having two sinks allows two people to work in the kitchen at the same time. It's nice to space the second sink away from the main sink, but close to the cooking surface. Secondary sinks are typically used for washing fruits and vegetables while cooking. They are also commonly used if the kitchen has a separate bar area. One thing to keep in mind is the size of the second sink. If a disposal needs to be added to this sink, be sure the sink selected is larger than 12 by 12 inches to accommodate one. Sinks this small can also have a problem with water splashing.

TYPES OF SINKS

As with the various materials discussed previously, there are also many options to choose from when selecting a sink. We will discuss the different styles and shapes of sinks available. As far as materials go, the most popular are stainless steel, cast iron, and fireclay. In addition, copper, stone, solid surface, and other metals are also seen. When selecting a stainless steel sink it is important to pay attention to the **gauge**. Better sinks will have 18-gauge stainless steel or lower. The higher the gauge number, the thinner the steel, and the less the quality will be. Cast iron is a very heavy and strong material. It comes in a wide range of colors and can tolerate abrasive cleaners. It can chip with forceful impact, but will last for a very long time. It is also important to be aware of how many holes are on the back ledge of the sink. It's possible to run out of holes if specifying additional water dispensers or spouts. Sometimes extra holes may be added, but it may be expensive and risky to the sink.

Undermount

Undermount has been the most popular style for sinks lately. They are mounted to the underside of the countertop material (Figure 7.23). Because the edge of the sink cutout will be exposed, the counter material will need to be consistent throughout. A laminate countertop could not have an undermount sink. Many people like this style of sink because it makes cleanup a little easier. There is no rim for food and dirt to accumulate in. Debris may be wiped directly into the sink from the adjacent counter.

Figure 7.23 Undermount sinks have been very popular in kitchens lately, probably because of the sleek look and ease of cleaning. *Photograph courtesy of Kohler Co.*

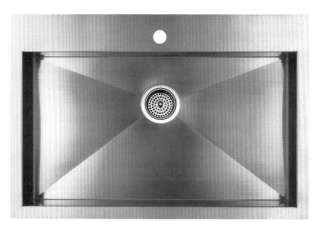

Figure 7.24 Self-rimming sinks are installed by being dropped into the countertop opening. *Photograph courtesy of Kohler Co.*

Self-Rimming

Self-rimming sinks may also be called overmount or drop-in (Figure 7.24). These sinks are mounted on top of the counter material. Because they are on top, a rim is formed around the sink. The disadvantage of this style is that there's a chance for dirt to build up where the sink meets the counter.

Apron

Apron sinks may also be referred to as farm sinks (Figure 7.25). This style sits entirely on top of a cabinet. The cabinet is ordered at a lower height than standard to accomodate the sink's height. The front of this sink is finished, because it is exposed. Although this style was at one time considered traditional, there are now contemporary versions of this style available in stainless steel.

Integrated

Integrated sinks are available when using solid surface material for the countertops. The manufacturer simply makes a sink of the same material and it is part of the countertop. Like the undermount sink, this is a convenient option for easy cleanup. Although it is functionally sensible, this style has not been as popular lately because solid surface has not been a popular counter material to use.

Single Bowl

The single-bowl sink is just as described, one bowl. Single-bowl sinks are typical when using a secondary sink; however, many people even like their main sink to be single bowl. Most of the apron sinks available will be a single-bowl style. The advantage to this sink, like the bowl and a half, is the opportunity to be able to put large stock pots in the sink without trouble.

Double Bowl

A double-bowl sink simply refers to a sink that has two equal-sized bowls. This is a style that has been around for a long time. The double-bowl sink has been dropping in popularity because of the other options available in sinks, such as one large-bowled apron sink or a bowl and a half sink.

Bowl and a Half

The bowl and a half sink has become a popular option for kitchens (Figure 7.26). The benefit of this sink is that the large bowl is typically larger than the bowls in a double-bowl sink. Homeowners like this because they can fit large stock pots into the bigger bowl. The smaller bowl is also beneficial for washing fruits and vegetables while the dirty dishes may be stacked in the larger bowl. For this same reason, many homeowners prefer to have a garbage disposal in the small bowl.

Triple Bowl

There are a few options available for a sink style that has three bowls (Figure 7.27). Triple-bowl sinks are generally quite large, so would certainly require a kitchen large enough to accommodate their use.

Shaped Bowl

In addition to the basic variations in number of bowls, there are also specialty shaped-bowl sinks available. Martini glass and long squiggly sink shapes are just a couple that are offered.

SINK ACCESSORIES

It has become common for sink manufacturers to offer various sink accessories that may be purchased to work with the sink. One option is a bottom grid, which is a grid that sits at the bottom of the sink bowl to help protect it from scratches. Another is a cutting board. The sink manufacturer makes these to fit perfectly in their sink bowls. This makes prepping and cleaning very easy. Rinsing baskets are an additional option. These baskets fit inside the sink bowl to help organize dishes for washing and drying. Strainers are not typically included with the sink. If a disposal is not being used for a drain, be sure to order a good-quality strainer. Drainboards are another accessory option for the sink. Some sinks are available with a drainboard attached, which is a useful feature for those who cook with a lot of fresh food.

Figure 7.25 Apron sinks are available in many styles from traditional to contemporary. *Photograph courtesy of Kohler Co.*

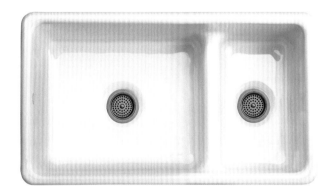

Figure 7.26 Bowl and a half sinks are used frequently because the larger bowl allows bigger stock pots to fit. *Photograph courtesy of Kohler Co.*

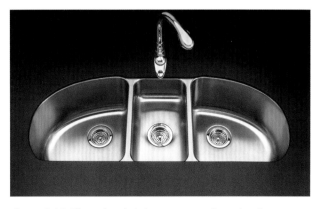

Figure 7.27 Three-bowl sinks are generally rather large. *Photograph courtesy of Kohler Co.*

FAUCETS

Several different styles of faucet are available for the kitchen sink. Faucet styles include single-control, pull-out spray, 8-inch spread, bridge, gooseneck, wall-mounted, bar, touch faucet, professional style, and pot filler. Although these are the basic styles of faucets, any of them may be found in traditional, transitional, or contemporary styles and with numerous finishes. Faucets also may be selected with sustainable or universal design in mind. Faucets with an aerator will mix air with the water flow, making the pressure feel the same but using less water, making them sustainable. The touch faucet option could be used when universal design is a concern. Sustainable and universal design are discussed further in Chapter 3.

Single Control

The single-control faucet is typically the most economical choice for the kitchen. The single-control faucet simply has a handle that is moved to turn the water on and to adjust the temperature. Less expensive versions of this style will occasionally include a plate that sits at the base of the faucet. The plate is necessary for sinks that have three holes to hide these extra holes.

Pull-out Spray

A new addition to the single-control faucet is the pull-out spray option (Figure 7.28). This has become a very popular style for the kitchen faucet. It allows the user to pull out the faucet to use it as a spray as well, instead of having a separate side spray. The pull-out spray has a button or other control to change the spray pattern. They may have a few different water spray patterns as well. Minimally, it will have spray and single-stream options.

Eight-Inch Spread

The handles of an 8-inch spread faucet have 8 inches between them. It provides a clean look, with no plate

Figure 7.28 The pull-out spray faucet is used frequently because it is very functional. This sink also has a bottom grid for protection from scratches. *Courtesy of Abt Electronics by Brad Wilkening.*

Figure 7.29 The bridge faucet is typically a traditional style. *Courtesy of Allied Plumbing by Brad Wilkening.*

sitting on the countertop. It also allows enough space for the handles so that it does not feel cramped when turning the faucet on and off.

Bridge

The bridge-style faucet is usually considered a more traditional style of faucet, although some contemporary versions can be found (Figure 7.29). This type has its handles connected to the spout, forming a bridge. This style will usually have a coordinating side spray included with it.

Gooseneck

A gooseneck faucet is tall with a high arc (Figure 7.30). The advantage of the gooseneck style is that it allows plenty of space beneath it. A gooseneck is deck mounted and typically will swivel.

Figure 7.30 The gooseneck faucet has a high arc. *Courtesy of Abt Electronics by Brad Wilkening.*

Wall Mount

Wall-mounted faucets are simply faucets that are mounted from the wall instead of the deck. They can be found in either traditional or contemporary styles.

Bar Faucet

Bar faucets are smaller faucets that are best used in a bar area or for a secondary sink. Because they are smaller, they generally are not used on a main sink (Figure 7.31). The handles are usually closer together and the spout may not reach as far. Many companies selling faucets will have collections in which bar faucets are an option so they may coordinate with the larger main sink faucet.

Figure 7.31 Bar faucets are typically the smallest available. *Photograph courtesy of Kohler Co.*

Professional Style

Along with the trend toward professional-style appliances also comes the trend toward professional-styled faucets (Figure 7.32). These are larger faucets that look like they might be found in a restaurant. They are generally tall with a high gooseneck. The size of this faucet should be considered when deciding on its location, because of its aesthetic. Its size may also require additional support.

Pot Fillers

A pot filler is a specialty faucet used specifically to fill large pots. Pot fillers are typically placed by the cooking surface so that large pots may be filled as they are sitting on the cooking surface (Figure 7.33). These faucets generally have an elbow or two so they can be pulled out above the pot for use and pushed back out of the way when not in use. These faucets may be wall mounted above the cooking surface or deck mounted on the countertop next to the cooking surface.

Touch Faucet

A newer technology in faucets is the touch faucet (Figure 7.34). There are only a few companies making these faucets, but they are a great consideration for universal design. These faucets turn on and off by simply touching the faucet a certain way. They do require power, so if used be sure to mention it on the electrical plan.

DESIGNER'S DIALOGUE 7.3
"You can sell a faucet for $2,500 or $250, so understand your client's needs and pick something appropriate. It's important to know what pricing is." —*Joanne Giesel, Kitchen and Bath Designer*

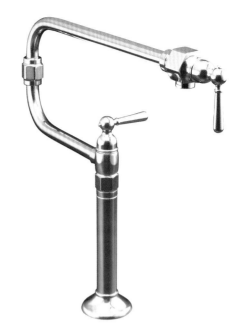

Figure 7.32 Professional faucets are usually rather tall. *Photograph courtesy of Kohler Co.*

Figure 7.33 This is a deck-mount pot filler, but they are also available as wall mount. *Photograph courtesy of Kohler Co.*

Figure 7.34 A touch faucet is a great newer technology, which allows the user to simply tap it to control the flow. *Courtesy of Pamela Polvere Designs and Dennis Jourdan Photography Inc.*

FAUCET ACCESSORIES

Several additional accessories may be specified for use by the sink and faucet. Soap or lotion dispensers, hot water dispensers, and point-of-use water filtration are convenient features to add to a sink area. These accessories have become very popular for kitchen use.

Soap or Lotion Dispensers

Soap or lotion dispensers are a desirable accessory to add. These are installed with a pump at the sink level and a bottle below the sink that holds the soap or lotion (Figure 7.35). This feature can be used to help keep the sink area clean, so the user does not need to store multiple bottles on the countertop.

Hot Water Dispensers

Hot water dispensers are popular with homeowners who like to drink a lot of tea. They are also nice for instant coffee or soups. The water is brought in from the cold water line and heated in a tank located under the sink. The tank stores hot water so it is ready in an instant for use.

Point-of-Use Water Filtration

Before selecting a point-of-use water filtration device it is important to determine the client's goals. There are several types of technologies for these devices and not one will remove all contaminants. It is important first to test the quality of the water to know which contaminants are present if any. The main types of water filtration are distillation, reverse osmosis, ultraviolet treatment, softeners, and filtration filters (Figure 7.36). Any of these systems will require maintenance. It is important to read the manufacturer's guide regarding maintenance.

Figure 7.35 Soap and lotion dispensers are a nice accessory to keep the sink area clean. *Photograph courtesy of Kohler Co.*

Figure 7.36 Point-of-use water filtration is a luxury in the kitchen. *Photograph courtesy of Kohler Co.*

DISTILLATION

Distillation systems heat water until it is steam and collects the water as it condenses, leaving the contaminants behind. This method is effective at removing heavy metals, but some contaminants that vaporize with the water may be carried over with the water vapor. This method is still considered beneficial. Some think the taste is not ideal because the water has no minerals. It can also be one of the slower systems for water filtration.

REVERSE OSMOSIS

Reverse osmosis passes the water through a semipermeable membrane. The membrane allows the water to pass through, but not the impurities and contaminants. The impurities and contaminants are flushed down the drain. Most reverse osmosis systems will also have pre- and postfilters. Replacement of the various cartridges may require a lot of maintenance. Filters with this system may also work slowly.

ULTRAVIOLET TREATMENT

This filtration system uses ultraviolet light to disinfect water. It kills harmful biological contaminants; it does not remove metals, chlorine, or other chemical contaminants. It is best combined with another type of filtration.

SOFTENERS

This type of filtration may also be referred to as *ion exchange*. Basically, it is used to soften hard water. Hardness is caused by a higher concentration of calcium and magnesium. These ions are replaced with sodium or potassium ions to soften the water. When using a softener, the homeowner will occasionally need to add salt to the tank.

FILTRATION FILTERS

Filtration filters are another commonly used way to filter water. In this method, liquids, gases, and matter attach to an absorbent piece. Carbon filters, the most popular filtration filters, reduce bad taste, odor, chlorine, lead, and volatile organic chemicals. They do not remove bacteria, however. They have filter cartridges that need to be replaced periodically.

SUMMARY

It is important to know the basics about household plumbing when assisting clients to select the various plumbing fixtures. It is also necessary to know about the different options that are available for the kitchen and bath. The plumbing fixtures play a big part in the aesthetic and function of the bathroom and kitchen. As with all parts of the kitchen or bath project, it is best to stay up to date with what new things are being offered. Knowing about the newest trends and technologies is the designer's responsibility to the client, and these things are constantly changing and improving.

CHAPTER 7 EXERCISES

I: Specify all the plumbing fixtures and fittings that you would recommend for the Kings, mentioned at the beginning of the chapter. Be prepared to explain why the selections you made are the most appropriate for their situation.

II: Specify all the plumbing fixtures for your dream bath.

CHAPTER 7 DISCUSSION QUESTIONS

1. What is the benefit to a bowl and a half kitchen sink?
2. What are three types of shower control system?
3. How many GPF should a toilet be, based on code?
4. What's a disadvantage of most pedestal sinks?
5. What needs to be done if the existing water heater will not be sufficient?
6. Why is it mandatory that each plumbing fixture be vented?
7. What are the advantages and disadvantages of a two-piece toilet versus a one-piece toilet?

REFERENCES

Godsey, Lisa. *Interior Design Materials and Specifications*. New York, NY: Fairchild Publications, Inc., 2008.

NSF International (2004). Available at http://www.nsf.org. Accessed June 19, 2012.

ADDITIONAL RESOURCE

According to the NSF website, "NSF International is an independent, not-for-profit organization that provides standards development, product certification, auditing, education and risk management for public health and the environment." This website (http://www.nsf.org) has additional information regarding specifics about water filtration.

___ Will the project's existing water heater be sufficient for the new installation?

___What style of faucet is appropriate for the homeowner?

___What style of sink is appropriate for the homeowner?

___What toilet would be the best choice for the homeowner's comfort and cleaning needs? What would be the ideal flushing system for it?

___Would a bidet or bidet seat be a fixture to recommend for the client?

___What would be the ideal type, shape, and material for the tub?

___If an air tub or whirlpool tub is used, be sure to allow access to the pump or motor.

___Does the budget require a shower pan base or can the shower be custom with tile?

___Which system should be used for the shower: pressure balance valve, thermostatic, or electronic?

___Will the shower be a steam shower? If so, be sure to include the steam generator, glass to the ceiling, a rainhead, and a place to sit.

___Should any accessories be specified for the kitchen sink, such as a water purifier, heater, or chiller?

___Does the cooking style of the client require a pot filler to be near the cooking surface?

KEY TERMS

Branch lines: Branch lines are the plumbing lines that run from the plumbing fixtures to the main plumbing line.

Gauge: The measurement of the thickness of stainless steel. The higher the gauge number, the thinner the stainless steel and the less quality it has.

GPF: Gallons per flush, a term used when describing how much water a toilet uses per flush to remove waste.

Integrated sink bowl: A sink bowl that is incorporated into the counter material, making one smooth piece of counter with the sink bowl integrated as part of the counter.

Soil stack: A soil stack is where the waste from plumbing fixtures exits the home. Waste lines run to the soil stack, which removes it to the building drain, which then goes to the sewage line and on to the septic system or public sewer.

Solid surfacing: Man-made material, typically consisting of bauxite, acrylic, or polyester resins, and pigment.

Trench drains: Long trough drains used for zero threshold showers to keep water from flowing into the bathroom.

Water softener: An appliance used to soften water by reducing the amount of calcium, magnesium, and other ions found in hard water.

OBJECTIVES

After reading this chapter, you will:

- Understand the industry standards for drafting kitchen and bathroom floor plans and elevations.

- Be familiar with the variety of software options used to draft kitchen and bathroom drawings.

DESIGN SCENARIO

You have prepared two layout options for the McManus kitchen (refer to Chapter 2). You are now ready to formally draft the plans for the presentation of these layouts. Once the family decides on the proceeding plan, you then will provide elevation drawings so the family members can better visualize the space. Ultimately, the plans drawn also will be used for the installation of the new kitchen. These multifunctional drawings are an essential part of the kitchen project as they will communicate the design to everyone involved, so they must be easy to understand.

1. What scale do you need to draft these drawings in?

2. What is the proper way to draft floor plans and elevations?

3. What software might you use to draft these drawings?

Floor plans and elevations are standard drawings used in kitchen and bath design to communicate the design. Providing clear and concise drawings for the client and installer is crucial to minimize issues that could arise later in the project.

FLOOR PLANS

Floor plans are used for multiple purposes. They convey to the client what the completed kitchen or bath is going to look like. They also serve as construction documents for the installer so that it is clear how to install the project. Some design firms do not initially provide the client with dimensioned floor plans if they have not yet signed a contract with the client. This is done to protect the designer from the client simply taking the design and going elsewhere to purchase the cabinets.

Kitchen and bath drawings are typically drawn at ½-inch scale. This is the best scale because a single room drawn at ½-inch scale typically fits on a page, and allows for the proper amount of detail. Generally, the more detail to be shown, the larger the drawing should be. This is why details are generally shown at either ½- or 1-inch scale, or at an even larger scale. If it is a particularly large kitchen and the floor plan does not fit on a page a smaller scale, such as ¼ inch, can be used.

DESIGNER'S DIALOGUE 8.1

"Any drawings before selling a job should not have dimensions; keep the detail out. Once you get a retainer you can add the dimensions and details. When you're in the design process you should tell the client what is in each cabinet, it gives value to them. You should record this on the drawings because it's nice for them so they can reference it. In a meeting you might be going through everything but after they leave they may forget. They take the drawings home and look at them the next morning and you're not around to discuss it."

—*Lisa McManus, ASID, Kitchen and Bath Designer*

LINE WEIGHTS AND LINE TYPES

Line weights are an important aspect of the kitchen or bath plan because they communicate what is happening in the space. Walls should have the heaviest line weight whereas fine details, such as a pattern on a glass or tile, should be the lightest line weight. Ideally, a drawing should have a minimum of three different line weights. Having various line weights helps the drawing be clear to read.

Types of lines used in kitchen and bath drawings are slightly different from those shown for a kitchen layout from a general interior designer. General interior designers show the wall cabinets as dashed lines, solid countertops as lines, and none of the individual cabinets. The kitchen and bath designer needs to show each individual cabinet that will fit in the space. This is important so that the proper cabinets are ordered and they are installed correctly. In this method of drawing, base cabinets, or anything hidden under the countertop, are shown with a dashed line. Wall cabinets, tall cabinets, and countertops are shown with a solid line. Items on the ceiling, such as skylights or soffits, are shown with a lighter dashed line than the hidden objects (Table 8.1).

CENTERLINES

Centerlines are a component of the plans that are very helpful for both the designer and the installer. When drafting a floor plan it is ideal to centerline windows, plumbing fixtures, and appliances. The window centerlines are helpful to the designer when space planning. If the designer wants to center an item, such as a sink on a window, it makes the math simpler to determine what cabinetry will fit correctly. Window centerlines are important to the installer especially if new windows are being installed. Plumbing fixture and appliance centerlines are beneficial to the installer so that they have less chance of error in locating these items. When the designer provides the appliance centerlines along with the appliance specifications, as described in Chapter 6, it makes the installation process easier and more seamless.

TABLE 8.1 LINE WEIGHTS	
Line Weight	Where to Use Line Weight
Lightest	Fine details such as glass, wood grain, seams on cabinet doors, patterns on tile
Medium thickness	Cabinets, countertops, furniture, sinks, appliances, notes, and dimensions
Thickest	Walls and windows
Dashed	Hidden objects such as base cabinets or undercounter appliances
Lighter dashed	Soffits, walls removed, skylights or other items on the ceiling

DIMENSIONS

Dimensions are a crucial part of the floor plan. In kitchen and bath design, dimensions for plans should be in inches instead of feet and inches. There are typically three levels of dimension stringers on a wall with multiple dimensions. The first stringer is closest to the wall, dimensions walls, windows, and doors. The second stringer out should dimension all the necessary centerlines. The third stringer is away from the wall, and should give an overall wall dimension. Aisles and walkways should be dimensioned. Although sometimes unavoidable, it is important when dimensioning to keep the dimension stringers out of the drawing as much as possible. Leaving dimension stringers to intersect with wall lines makes the drawing confusing to read.

NOTES AND CABINET INFORMATION

Final kitchen or bath floor plans should include the **nomenclature** for all of the cabinets. Cabinet nomenclature is discussed in detail in Chapter 5. It is best to include this information on the floor plan so that it is very clear where to place cabinets and accessories.

For the bathroom drawings, items such as whirlpool tubs or steam showers should be noted. This emphasizes

that these items are included, making it easier for any electric and/or plumbing that these appliances require to be located properly. It is useful to note the sizes of the shower and/or tub on the plan. It is helpful for the client, who may take the drawings home and forget what was discussed in the meeting with the designer.

It is also beneficial to make other notes on the plan about any construction or changes needed. If walls are being added or removed a key should be provided indicating these walls. Heights of new walls should be noted because they can be full height, or half height. Construction changes, such as removing soffits or relocating vents, should be noted. The ceiling height is important to note. In the bathroom this becomes important for the designer when considering how high to take tile in a shower or how high glass will be for a steam shower. In the kitchen the ceiling height is important with regard to the height of the wall and tall cabinets.

Other items that should be included on the floor plan are elevation tags and room labels for spaces adjacent to the kitchen or bathroom. This helps the person reading the plan orient where everything is located. Some designers like to include a north-pointing arrow to indicate direction as well, but this is not mandatory.

FLOOR PLAN EXAMPLES

Let's take a look at some examples of finished floor plans for the kitchen and bath.

An example of a finished floor plan for a kitchen is shown in Figure 8.1. Another example of a kitchen floor plan is presented in Figure 8.2.

Figure 8.3 is an example of a finished floor plan for a bathroom. It has the key components described earlier. The windows and plumbing are centerlined. There are three levels of dimension stringers. All the cabinet information is included on the floor plan. Proper line weights and types have been used. Adjacent rooms are labeled and elevation tags are shown.

Another example of a finished floor plan is shown in Figure 8.4. It too has all the elements discussed previously.

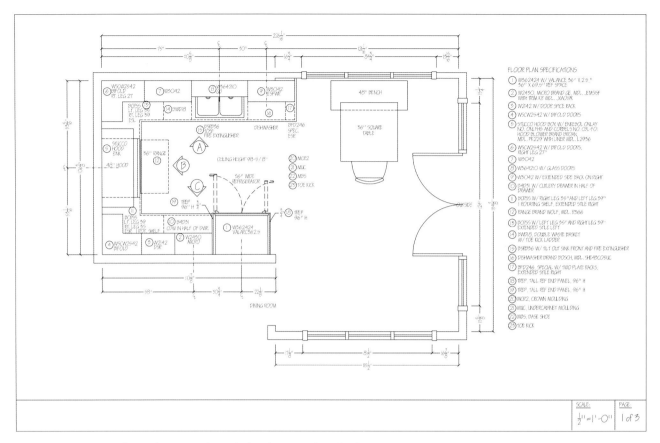

Figure 8.1 A kitchen floor plan example with the elements described.

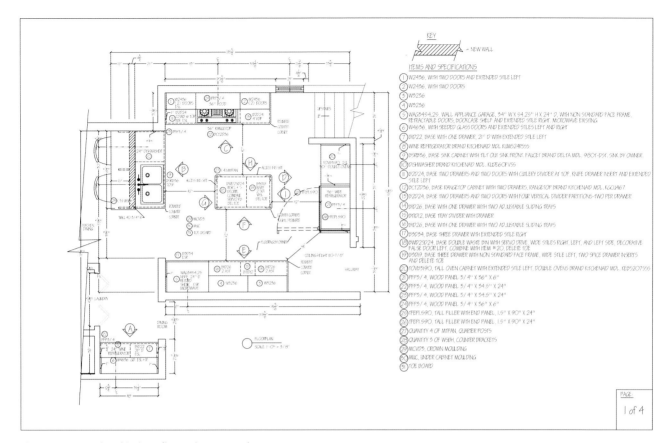

Figure 8.2 Another kitchen floor plan example.

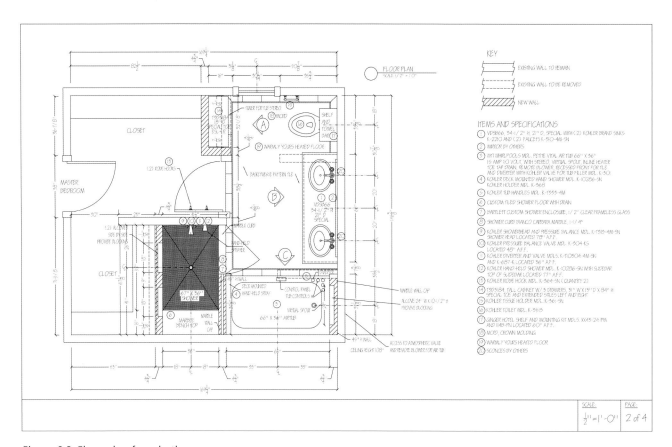

Figure 8.3 Floor plan for a bathroom.

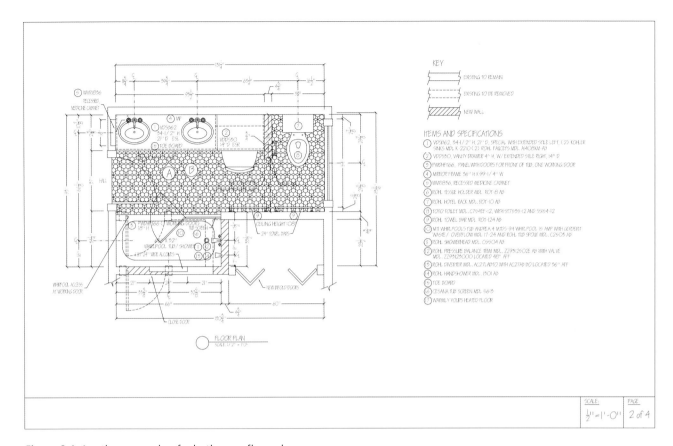

Figure 8.4 Another example of a bathroom floor plan.

ELEVATIONS

Elevations commonly are used to convey what the completed design should look like. Combined with floor plans, the client and installer can have a thorough understanding of what the space will look like.

Elevations show the exact door style that will be used for the cabinetry in the space. This is very useful to show the clients, so they can see how the look of the door style may change on different cabinet sizes.

It is also standard that each individual cabinet will be dimensioned. This is helpful not only for the client, but for the installer as well. The cabinets will need to be sorted when delivered to the job site. This makes the task of locating the cabinets much easier.

Elevations also should show centerlines for the windows, plumbing fixtures, and appliances, as the floor plan does. This again makes it very easy for the installer to locate exactly where these items need to be placed.

Elevations in kitchens often end up showing a section. When showing the full wall of cabinets, a section is shown if the cabinets turn the corner.

ELEVATION EXAMPLES

Let's look at some examples of elevations. In Figure 8.5, notice how elevation B is showing two sections, one at each corner. These sections are simply part of the elevation. They are showing that the cabinetry turns the corner and is coming toward the viewer. In these sections, we see the profile of the crown molding and undercabinet molding. An *X* is drawn in the wall and base cabinet to indicate that it is a section, and not a side view of the cabinetry. We also see the countertop overhang on both sides as the countertops also turn the corners and come toward the viewer. Notice that while dimensioning these corner cabinets, each entire cabinet's width is dimensioned. It is not necessary to dimension the cabinet depth because each is a standard 24-inch deep cabinet. If they were custom or special-depth cabinets it would be a good idea to give their dimensions.

Look at elevation E in Figure 8.6. Notice that the wall cabinet to the far right is showing what is happening in the interior. This is a custom cabinet with a fixed shelf inside. For this instance, it was helpful to show this information so the client and installer could see it. Both elevations are also showing the appliances centerlined, making it easy for the contractor and installer.

Figure 8.7 is an example of two elevations from the bath project shown previously in Figure 8.3. Elevation B shows the vanity area and elevation C shows the tub and shower areas.

Figure 8.8 is an elevation from the bath project shown previously in Figure 8.4. The "R.O." listed on the left-side dimension stringers is indicating the rough opening for the recessed medicine cabinet.

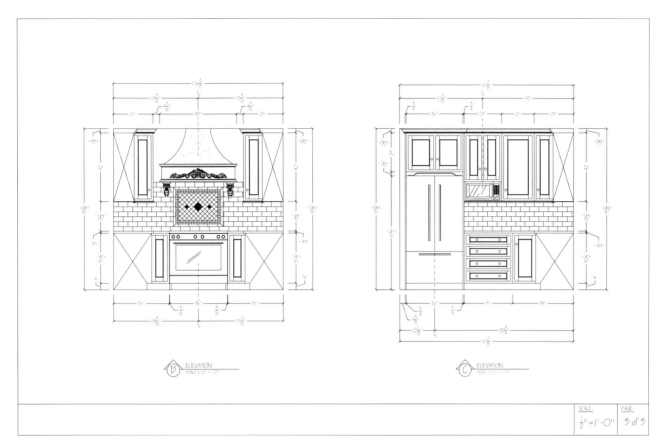

Figure 8.5 Elevations for the floor plan from Figure 8.1.

Figure 8.6 Elevations for the floor plan in Figure 8.2.

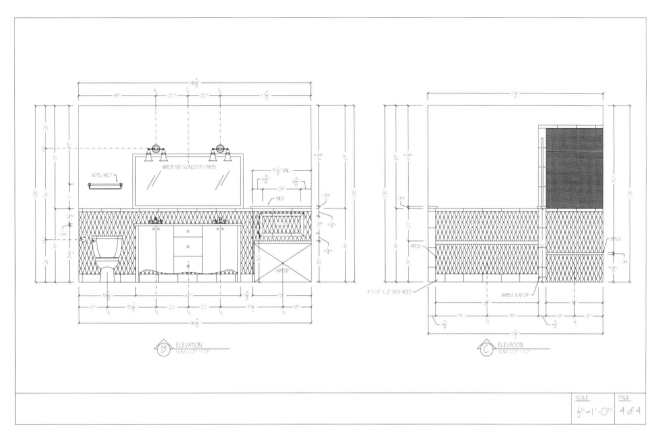

Figure 8.7 Elevations for the floor plan in Figure 8.3.

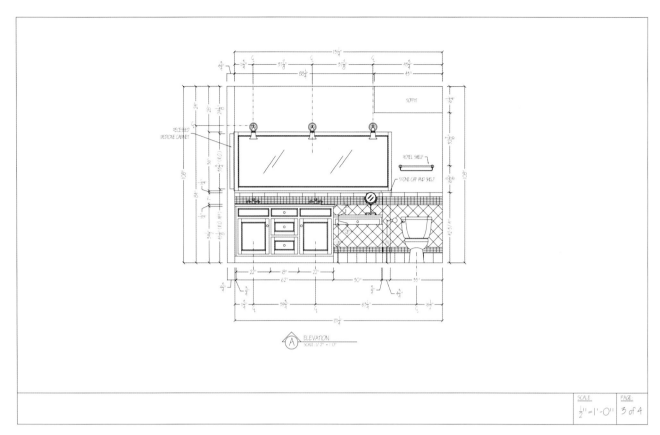

Figure 8.8 Elevations for the floor plan in Figure 8.4.

PERSPECTIVES

Perspectives are not as commonly used for kitchen or bath design as floor plans and elevations. When they are drawn, it is typically by using software with three-dimensional capabilities. Some designers may sketch a perspective in front of a client to communicate a design. Formal rendered perspectives are rarely drawn because of the time required to produce them. Having the ability to sketch a perspective in front of a client is a useful skill to have (Figure 8.9). As with anything, it takes practice to improve one's ability to sketch perspectives.

DESIGNER'S DIALOGUE 8.4

"If you have the opportunity, three-dimensional drawings can help the client visualize your ideas better. They can imagine it easier than from a floor plan or elevation."

—*Gladys Schanstra, CKD, CBD, Allied ASID, Kitchen and Bath Designer*

Figure 8.9 An example of a hand-drawn perspective with rendering. Although not frequently used, this really helps the client visualize the space. *Perspective courtesy of Lisa McManus, ASID.*

STANDARD SOFTWARE

Software is being used more and more for kitchen and bath plans. Those still doing hand-drafting are typically the designers who have been in the business for a long time. The younger generation of designers is entering the work force with a strong knowledge of these technologies and putting them to use to provide professional drawings to their clients.

One of the major benefits of using software for drawings is the ability it gives to easily make revisions. It is much more difficult to make revisions when working with hand-drafted plans and elevations. In addition, if the client changes his or her mind after revisions have been made and decides to go back to the original plan, the designer will have all versions of the plans saved and be able to easily retrieve them.

Remember that software should be used to draft the plans; however, it should not be used for space planning. As mentioned in Chapter 2, it is always better to determine the design by hand on trace paper. Work out a functional design first before formally drafting it for presentation.

AUTOCAD

Computer-aided design (CAD) is frequently used by design firms for drafting plans. A popular program for this purpose is **AutoCAD**. One major benefit of using AutoCAD is the ability to work with an architect's plans. It is common for the architect to e-mail a building shell so that the designer can space plan on the basis of the shell. The designer can then return the plan to the architect with the kitchen or bath design, so that he or she can include it in with the plan set.

Another benefit to using AutoCAD is the number of blocks available. Some manufacturers provide Auto-CAD blocks of their products on their websites, making it very easy to show exactly what the space will look like. Many cabinet companies have blocks of their cabinets, door styles, moldings, and other items. Appliance manufacturers provide plan and elevation views of their products. Plumbing fixture companies offer blocks of their sinks, tubs, and other items. For designers using AutoCAD, it is a good idea to develop and maintain a library of the blocks most frequently used, which makes it easy to quickly draft a detailed plan.

20-20

20-20 software is used in the kitchen and bath design industry. 20-20 is commonly used by designers who work with stock or semicustom cabinetry. However, designers who work primarily with custom cabinetry often decide not to use 20-20 because it is not as useful a tool when including custom components. This software is capable of providing not only floor plan and elevation views, but also three-dimensional views. Some manufacturers have drawings of their products available to import into 20-20 drawings. AutoCAD files can be imported into 20-20 as well. Another benefit of this software is its pricing capabilities. A project can be estimated and have an itemized list of products. This is another reason why designers with custom cabinetry do not often use this software; custom pieces require a special quote, which would not be available from this software.

CHIEF ARCHITECT

Chief Architect produces software that some kitchen and bath designers choose to use. This software has both two- and three-dimensional capabilities. It can also help with cost estimates because it has a materials list feature.

SUMMARY

Clear and concise floor plans and elevations are essential to successfully communicate a kitchen or bathroom design to the client and the installer. The drafting style used for kitchen and bathroom drawings is different from that used by general residential interior designers because these drawings need to be more detailed. Although the general industry standards have been discussed here, you may find that drafting styles vary slightly from design firm to design firm. What is most important is that everyone involved understands exactly what the drawings are intending to convey.

CHAPTER 8 DISCUSSION QUESTIONS

1. Why is ½-inch scale used for kitchen and bath drawings?
2. Why is it a good idea to show the actual door style in the elevations that is going to be used?
3. Why is it a good idea to include centerlines for appliances and plumbing fixtures?
4. What is the benefit of drafting the drawings with computer software?
5. What is another good resource for drawing standards for the kitchen and bath designer?

CHAPTER 8 EXERCISES

I: Review the two options you designed for the McManus family in Chapter 2. Select the better of the two floor plan options and draft the floor plan and elevations according to the standards discussed in this chapter.
II: Look at the two options you designed for Mr. Amezquita in Chapter 2. Select the better of the two floor plan options and draft the floor plan and elevations according to the standards discussed in this chapter.

ADDITIONAL RESOURCE

Newton, David with Kelly Hayes. *Kitchen and Bath Drawing*. Hackettstown, NJ: NKBA, 2006. http://www.nkba.org

CHAPTER 8: FLOOR PLAN CHECKLIST

___Floor plans and elevations are drafted at ½-inch scale.

___Centerline dimensions for all appliances and plumbing fixtures have been included.

___Dimensions are included for all walls, doors, windows, and aisles.

___Dimensions are written in inches.

___All necessary elevation tags and keys have been included.

___The items and specifications list has been included on the floor plan.

___The exact door style being used for the project is shown on the elevations.

___All appropriate construction notes are included.

KEY TERMS

AutoCAD: Computer-aided design software used by design firms for drafting plans.

Centerlines: Important focal points in a design plan for accurate installation of fixtures and appliances in a space.

Dimensions: A crucial part of the floor plan measured in inches instead of feet and inches.

Elevations: A view looking straight at a structure or group of objects to convey what the completed design should look like.

Floor plans: Layout of a space to show the detailed specifications usually drawn at ½-inch or 1-inch scale.

Line weights: Types of lines used in kitchen and bath drawings to indicate the details of the space.

Nomenclature: Abbreviations used in the cabinet industry to refer to specific types of cabinets.

Perspectives: Three-dimensional drawings that can help clients visualize the designers ideas and plans.

CHAPTER 9 KITCHEN AND BATH DESIGN: LIGHTING AND ELECTRICAL PLANS

OBJECTIVES

After reading this chapter, you will:

- Recognize the various types of lighting that make for a well-designed lighting scheme.

- Grasp electrical requirements for a kitchen and bathroom project.

- Know how to effectively communicate the lighting and electric information on a plan to the electrician.

- Be familiar with electrical code requirements for the kitchen and bath.

DESIGN SCENARIO

You've been working with your clients, the Larsens, who have decided on their kitchen layout. They now need to know what type of lighting and electrical work will be required for the space. It is your responsibility to plan this for them and communicate it by a lighting and electrical plan for the electrician. The Larsens are a family of five, who prepare a great number of home-cooked meals. Everyone in the family helps out, including Grandma, who frequently visits. The Larsens want lighting that will accommodate the various users, but that also makes a design statement.

1. What types of lighting do you need to include?

2. What can you do to help Grandma see sufficiently while helping?

3. What can you do to make a statement with their lighting?

ighting and electrical are an essential aspect of the kitchen or bath project. Many tasks occur in kitchens and baths, which require more lighting than other rooms in the home. These items have a significant effect on the result of the overall design of a space. Ambient, task, and accent lighting must be provided for any space. In addition, outlets, switches, and any special power needs must be communicated to the electrician. Local building codes need to be followed to be in compliance. All of these items are shown on the lighting and electrical plan, so that the installation can move along as smoothly as possible.

MEASURING LIGHTING LEVELS

Measurements of lighting are done in **lumens** or **foot-candles.** Watts are not an accurate measure of light because they indicate the power used, not the light output. Derived from the International System of Units (SI), a lumenisa unit that measures the amount of light perceived by the human eye. A foot-candle is a non-SI unit that measures luminance or light intensity. These measurements are based on a light source striking a surface. A foot-candle is equal to 1 lumen per square foot, that is, it is equivalent to 1 lumen spread evenly over a 1-square-foot area.

It can be beneficial to work with a lighting specialist on larger and more complicated projects.

LIGHT COLOR TEMPERATURE

Before we discuss the specific types of lighting that should be accounted for in any space, let's look at some general considerations. First, the light color temperature used should be selected so that it is similar to the temperature of the lighting throughout the house. A noticeable difference in lighting temperature from room to room is not pleasing to the eye. Next, think

Comparing Lighting Sources					
Type	Output, lumens	Color Temperature (•K)	Efficiency, Lum/W	Pros	Cons
Incandescent	126 (15W) – 1380 (100W) 6100 (300W)	2550 – 2800	8.4 13.8 20.3	Low initial cost. Good color. Convenient. Dimmable. Many lamp sizes & shapes.	High ultimate cost. Short life. Energy Produces heat.
Fluorescent (straight tubes)	1350 (24") – 2900 (48")	3000	58 – 85	Efficient. Long life. Choice of light color. Distributes light evenly. Choice of lamp sizes & shapes.	Magnetic ballasts noisy, flicker and not dimmable.
Compact Fluorescent	900 – 1100	2700	40 – 60	Efficient. Long life. Choice of light color. Choice of lamp sizes & shapes.	First cost expensive, compared to incandescent.
Halogen	2500 (100W) –	2850 – 3000	25 –	Efficient. Full-spectrum white color similar to sunlight. Small shapes.	High first cost than incandescent. Low-voltage halogen lamps need a transformer.
Xenon (festoon mini-bulbs)	50 (5W) 120 (10W)	3000	10 12	Full-spectrum white color similar to sunlight. Small shapes work with under-counter applications.	High first cost than incandescent. Need transformer.

Color Temperature of Light Sources

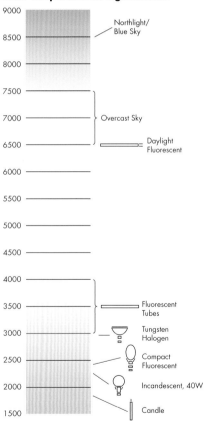

Figure 9.1 Degrees Kelvin are used to describe the color temperature of light in comparison with daylight.

about the colors of the main surfaces in the space. Darker finishes absorb more light, just as lighter finishes reflect more light. This means that if a kitchen is all white, it requires much less light than one with dark wood cabinets.

Lamp temperature is measured in degrees **Kelvin.** The temperature is a description of the whiteness of light. Bluish-white light has a high color temperature and yellowish-white light has a low color temperature. Higher degrees Kelvin indicate cooler light and lower degrees Kelvin correlate with warmer light. Daylight is the best type of light to use for determining the true color of materials. Light sources other than daylight are rated in comparison with true daylight. The **Color Rendering Index** (CRI) is the rating used to score how similar a light is to daylight. Daylight scores as 100 percent and the more similar a light source is to daylight the higher its CRI score. A light source with a 90 percent rating is considered high.

The lamp temperature should be considered not only at the stage of designing the lighting scheme, but before that, when the materials are being selected. As mentioned previously, it is best to maintain consistent lighting throughout the home. Be sure to take this into consideration when viewing finish samples, because the lighting at the showroom where you meet the clients may be different from in their home (Figure 9.1).

ADDITIONAL LIGHTING CONSIDERATIONS

Think about the reflectance of the various surfaces of fixtures in the space; the light will bounce off smoother surfaces, such as a mirror. This can affect the type of mood that you would like to evoke. Flexibility in lighting should also be provided. While considering the options of lighting for various moods, don't forget about the overall goal of the lighting scheme.

AMBIENT LIGHTING IN THE KITCHEN OR BATH

Ambient, or general, lighting is needed in any space. The purpose of this type of lighting is simply to light the space enough so that users may move about the area without bumping into anything or hurting themselves. These are typically the lights that are first turned on when entering a room (Figure 9.2).

The most popular fixtures used for ambient lighting in residences today are recessed downlights. They are clean looking and provide even light distribution. A

Figure 9.2 The recessed incandescent lights in this kitchen are acting as ambient lighting. *Courtesy of Pamela Polvere Designs and Dennis Jourdan Photography Inc.*

general rule for recessed downlight location is to place them 18 to 36 inches from the wall. Although not as popular, surface-mount fixtures are also used. In the past, track lights were popular for ambient and task light, but this type is ideal for accent. Track lights are a poor option for ambient lighting because they cast shadows.

Another option for ambient lighting is linear **luminaires** mounted above the cabinets. This type of lighting is considered indirect because the light is directed toward the ceiling and then bounces off it, creating light for the space.

The ambient layer of light works well to fill in any areas not covered by the task or accent lighting, which helps to minimize shadows. When working on a lighting scheme, it is usually beneficial to fill in the ambient lighting after the task and accent lighting have been accounted for. Because bathrooms are typically small spaces, they do not usually require a large quantity of ambient lights.

TASK LIGHTING IN THE KITCHEN

Task lighting is lighting that provides illumination for performing tasks. In the kitchen, where many sharp and potentially dangerous items are used, adequate task lighting is crucial (Figure 9.3).

Figure 9.3 This kitchen has task lighting via undercabinet lights as well as strategically placed recessed incandescents. *Courtesy of Pamela Polvere Designs and Cindy Trim Photography.*

If downlights are being used for task lighting it is important to consider the location to avoid shadowing. If used, downlights should be placed in front of the person, directly above the work surface. Downlights located above or behind where a person may be standing will cast shadows.

Undercabinet lights, those applied to the underside of wall cabinets, are a good option for task lighting. These fixtures light the work surface directly. They are available in many different styles and lamp sources. These lights can be found as linear or puck light models. When using incandescent linear lights, it is important to know that they will produce heat that could affect items stored on the bottom shelf. If using this type of lighting, be sure to inform the client so they know not to store perishable items on the bottom shelf.

When placing undercabinet lights, how reflective the backsplash and countertop are should be considered. If the countertop has a matte finish, it is ideal to locate the undercabinet lights toward the front of the cabinet. This way the light may send light toward the backsplash, which will then bounce the light on the work surface without a glare. When both the backsplash and counter are shiny, the undercabinet lighting becomes more challenging because the shiny surfaces will cause much light reflection. These lights can be recessed into the cabinet and have louvers covering the face of the lamps.

DESIGNER'S DIALOGUE 9.1

"When providing task lighting by a seating area where you have a two-level island and are using a mini, the light has to land in between both surfaces or you'll get a glare. It also ensures that the lighting is not directly overhead."
—*Lisa McManus, ASID, Kitchen and Bath Designer*

TASK LIGHTING IN THE BATH

Again, task lighting is lighting provided for a specific task. In the bathroom, several tasks require sufficient lighting (Figure 9.4). Shaving, applying makeup, brushing teeth, and blow-drying hair are just a few of the more common tasks performed in the bathroom.

Most of these tasks typically take place at the mirror. Having a well-lit mirror, generally above the sink, is very important. The best type of lighting at a mirror is when the light is at the side of the user's face, approximately at cheek level. Although average heights can be used, it is best to determine the measurement based

Figure 9.4 Lighting located at the side of the user's face makes the most ideal task lighting for a bathroom mirror. *Courtesy of Pamela Polvere Designs and Dennis Jourdan Photography Inc.*

on the client's height. Public spaces that are used by a variety of people of different sizes typically use average heights. Alternatively, the homeowner will inform the designer who exactly uses the bathroom, so the space can be planned accordingly. It also is important to have a thorough understanding of the tasks done in the bathroom that are specific to the homeowner. This information should be gathered in the beginning stages of the project with the client survey as discussed in Chapter 1.

Figure 9.5 This kitchen has accent lighting inside the wall cabinet above the sink, to highlight its contents. *Courtesy of Pamela Polvere Designs and Dennis Jourdan Photography Inc.*

ACCENT/FOCAL LIGHTING

Accent, or focal, lighting is the third layer of lighting found in any space. Accent lighting can be used to highlight architectural details or decorative items (Figure 9.5). Many homeowners have collections that they like to display in their kitchens. Be sure to highlight these collections as these are what make each space unique and personal.

The kitchen or bath may have a textured surface, such as a brick wall, that would be nice to highlight. To show off the texture, place light directed at a small angle onto the surface. If the light is placed too far away the brick wall will appear smooth, not accenting the texture.

DESIGNER'S DIALOGUE 9.3

"The designer has to consider the effects of the lighting. A recessed can less than a foot away from a cabinet will cause a scallop on the cabinet. Sometimes a contemporary kitchen may call for that, but a traditional kitchen may not and you're adding a glare of light. If you are placing a can and want to avoid the scallop effect place it 18 inches or more away."
—*Lisa McManus, ASID, Kitchen and Bath Designer*

LIGHT SOURCES

Now that we know the various layers of lighting that should be accounted for, let's look at the specific types of light sources that can be used to accomplish these lighting layers and our overall lighting scheme. As mentioned earlier, the color of the light source is a crucial consideration. What light source is used should be determined on the basis of the existing lights in the home, the purpose of the light, what it will be lighting, the overall lighting scheme goal, and any pertinent codes. The major types of lighting used for a kitchen include incandescent, fluorescent, compact fluorescent, halogen, xenon, and light-emitting diodes (LEDs) (see Table 9.1).

INCANDESCENT

Incandescent lights have traditionally been the most common type of lamp used in households. These lamps are easily dimmed and inexpensive. They have many shapes and wattages available to choose from. The disadvantages are that they have a short life and they are the least efficient of the lamp options.

FLUORESCENT

Fluorescent lamps create light by way of electricity that passes through mercury and inert gases inside a glass envelope. They require a ballast to start the lamp and regulate the current. New, electronic ballasts have increased the energy efficiency of fluorescent lamps and eliminated the hum or flickering often associated with these lights. Fluorescent lamps last much longer than incandescents and use less energy to render the same amount of illumination. They also do not give off as much heat as incandescents and have more color variety. When dimmed, they do not change color as much as incandescents do. The disadvantages are that some will hum due to inferior ballasts. They are generally larger light sources, and typically will not be used for situations needing a concentrated beam. They also have difficulty lighting in cold temperatures. They may take several minutes to warm up to provide their full output.

COMPACT FLUORESCENT

Compact fluorescent lamps, referred to as CFLs, are smaller versions of fluorescents. They are more energy efficient and last longer than incandescent lamps. CFLs cost more, but will last longer. Turning them on and off frequently will lessen their life.

HALOGEN

Halogen is a type of incandescent lamp. Although halogen has a whiter light when fully on, it becomes more yellow, similar to a standard incandescent, when it is dimmed. Halogen lights are smaller than standard incandescents and produce more light. They too come in a variety of shapes and sizes and provide better control than other sources. Halogen lights also are capable of a variety of **beam spreads.** The disadvantages of halogen lights are that dimming them may shorten their life; the glass envelope must not be touched without wearing gloves; and they have to be shielded in a glass envelope to protect users from its heat.

XENON

Xenon lamps contain xenon gas inside a glass envelope. They are similar to halogen lamps in size, but are cooler to the touch. Xenon lamps are dimmable, provide ample light output, and are available in **line-voltage** or low-voltage systems.

LEDS

LEDs are being used more and more in residences as the technology is being continuously improved. It is a preferable light source for its energy efficiency, long life, and color temperature. As they continue to gain popularity, the price is decreasing, which combined with a long life makes them a very good choice.

LAMPS

The various types of lamps described in the preceding sections also are available in many different sizes, configurations, and wattages. Which type of lamp is used depends on the fixture (Figure 9.6).

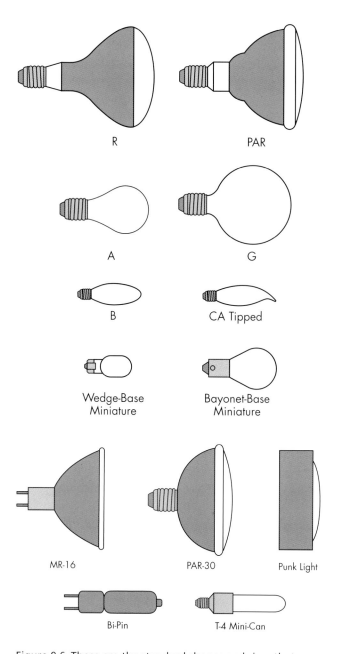

Figure 9.6 These are the standard shapes and sizes that can be found for incandescent and halogen lamps.

TABLE 9.1 LIGHTING SOURCE COMPARISON

Type of Light	Pros	Cons
Incandescent	1.Inexpensive initially 2. Good color 3. Dimmable 4. Available in many lamp shapes and sizes	1. Short life 2. Inefficient 3. Produces heat
Fluorescent	1. Efficient 2. Long life 3. Good choice of color 4. Good selection of lamp shapes and sizes	1. Initial cost more expensive than incandescent
Halogen	1. Efficient 2. Color similar to sunlight 3. Small lamp shapes	1. Initial cost more expensive than incandescent 2. Low-voltage version needs transformer
Xenon	1. Color similar to sunlight 2. Small lamp shapes	1. Initial cost more expensive than incandescent 2. Requires transformer
LED	1. Long life 2. Efficient 3. Dimmable 4. Variety of color temperatures available	1. Initial cost more expensive than incandescent

Abbreviation: LED, light-emitting diode.

NATURAL LIGHT

Natural lighting is another important consideration when planning the lighting scheme. Before deciding on the type and location of lights to be used, consider what type of daylight the space receives. Using natural light as much as possible helps to conserve energy (Figure 9.7). If the project budget and design allow, it can be beneficial to consider adding windows. Light fixtures can then be specified to make up for less light on overcast days or at night. Windows can be added in many creative ways besides the standard windows typically seen. Clerestory windows, which are located high on the wall, allow daylight to enter while maintaining privacy. Smaller windows can even been installed within a kitchen backsplash, allowing for a potentially wonderful view from the kitchen. When factoring the daylight, be sure to consider the direction of the exposure. Warmer light will be seen from western and southern directions, and cooler light will be seen from eastern and northern directions.

Figure 9.7 This kitchen is maximizing the use of natural light with its generous windows. *Courtesy of Pamela Polvere Designs and Dennis Jourdan Photography Inc.*

LIGHTING CONTROLS

The lighting controls allow the user to turn the lights on and off or to dim them. Most commonly, switches are used, although there are other systems. Be sure always to locate switches on the unhinged side of the door: It is not ideal for the user to have to reach around the back of a door in a dark room to find a switch. It is best that the lighting scheme provide flexibility for the users of the space. Having the three main types of lighting contributes to this but is not enough. It is best to specify lights and switches that are dimmable to allow for different light levels in the space. Having dimmable switches also helps to provide a more energy-efficient lighting scheme. It is also nice to provide multiple switches so that certain lights may be turned on and off independent of other lights.

In addition to dimmable switches, three-way or four-way switches also should be considered. These switches allow the lights to be controlled from multiple locations. Three-way switches control the lights from two locations, and four-way switches control the lights from three locations.

Companies now have what they refer to as "scenes," which are preset lighting levels. The homeowner can set different "scenes" as they like to achieve different uses for the space. The lighting level for the whole family cooking together in the kitchen should be much brighter than the lighting level for an intimate dinner in the kitchen. This system of lighting can be controlled from a panel on the wall or even with a remote control.

DESIGNER'S DIALOGUE 9.4
"Lighting systems have become popular. Dimmable light fixtures are very popular. Too much lighting is better than not enough because you can always dim them." —Gail Drury, CMKBD, Kitchen and Bath Designer

LOW VOLTAGE

Low-voltage systems use less than 50 volts and need a **transformer** to change line voltage (120 volts) to these lower voltages. The most commonly used systems are 12 volts, but 6- and 24-volt systems are also used. Some low-voltage fixtures such as track lights or recessed ceiling lights include built-in transformers, but smaller fixtures become too small and need a remote transformer. The advantages of low-voltage lighting are the size and beam spread. They are available in very small sizes and come with a variety of beam spreads, from narrow to wide. The disadvantage of low-voltage lighting is when a remote transformer is used. The lights will become dimmer the farther away this transformer is placed. Code requires that the transformer be accessible in the event of a malfunction. All low-voltage systems will produce a hum that comes from the transformer, lamp, dimmer, or all three. Transformers can be installed in a remote location to avoid hearing this hum.

TRANSFORMERS

Transformers are used to convert house voltage to a low-voltage system. There are two types: magnetic and electronic. Magnetic transformers are larger and fail less often. Electronic transformers, on the other hand, are more compact and therefore used for small fixtures.

LINE VOLTAGE

Line voltage refers to the home voltage which uses the standard 120 volts. Transformers are not needed; the fixtures are connected directly to the line voltage.

DESIGNER'S DIALOGUE 9.5
"I like to think of the lighting as the jewelry. A simple piece can really draw the eye and make it a focal point. You can make a statement. I like to use fixtures in a nontraditional way such as a pendant over a vanity, work space, or something you want to accent." —Gladys Schanstra, CKD, CBD, Allied ASID, Kitchen and Bath Designer

OUTLETS

Outlets are needed in any space. In the kitchen and the bath, it is important that each outlet be a ground-fault circuit interrupter **(GFCI)**. This type of outlet is used in areas where water can come into contact with the outlet. If there is an imbalance in the outlet due to water, it automatically turns off to prevent electrical shock.

Companies are now making outlet strips. These are strips of outlets that can be installed on the underside of wall cabinets, at the back. These are convenient in kitchens because they keep the outlets from interfering with any specialty backsplash design.

For the bathroom, it is always important to consider the tasks that will need outlets. People commonly use hair dryers, hair curlers or straighteners, electric toothbrushes, and electric razors, to name a few. The designer should ask how many of these items are used at the same time to help determine how many outlets are adequate and where to locate them for the easiest convenience.

EXHAUST FANS

Exhaust fan are very important for bathrooms. They are used to remove both moisture and odor from a bathroom. The power of the exhaust fan is determined by its cubic feet per minute **(CFMs).** The CFMs refer to how much air is moved from the space. The minimum suggested air movement for a bathroom exhaust fan is 100 CFMs. For every square foot of the bathroom, at least 1 CFM is necessary. In the past, exhaust fans were always loud and likely annoying. Today, many exhaust fans are

Figure 9.8 Here is an example of a bath exhaust fan, which is required for all baths.

much quieter; some can barely be heard (Figure 9.8). There also are exhaust fans that automatically turn on when they detect a certain level of humidity. They may have a timer so that the fan will run for a certain length of time and then automatically shut off. Some are available with a light as part of the unit. The bath exhaust fan must vent outdoors. The designer should be aware of local codes, as there may be requirements regarding the amount of CFMs needed or how the fan is vented.

CODES

Codes are another important consideration when planning the lighting and electrical for a bath project. **The International Residential Code (IRC)** is an excellent general reference; however, local codes should always be checked to be sure the project is in compliance. The local codes may dictate items, such as the number of outlets required. Here are some codes from the IRC that are specific to the kitchen that need to be followed: IRC E 4001.6, IRC E 3903.2: At least one wall-switch-controlled light must be provided. That switch must be placed at the entrance of the bathroom or kitchen. IRC E 3901.6: At least one GFCI-protected receptacle must be installed within 36 inches of the outside edge of the sink. IRC 3902.1: All receptacles must be protected by GFCIs.

The IRC has several bath codes that should be followed when planning a bath project. IRC E 4001.6, IRC E 3903.2: At least one wall switch–controlled light must be provided. That switch must be placed at the entrance of the bathroom or kitchen. IRC E 4003.9: All light fixtures installed within tub and shower spaces should be rated and marked "suitable for damp/wet locations." IRC E 4003.11: Hanging fixtures cannot be located within a zone of 3 feet horizontally and 8 feet vertically from the top of the bathtub rim or shower stall threshold. IRC E 3901.6: At least one GFCI-protected receptacle must be installed within 36 inches of the outside edge of the sink. IRC 3902.1: All receptacles must be protected by ground fault circuit interrupters (GFCI). IRC 4001.7:

Switches shall not be installed within wet locations in tub or shower spaces within reach while standing in the tub or shower unless installed as part of the listed tub or shower assembly.

THE LIGHTING AND ELECTRICAL PLAN FOR THE KITCHEN

The lighting and electrical plan is an important part of the plan set for the kitchen project. This is what the electrician will use to locate outlets and power for the various items in the kitchen. It should be drafted at the same scale as the floor plan. Because ½-inch scale is the ideal scale for a kitchen or bathroom, the lighting and electrical plan should typically be at this scale as well.

It is important to show only those notes relevant specifically to the lighting or electric plan. Oftentimes the contractor will hire a electrician to do the electrical work. The electrician does not typically need extra information that does not pertain to the work he or she will be doing. The plan should be easy to understand so that the electrician does not waste time deciphering the plan.

The basic components that this plan should include the lighting, outlets, switches and circuitry, and any specialty item needing power. The plan also should have a legend explaining what the various symbols represent. It is important to label the locations of all appliances, as these items need power. It is also best for the designer to provide the contractor or electrician with specifications for all the appliances, as these will include information about their power requirements and locations.

It is also ideal to dimension the centerlines of fixtures and equipment whenever possible to make the installation easier for the electrician. Centerline dimensions should be taken from walls.

Figure 9.9 shows examples of standard symbols used in the industry; they are not the only symbols that

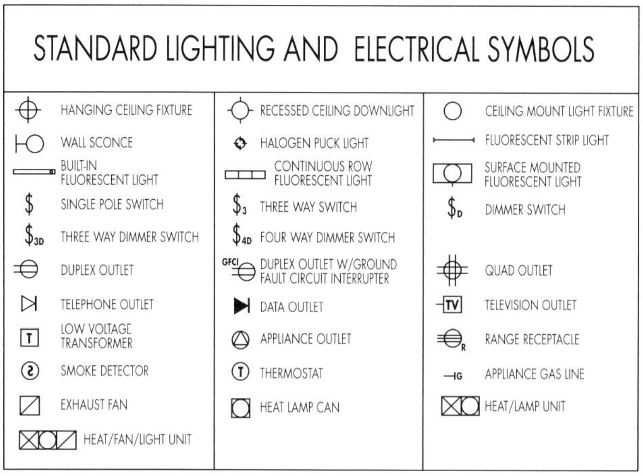

Figure 9.9 Examples of standard symbols used in the design industry.

may be seen. Different design firms may use slight variations on these symbols, and may also have additional symbols for other items. The most important thing to remember is to include a legend explaining what the symbols represent.

Figure 9.10 is an example of an electric and lighting plan. This kitchen has the three main layers of lighting in addition to the required outlets. The undercabinet lights and the recessed incandescent lights at the counters are acting as task lighting. The puck lights inside the wall cabinet above the sink and the sconces by the door are acting as accent lighting. The remaining recessed incandescent lights are acting as ambient; they light the space enough so people may move about safely.

TRADE TALK 9.1

"Inform the client that you will provide a lighting plan, but need to work within how the house is framed. If there is a ceiling joist in the way where a recessed incandescent is planned, we will do our best to get it close. Tell the client we will know as soon as the space is gutted what will work and that we'll be on site if there's a problem. The designer and contractor will meet the client on site to work it all out."
—*John Gruszka, Jr., President, Fair Oaks Contractors*

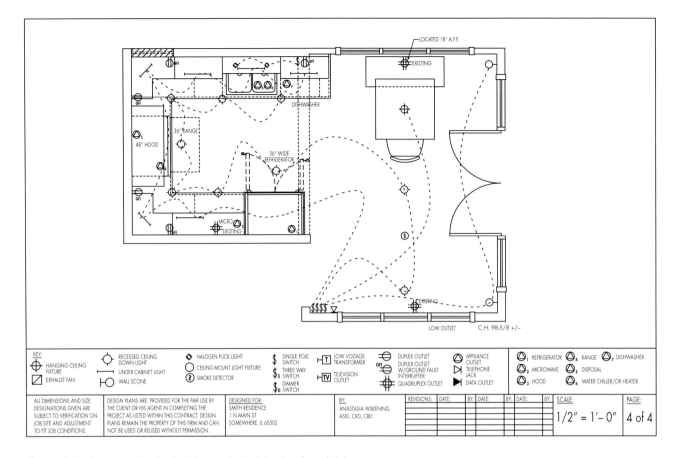

Figure 9.10 An example of a lighting and electric plan for a kitchen.

THE LIGHTING AND ELECTRICAL PLAN FOR THE BATH

The lighting and electrical plan is an important part of the plan set for a bath project. This is what the electrician will use to locate outlets and power for the various items in the bath. It should be drafted at the same scale as the floor plan. Because ½-inch scale is the ideal scale for a kitchen or bathroom, the lighting and electrical plan should typically be at this scale as well. As mentioned previously, it is important to show only notes relevant specifically to the lighting and electrical plan.

The basic components that this plan should include are the lighting, an exhaust fan for baths, outlets, switches and circuitry, and any specialty items needing power. The plan should have a legend explaining what the different symbols represent. See Figure 9.9 for an example of a lighting and electrical plan legend. Figure 9.11 shows an example of a lighting and electrical plan for a bath project.

WHIRLPOOLS, AIR TUBS, AND STEAM SHOWERS

Because whirlpools and air tubs require power to operate, they need to be noted on the lighting and electrical plan. The same is true for steam showers. Steam showers require a generator for power, so it is important to note this on the lighting and electrical plan. Typically, if the designer is providing these items, the specifications should be provided to the electrician.

He or she needs to know what type of power is required because these items may need a special dedicated circuit. The electrician will also need to know where to locate the power for these items; these locations should be shown on the designer's drawing and described in each item's specifications. It should also be noted on the plan where the access will be in the event that any of these items need to be repaired or replaced.

TOILETS OR BIDETS WITH ELECTRICITY

Some contemporary toilets and bidet seats also require electricity. Tankless toilets require electricity because they use an electric pump to power the flush. Although not all bidets require electricity, most bidet seats will. Again, this should be noted on the electric and lighting plan. As with the other specialty items discussed, the designer should provide the specifications for the

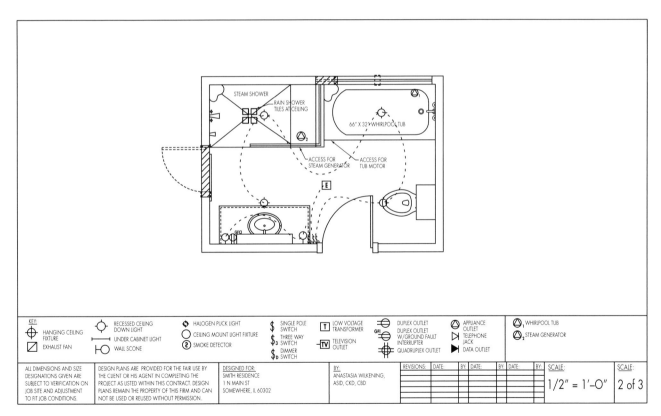

Figure 9.11 An example of a lighting and electric plan for a bathroom.

contractor and electrician, as they may require special dedicated outlets.

MIRROR DEFOGGERS, TOWEL WARMERS, AND HEATED FLOORS

Mirror defoggers, towel warmers, and heated floors are a few additional features often found in baths that may require power. Hydronic versions of these items work by way of hot water, but electric versions are commonly used as they are easier and more flexible to install. Again, the specifications will need to be provided, and a note on the plan should explain where controls or access needs to be located.

SUMMARY

There are many things to consider when designing a lighting and electrical layout. It is important to think about the big goal first and then to consider the finer details, such as codes, lighting temperature, and natural daylight. Always be sure to account for the three layers of lighting: task, accent, and ambient. Once the lighting and electrical is decided, it is communicated by the lighting and electrical plan. It is crucial that this plan be accurate, so that the electrician knows what needs to be installed and where. As with any other aspect of a kitchen or bath project, it is important that the designer be available to answer questions should there be any confusion or unexpected issues that may arise.

CHAPTER 9 EXERCISES

I: Look at the following floor plan layout for the Larsen's kitchen (Figure 9.12). Create a lighting and electrical plan for them, taking into consideration their situation discussed at the beginning of the chapter.

II: The Larsens have asked that you help them determine preset scenes for their kitchen. What are three different scenes that you would recommend for the lighting and electrical plan you designed? Describe the various lights used, the levels of brightness, color, and so on. Why are these three scenes best for the Larsen family?

III: You've been working with your clients, Mr. and Mrs. Chaney-Soto, on their bathroom project. The layout has been decided and now you need to plan and communicate the lighting and electrical for the space. Mr. Chaney-Soto wakes up much earlier for his job and is finished and out of the house before Mrs. Chaney-Soto needs to get ready in the morning. They are interested in the newest technology and like the idea of motion sensor lights. You need to take these facts into consideration for the electrical and lighting plan. Look at the following floor plan layout for the Chaney-Soto bath (Figure 9.13). Create a lighting and electrical plan for them, taking into consideration their particular situation.

IV: The Chaney-Sotos have asked that you help them determine preset scenes for their bath. What are two different scenes that you would recommend for the lighting and electrical plan you designed? Describe the various lights used, their level of brightness, color, and so on. Why are these two scenes best for Mr. and Mrs. Chaney-Soto?

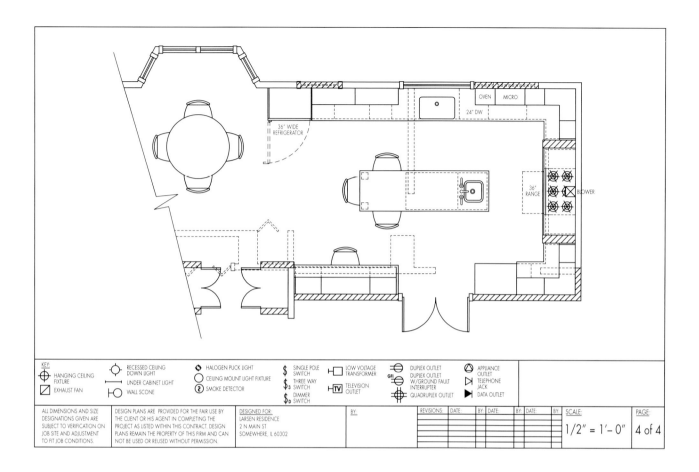

KEY:

⊕ HANGING CEILING FIXTURE
▢ EXHAUST FAN
⬥ RECESSED CEILING DOWN LIGHT
⊢● UNDER CABINET LIGHT
⊢○ WALL SCONE
◆ HALOGEN PUCK LIGHT
○ CEILING MOUNT LIGHT FIXTURE
② SMOKE DETECTOR
$ SINGLE POLE SWITCH
$₃ THREE WAY SWITCH
$ᴅ DIMMER SWITCH
⊟ LOW VOLTAGE TRANSFORMER
TV TELEVISION OUTLET
⊖ DUPLEX OUTLET
GFI DUPLEX OUTLET W/GROUND FAULT INTERRUPTER
⊕ QUADRUPLEX OUTLET
△ APPLIANCE OUTLET
▷ TELEPHONE JACK
▶ DATA OUTLET

ALL DIMENSIONS AND SIZE DESIGNATIONS GIVEN ARE SUBJECT TO VERIFICATION ON JOB SITE AND ADJUSTMENT TO FIT JOB CONDITIONS.

DESIGN PLANS ARE PROVIDED FOR THE FAIR USE BY THE CLIENT OR HIS AGENT IN COMPLETING THE PROJECT AS LISTED WITHIN THIS CONTRACT. DESIGN PLANS REMAIN THE PROPERTY OF THIS FIRM AND CAN NOT BE USED OR REUSED WITHOUT PERMISSION.

DESIGNED FOR:
LARSEN RESIDENCE
2 N MAIN ST
SOMEWHERE, IL 60302

BY:

REVISIONS: DATE: BY: DATE: BY: DATE: BY:

SCALE:
1/2" = 1'– 0"

PAGE:
4 of 4

Figure 9.12 Larsen floor plan for exercise I.

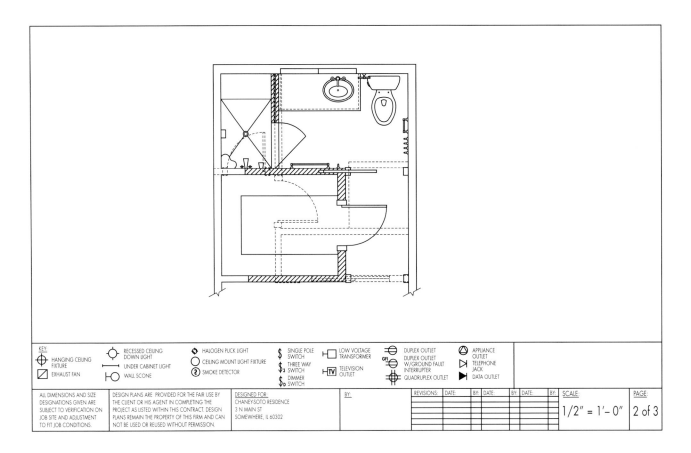

Figure 9.13 Chaney-Soto floor plan for exercise III.

CHAPTER 9 DISCUSSION QUESTIONS

1. What are some creative ways to incorporate accent lighting?
2. What is the best type of task lighting in a kitchen?
3. Where is task lighting most important in the bath?
4. What are the advantages of LED lighting?
5. What scale should the lighting and electrical plan be in?

REFERENCES

International Code Council. *International Residential Code*. Country Club Hills, IL: International Code Council, Inc., 2009.

Whitehead, Randall. *Residential Lighting*. Hoboken, NJ: John Wiley & Sons, Inc., 2004.

CHAPTER 9: LIGHTING AND ELECTRICAL CHECKLIST

___Have you included all three types of lighting: ambient, task, and accent?

___What type of lighting makes the most sense for your client (e.g., incandescent, fluorescent, xenon, LED, etc.) ?

___Were dimmable switches specified to allow for more flexibility?

___Are the appropriate outlets labeled GFCI?

___Does the lighting and electrical plan show only those items relevant to the electrician?

___Is an appropriate key included on the lighting and electrical plan?

___Have any special electrical requirements such as air tubs, steam showers, or electric-powered cabinets been labeled?

KEY TERMS

Accent lighting: Lighting that accents something, such as an architectural detail or a decorative item. Also called *focal lighting*.

Ambient lighting: Overall illumination; also called *general lighting*.

Beam spread: The beam pattern of the light from a lamp. Manufacturers typically have graphs or charts to show the beam spread of their light fixtures.

CFMs: Cubic feet per minute; refers to the measurement of air moved by an exhaust fan in a bathroom. The minimum CFM recommendation for a bath is 100.

Color Rendering Index: Also known as CRI rating; the CRI measures the score of light color compared with daylight, which scores 100 percent. The higher the CRI score, the closer the light color is to daylight.

Foot-candles: A foot-candle is a non-SI unit that measures luminance or light intensity.

GFCI: A GFCI, or ground fault circuit interrupter outlet, is an outlet that automatically turns off to prevent electrical shock if it senses an imbalance due to water.

International Residential Code (IRC): A model building code, created by the International Code Council, that has been adopted by most of the United States.

Kelvin: A unit of measurement for color temperature of light.

Lamp: The correct term for a light bulb.

Line voltage: Refers to the home voltage, which is 120 volts.

Lumens: A lumen is an SI-derived unit that measures visible light, that is, the amount of light perceived by the human eye.

Luminaire: Also called a light fixture, a luminaire is a device that creates illumination.

Task lighting: Lighting that provides illumination for a specific task.

Transformer: A transformer is magnetic or electronic, and converts the house line voltage to low voltage so that low-voltage lighting can be used.

10 PROJECT MANAGEMENT FOR
KITCHEN AND BATH

OBJECTIVES

After reading this chapter, you will:

- Act in a professional manner while overseeing the installation of the project.

- Learn about visiting the job site regularly and why it is important.

- Understand why direct and open communication is one of the most important aspects of accomplished project management.

DESIGN SCENARIO

You have designed, drafted, and specified everything for your client, the Dabrowski family. They have signed the purchase agreement and are ready to get started with the order and installation of their project.

1. What is the standard list of events that will happen during the installation?

2. What actions are considered good practice while working on the project?

3. What is your responsibility as the designer?

Once the kitchen or bath has been designed, the management aspect of it has only just begun. Project management ends up being a large part of the designer's job. It is important that the designer be professional and timely, and have proper communication skills.

THE DESIGNER AND THE PROJECT MANAGER

How much the designer is involved during the project installation depends on the structure of the design firm. A larger design firm may have multiple employees with roles during the installation. Some design firms have specific project managers or people for placing orders. The idea is that if the designer does not need to spend his or her time managing the installation, there will be more time to generate new sales. The problem with having a separate project manager on a project is that it ends up being an opportunity for potential problems in communication and loss of details from the designer. The designer who is managing the project throughout also will have a better understanding and relationship with the client. We discuss the designer's role in this chapter, assuming he or she does not have these additional resources and is responsible for all aspects of the design project.

DESIGNER'S DIALOGUE 10.1

"If there is another separate project manager, he or she needs to be familiar with your job. Have your client meet the project manager before the job starts so they don't have some stranger walking in their home."
—Lisa McManus, ASID, Kitchen and Bath Designer

COMMUNICATION

Communication is extremely important during the project's installation. The designer should be in contact with the contractor and the client on a regular basis. Being in contact helps resolve any issues as quickly as possible. Always be open, direct, and professional with the client and contractor. The designer's goal is to make the installer's job as easy as possible and the client as happy as possible.

PROJECT ORGANIZATION

Different designers use different methods to keep all the paperwork organized for a project. Some designers prefer to use a file folder with tabs to organize the various types of paperwork. Some like to have a book they keep on the project site, which allows everyone access. There is no one right way to be organized. Whatever makes the most sense to the designer, or whatever procedures a firm has in place that works for him or her, is fine. It is best to have some method, though. For example, when the designer receives an invoice and wants to confirm that the correct amount is being billed, it would be a waste of time to spend an hour trying to locate the original quote.

PROJECT SCHEDULE

A schedule for the installation of the project is typically provided by the contractor. As mentioned in Chapter 1, a contractor can be employed by the design firm or the client may hire the contractor directly. There is a large variance in the manner that contractors work. Some will provide a schedule and some may just give a vague estimate of the length of time. It is best when the contractor provides a detailed schedule; everyone is then aware of the plan and about what is happening when. It is also helpful to the designer, so that he or she knows when the materials need to be at the site and when measures can be scheduled for the countertops and custom shower doors if needed.

INITIAL INSTALLATION MEETING

A valuable practice for the designer is to schedule a pre-installation meeting. This habit helps ensure minimal problems with the installation. This meeting should minimally involve the designer, contractor, and client. The final plans should be provided and reviewed to make sure everything is clear and to answer any questions. This also is a good time to discuss the proposed schedule. Having this meeting helps lay the groundwork for good communication during the project; this is crucial to a successful installation.

The initial consultation is an ideal time for any additional questions regarding the job site or how everyone will work. Some designers have company yard signs they may ask to put up. There may be limited parking to consider, or a security system or lockbox that requires access. All of these concerns should be discussed ahead of time with the client. In multiple-housing buildings such as condos, there may be restrictions as to when the elevator can be used to move materials in and out of the project. If children or pets are around during the construction it is important to know how to handle the intrusion.

WORKING ON A REMODEL VERSUS NEW CONSTRUCTION

There are more considerations when a project is a remodel versus new construction. When the kitchen is being remodeled, the homeowner will require a temporary kitchen. Items that were stored in the kitchen will need to be stored elsewhere during the remodel. Dust barriers typically need to be set up to help minimize dust moving throughout the home. In general, keeping the work area clean is more important than at a new construction project.

When a bathroom is remodeled, the room is unavailable and unusable for 3 to 4 days. Even when it is usable, it will not necessarily be finished. The client should be informed of this ahead of time so as to be prepared.

BUILDING CODES AND PERMITS

Obtaining permits is typically the responsibility of the contractor or homeowner. The designer needs to be aware of building codes while planning the space. If the inspector finds a problem that needs to be corrected, the designer needs to fully understand how it is to be corrected.

VISITING THE JOB SITE

During installation, it is a beneficial practice for the designer to make regular visits to the job site. Regularly seeing the progress of the project allows the designer to catch any problems with the products or installation. It also makes communication faster and easier, because the designer will be a familiar face to the contractor. If the contractor runs into any questions that require a decision, the designer can easily be asked while on site.

SCHEDULING DELIVERIES

The task of scheduling deliveries is the designer's responsibility for any material he or she is providing. Most materials can be delivered directly to the job site, but in some cases they may need to be delivered to the designer or to a warehouse. Different designers have different methods for their deliveries, which also can be affected by the contractor for the project. Some contractors prefer that all the materials be at the job site before starting the project at all. Other contractors will begin the project knowing they have several weeks of work before the materials are even needed. Even if the contractor starts the project before all the materials arrive, the designer should be aware of what will be needed first for the specific project. Typically, any new flooring material will be needed early on. Rough-in valves for the bathroom plumbing also will be needed early in the project.

Cabinetry deliveries typically do not allow for any variation in their scheduled delivery. When the cabinet order is placed the cabinet company provides an exact date or an estimated date for the delivery. Although there are exceptions, generally once the cabinet company provides a date for the delivery it cannot be changed. Cabinet companies send their delivery trucks on the basis of what orders they have to deliver. They may have several different projects' cabinets in one truck for delivery. Because the deliveries are based on these locations, requesting a different delivery date may interfere with their scheduling. Ideally, the cabinets will arrive when the contractor is already working at the job site. It is also very common that the cabinet delivery truck driver will not unload the cabinets. They will only carry the cabinets to the truck opening so they can be unloaded. If the contractor is not at the job site when the cabinets arrive, the designer may need to hire someone to unload the cabinets. It is best for the designer to make the delivery arrangements far enough in advance so as to be aware if there will be this extra charge. Ideally, if the designer needs to hire someone to unload the cabinets, this cost will be accounted for in the client's purchase agreement.

Tile, plumbing fixtures, and appliances are other items that may require unloading once delivered to the job site. Whether the driver will unload these items depends on the company from which they were ordered. Sometimes, for these pieces, the truck driver will bring them inside. It is important for the designer to find out ahead of time so as to be prepared.

Smaller or breakable items, such as hardware or glass pieces, might be better delivered to the designer. Small items may be lost on the job site and fragile items may be broken. Because the designer should be visiting the job site regularly in any case, he or she can simply bring these pieces along on one of these visits. Some larger design firms may have a company vehicle for making these deliveries, but most often the designer will simply drive his or her own car to the job site. Some designers, who have been in the business for some time, may choose to own a larger car to accommodate needed job site deliveries.

Sometimes warehouses need to be used for a project. If the project is new construction there may not be anywhere safe to store the project materials. Keep in mind that if a warehouse is used there will be an additional charge for storing these items. When selecting a warehouse be sure to take into consideration whether they do deliveries. It is easiest to use a warehouse that will redeliver the items, so that there is one less person or company to work with. It is also important to hire a company that is licensed and insured in the event of any damage to the goods. The best warehouse companies will be those frequently used by high-end designers. Ask the warehouse company for referrals or ask well-established designers who they like to use.

CHECKING A PROJECT'S MATERIALS

It is always sensible practice for the designer to check the materials received as soon as possible. Sometimes materials may arrive damaged or incorrect. The sooner these problems are caught, the faster they can be resolved.

DESIGNER'S DIALOGUE 10.2

"Inspect the products when they arrive; don't wait until the installation."
—*Gladys Schanstra, CKD, CBD, Kitchen and Bath Designer*

MEASURING FOR COUNTERTOPS AND CUSTOM SHOWER DOORS

Certain items, such as the countertops and custom shower doors, are typically measured on site before fabrication. As the designer, it is important to know when it is expected that the site will be ready for these measurements to be taken. It is best to know in advance so that the measuring can be scheduled. Some companies may be solidly booked, and if contacted at the last minute will not have immediate availability to measure on site. A delay in measuring means a delay in fabrication and project completion. Countertops can be measured when all the base cabinets have been installed. Custom shower doors can be measured once the tile and curb have been installed. The installer typically wants to know when the countertop measure is scheduled so that the plumber can then be scheduled to hook up the sink and faucet.

RUNNING INTO UNEXPECTED ISSUES

Various issues commonly arise during an installation. The designer can never know where and when exactly these potential issues may arise. For example, errors can occur with any cabinet or other material order. Items can end up having longer lead times than expected. Contractors may make installation mistakes. Unexpected problems can arise when the contractor opens the walls to install the plumbing, electric, and other items. Although some clients handle these issues better than others, it is the designer's responsibility to remain professional and ethical. The designer's goal should be to make the client as happy as possible.

CHANGES

Sometimes, as issues arise on the job site, changes need to be considered and made. **Change orders** are used to make changes to the original contract. The designer should have a standard form to use and once the change order is typed it should be approved by the client in writing. If the change order causes additional payment it can be collected at the time of signing instead of adding it to the final bill.

PUNCH LIST

The **punch list** is an industry phrase used for the project's final "to do" list. This is a list of outstanding work that needs to be done. This list is typically composed when the project is close to completion. The designer walks through the project with the contractor and client to make a list of the remaining tasks. It is important to remember that punch list items are expected. It is best to start in one corner of the space and work around the room to inspect all aspects of the project.

having the discussion face to face if they are not comfortable. It is extremely beneficial to the designer to see these survey results to know what his or her strengths and weaknesses are. If there is something that upset the client that the designer was not aware of, the designer can take action to resolve the matter. It also helps the designer improve and do better on the next project. The survey is also beneficial to the business owner. When design firms have multiple designers it is difficult for the business owner to be everywhere. This gives the company owner clear insight into how the company designers and tradespeople are performing.

MAINTENANCE AND CARE FORMS

The designer must confirm that the client has received all the necessary care and maintenance forms for the materials used in the project. Often these forms will be included when the product arrives at the job site. The countertop installer should bring care instructions, as should the custom shower enclosure installer. The cabinetry will typically have a care kit with instructions. The designer should always keep extra copies of this paperwork, as this information can easily become lost on a job site. It would be ideal for the designer to send this information along at the same time as the postproject survey.

POSTPROJECT SURVEY

Many companies have a survey that is provided to the clients after a project has been completed. This practice is helpful for many reasons. It provides the clients with a means to share whatever they have felt about their project. A written survey is nonconfrontational, giving them an opportunity to be honest without necessarily

PROJECT MANAGEMENT SOFTWARE

For the tech-savvy designer, various types of project management software are available. Some programs or applications (or "apps," as they are commonly referred to these days) can be accessed conveniently via the designer's cell phone. This allows the designer to easily access project information anywhere from the office to the job site.

SUMMARY

Project management is the final stage of the kitchen or bath project. In general, communication is the most important factor for a successful installation. The designer should always be open, direct, and professional. Any issues should be communicated as soon as possible. Although potential problems can arise, work quickly to fix them and keep the project moving to a satisfactory completion.

CHAPTER 10 DISCUSSION QUESTIONS

1. Who is typically responsible for getting any needed building permits?
2. What items are typically best delivered to the designer instead of the job site?
3. Why does the designer need to know when the base cabinets will be installed?
4. What is a punch list?
5. What is the benefit of sending the client a postproject survey?

ADDITIONAL FEATURES

AT-A-GLANCE PROJECT BREAKDOWN EXAMPLE

- The client meets the designer and, after receiving the rough estimate for the project from the designer, decides to sign a retainer to hire the designer.
- The designer surveys the client for wants and needs, discusses the budget, and measures the existing space.
- The designer works up multiple options by hand and then drafts these plans to present to the client.
- The client selects the layout to move forward with, and the appliances and materials for the project.
- The designer drafts the elevations for the floor plan that the client selected.
- The client receives multiple quotes from various contractors for the labor needed to complete the project, using the drawings the designer has provided.
- All the project selections are finalized.
- The designer obtains quotes and pricing for all items and then works up a detailed purchase agreement for everything being provided to the client.
- The client signs the purchase agreement, makes a payment deposit, and selects the contractor who will do the work.
- The designer starts ordering everything for the project.
- The designer has an initial installation meeting with the contractor and client.
- The contractor starts working on the project.
- The designer schedules the needed deliveries to the job site or to the designer.
- Typically, the client pays the second purchase agreement payment when the cabinets are delivered.
- The designer visits the job site regularly to ensure that the installation is progressing as planned and to answer any questions.
- When ready, the designer schedules on-site measures needed for fabrication of countertops or custom shower enclosures.
- The designer does a walk-through with the contractor and client to assemble the punch list.
- The project is complete and the designer invoices the client for the final outstanding amount.
- The designer sends the client any maintenance and care information along with a postproject survey.

KITCHEN REMODEL BREAKDOWN EXAMPLE

Although there may be slight variations, based on the contractor working on the project, the following is an example of a typical kitchen installation order of events:

- Demolition
- Rough construction, including plumbing, electrical, HVAC, (heating, ventilation and air conditioning) framing, and walls
- Preparation for wall surfaces
- Building inspection
- Walls are "closed"
- Building inspection
- Walls primed
- Flooring installed
- Cabinets installed
- Countertop measure
- Finish cabinet installation (including necessary moldings and details)
- Countertops installed
- Sink and faucet hooked up by plumber
- Backsplash installed
- Appliances installed
- Punch list
- Light fixtures installed
- Finish details, such as touch-ups and hardware
- Complete punch list items
- Final inspection

BATHROOM REMODEL BREAKDOWN EXAMPLE

Again, there may be slight variations, based on the contractor working on the project, but this is an example of a typical bathroom installation order of events:

- Demolition
- Rough construction, including: plumbing, electrical, HVAC, framing, walls, and custom shower
- Preparation for wall surfaces
- Building inspection
- Walls are "closed"
- Building inspection
- Walls primed
- Flooring installed
- Wall tile installed
- Cabinets, toilet, tub, shower base, and additional fixtures and fittings installed
- Countertop and custom shower enclosure measured
- Finish cabinet installation (including necessary moldings and details)
- Countertops installed
- Sink and faucet hooked up by plumber
- Accessories installed
- Punch list
- Light fixtures installed
- Finish details such as touch-ups and hardware
- Complete punch list items
- Final inspection

CHAPTER 10: PROJECT MANAGEMENT CHECKLIST

___Meet with the contractor and homeowner for the initial installation meeting.

___Provide the contractor and client with the final set of drawings.

___Be sure the contractor has your contact information in the event that any questions arise.

___Schedule all necessary deliveries.

___Determine who will unload the cabinetry.

___Organize the project paperwork.

___Schedule any needed measures for countertops, custom shower enclosures, and so on.

___Have the client sign off in writing, via a change order, any changes made.

___Do the final walk-through and compose the punch list with the contractor and client.

___Finish any needed tasks from the punch list.

___Send the client a postproject survey.

___Follow up with the client 3 to 6 months postoccupancy to see how the space is working out.

KEY TERMS

Change order: A written agreement between the designer and client outlining changes to the original contract.

Punch list: A list of outstanding tasks that need to be done to complete a project.

BASIC METRIC CONVERSION TABLE	
Length	
English	**Metric**
1 inch	2.54 centimeters
1 foot	0.3048 meter/30.38 centimeters
1 yard	0.9144 meter
Metric	**English**
1 centimeter	0.3937 inch
1 meter	3.280 feet
Weight	
English	**Metric**
1 ounce	28.35 grams
1 pound	0.45 kilogram
Metric	**English**
1 gram	0.035 ounce
1 kilogram	2.2 pounds

General formula for converting:
    Number of Units × Conversion Number = New Number of Units

To convert inches to centimeters:
    [number of inches] × 2.54 = [number of centimeters]

To convert centimeters to inches:
    [number of centimeters] × 0.3937 = [number of inches]

To convert feet to meters:
    [number of feet] × 0.3048 = [number of meters]

To convert meters to feet:
    [number of meters] × 3.280 = [number of feet]

To convert yards to meters:
    [number of yards] × 0.9144 = [number of meters]

To convert ounces to grams:
    [number of ounces] × 28.35 = [number of grams]

To convert grams to ounces:
    [number of grams] × 0.035 = [number of ounces]

To convert pounds to kilograms:
    [number of pounds] × 0.45 = [number of kilograms]

To convert kilograms to pounds:
    [number of kilograms] × 2.2 = [number of pounds]

INDEX

Balance, 30–31

Bamboo
    in cabinetry, 122, 123
    in flooring, 108
    sustainable design and, 80, 82

Bar faucet, 190

Barrier-free design, 74
    See also Universal design

Bathroom floor plan, 202–3, 230
    elevations for, 207–8

Bathroom plumbing, 53, 165–84
    bathtubs, 36–40, 43, 78–79, 172–79
    bidets, 171–72
    code requirements for, 36–40
    lavatory faucets, 165–66
    showers, 37–39, 43, 78, 179–84
    sinks, 166–68
    spa experience, 176–79
    toilets, 77, 82, 168–71
    urinals, 172

Bathrooms
    accessories in, 41, 43–44, 53
    ADA codes for, 36–41
    alcoves in, 43–44, 174
    appliances in, 157
    balance in design of, 30
    cabinetry, 133–34
    chromatherapy in, 179, 183
    electrical outlets in, 224
    estimating floor tile, 111
    estimating remodel costs, 9
    grab bars in, 39, 43, 78
    lighting and electrical plan for, 226–27, 230
    relaxing in, 3
    remodel, 240
    rhythm in design of, 31
    spa experience in, 176–79, 183–84
    task lighting in, 217–18
    universal design in, 77–79
    vanities, 78, 115
    ventilation in, 41, 224

Bathroom sink. *See* Lavatory

Bathroom space planning, 42–44, 51–55, 60
    bidet, 42–43
    code requirements, 35–41
    doorways, 35–36
    lavatory, 42, 37
    showers, 37–39, 43
    surveys, 52–53, 61–66
    toilet, 42–43

Bathtubs, 172–79
    air tub, 176, 177, 227
    alcove/corner, 174
    cleaning systems for, 178
    code requirements, 36–40
    controls for, 38, 43
    drop-in, 175
    faucets for, 179
    freestanding, 172–73
    materials for, 176
    seating in, 38, 43
    standard sizes for, 176
    surround, 39
    undermount, 175
    universal design for, 78–79
    whirlpool tub, 176, 178, 227

Beadboard, 120, 136

Beam spread, in lights, 219, 220, 232

Beverage centers, 141, 142

Bidets, 171
    with electricity, 227

Birch wood, 121, 123

Blowers, 150, 162
    for bathtubs, 176

Body sprays, 180

Bottom grid, for sink, 187

Bowl-and-a-half sink, 187

Branch plumbing lines, 164, 195

Bridge faucet, 189

BTU (British thermal unit), 144, 146, 162

Building codes and permits, 17, 21, 235

    See also International Residential Code

Bullnose, 102, 112

Cabinet panels, 120, 129–30

Cabinetry, 113–36

    appliances in, 158

    in bathrooms, 133–34

    categories of, 114–20

    custom, 115–16, 136

    details, 125–34

    estimating, 9–11

    European (metric sizes), 118

    extended stiles and fillers, 125–26

    framed, 117–18

    frameless, 118

    full overlay, 117

    furniture pieces, 130–31

    hoods, 131–32

    kitchen, 48–51

    laminate, 125

    materials, 120–25

    moldings, 126–28

    nomenclature, 118–19, 199

    partial overlay, 117–18

    pricing and ordering, 120

    pull-out waste bins, 134

    scheduling deliveries, 236

    semicustom, 115, 116, 136

    stock, 114–15, 116

    sustainable design in, 83

    undercabinet lighting, 128, 217

    wide stiles, 126

    wood in, 120–24

Cast iron

    bathtubs, 176

    kitchen sinks, 185

Ceiling height

    bathrooms, 36

Centerline, 12, 25, 198, 212, 225

Ceramic tile, 103–4

    hand-crafted, 104

Certified aging-in-place specialist (CAPS), 74

CFMs (cubic feet per minute), 224, 232

Change orders, 237, 241

Cherry wood, 121, 123

China sinks, 166

Chromatherapy, in bathroom, 179, 183

Cleveland Clinic Heart Care at Home program, 79

Client interview, 16–17

Coffee systems, built-in, 156

Cold water dispenser, 155

Color, 30

    chromatherapy, 179, 183

Color rendering index (CRI), 215, 232

Commission, 3

Communication, 234–35

Compact fluorescent lamps (CFLs), 219

Computer-aided design (CAD), 210

Concrete countertops, 95, 99

Concrete flooring, 82

Contractors, 17

    appliance specs and, 158, 159–60

    delivery schedules and, 236

    installation errors and, 237

    recommended, 6–7

    schedule and, 234

Contrast, 31–32